CW00456750

TRANSPERSONAL PSYCHOTHERAPY

Related titles:

Robert Bor, Riva Miller, Martha Latz and Heather Salt: *Counselling in Health Care Settings*
Janice Brewi and Anne Brennan: *Passion for Life: Lifelong Psychological and Spiritual Growth*
Richard Nelson-Jones: *Creating Happy Relationships*
Michael Scott and Stephen Palmer (eds): *Trauma and Post-Traumatic Stress Disorder*
Frank Tallis: Changing Minds: *The History of Psychotherapy as an Answer to Human Suffering*
Elizabeth Wilde McCormick: *Change for the Better: Self-Help Through Practical Psychotherapy*

TRANSPERSONAL PSYCHOTHERAPY

Theory and Practice

Edited by Nigel Wellings and
Elizabeth Wilde McCormick

CONTINUUM

London and New York

CONTINUUM
Wellington House   370 Lexington Avenue
125 Strand   New York
London WC2R 0BB   NY 10017–6503

© 2000 Nigel Wellings, Elizabeth Wilde McCormick and the contributors

All rights reserved. No part of this publication may be reproduced or transmitted in any form or by any means, electronic or mechanical, including photocopying, recording, or any information storage or retrieval system, without prior permission in writing from the publishers.

First published 2000

British Library Cataloguing-in-Publication Data
A catalogue record for this book is available from the British Library.

ISBN 0–8264–4845–3 (hardback)
       0–8264–4846–1 (paperback)

Typeset by YHT Ltd, London
Printed and bound in Great Britain by T.J. International, Padstow, Cornwall

For Barbara Somers and Ian Gordon Brown, who established
transpersonal psychology in the UK, and for all
who will take it into the future

Contents

Foreword

Transpersonal psychology is still not fully accepted by all psychologists as a legitimate area for scientific investigation. Although there is no doubt that transpersonal experiences are frequently reported, the view of some critics is that they can be explained away as self-delusion arising variously from undue suggestibility, over-active imagination, wishful thinking or a form of psychosis. This is unfortunate. Failure to accord transpersonal states their due psychological legitimacy means that they have still not been subjected to appropriate scientific scrutiny, with the consequence that we know far less about them than we should. We do know, however, that such states can prove life-changing, exerting a profound and enduring effect upon subsequent behaviour, belief systems, self-understanding and life goals. They can also prove disturbing, presenting individuals with experiences that challenge their existing understanding and that may provoke crises of personal identity and threaten the stability of existing relationships. In the light of these effects, it is difficult to see how even the most committed behaviourist can deny the legitimacy of the states concerned, or ignore their importance for our understanding of the human mind.

There is also a sense in which transpersonal psychology is one of the most comprehensive of the various movements that go to make up psychological science, because although its focus is upon those aspects of experience and behaviour that lie beyond the confines of the individual ego, it addresses in addition the nature and meaning of this ego. There are two reasons for this latter undertaking. At the theoretical level, we cannot fully understand what lying beyond something really means unless we know what that something is. And at the practical level – of particular importance to the psychotherapist – we need to understand the relationship between the ego/personal self and the transpersonal if we are to facilitate movement from one to the other (and where necessary help strengthen the ego to the point at which such movement becomes possible).

Thus transpersonal psychologists and psychotherapists have a breadth to their theory and practice which is not always found in psychologists located in other areas of specialization. With this breadth goes not only an understanding of other approaches, but a readiness to combine them with transpersonal strategies when appropriate. Thus one can, for example, be both a transpersonal psychotherapist and a Jungian, a transpersonal psychotherapist and a neo-Freudian, a transpersonal psychotherapist and a Gestalt therapist. Further, it can be claimed that any psychologist or psychotherapist who sees men and women as more than complicated pieces of biological machinery is already venturing into the transpersonal.

It is self-evident to transpersonal psychotherapists that transpersonal concerns underlie many of the problems with which clients present. Sometimes these problems have to do with intensely mystical or spiritual episodes which clients have been unable to integrate into their psyches. At other times they spring from transpersonal experiences which appear disturbing or threatening – the so-called spiritual emergencies to which much attention has been drawn of late – or with those that distance the client from family or friends who fail to understand their significance. On yet other occasions the presenting problem may have to do with a client's perceived absence of a transpersonal dimension to life and with a consequent sense of meaninglessness and futility, or with his or her systematic attempts to repress transpersonal state as threatening or as incompatible with existing belief systems.

The prevalence of these presenting problems means that many psychotherapists, without labelling themselves as transpersonal, nevertheless find themselves using transpersonal techniques in their work. In fact, it is true to say that no psychotherapist who wishes to comprehend the full range of client issues can operate successfully without some knowledge of these techniques. Hitherto, however, there has been a scarcity of material that makes the transpersonal approach accessible to psychotherapists whatever their theoretical persuasion. The present text is thus particularly timely, both for those who identify specifically with this approach and for those who currently lack specialist knowledge.

In addition to proving timely, it represents a milestone in the formalization (if formalization is not too strong a word for an approach characterized by its sensitivity to individual client needs) of transpersonal psychotherapy, and demonstrates moreover the manner in which transpersonal psychotherapists are able to draw upon relevant techniques from other psychotherapeutic approaches. The range and quality of the contributions to the book, together with the rich humanity that informs them and the accessible language in which they are expressed, ensure that it will prove an invaluable addition to the libraries not only of psychotherapists but of all those interested in transpersonal psychology and its meaning for human thought and behaviour.

Nigel Wellings and Elizabeth McCormick and their collaborators provide us with what amounts to a detailed guide to all important areas of transpersonal psychotherapeutic theory and practice. They enthuse the reader with their own love for their subject, and with their own conviction of its critical importance. The wisdom and sensitivity with which they write, and the depth of experience upon which they are able to call, provide us with sufficient proof of the role that the transpersonal can play in our lives. These are writers who live their own message, who speak not only from their detailed work with others but from their work upon themselves. The book stands as a shining example of how psychotherapists can not only make their work comprehensible to readers, but can convince us of its ability to make a profound difference to the lives both of their clients and of themselves. There can surely be no higher commendation.

David Fontana
Distinguished Visiting Fellow of Cardiff University
Visiting Professor of Transpersonal Psychology at Liverpool John Moores University

Acknowledgements

The original idea for writing this book came from the desire to record the work initiated by Barbara Somers and Ian Gordon Brown, whose training for professionals, offering a transpersonal perspective, has been in operation since 1977. We offer our grateful thanks to Barbara and Ian for all their years of workshops and training programmes that have been completed by hundreds of people working in a wide variety of settings. We hope their creativity, generosity and spirit continues as the work develops.

Our grateful thanks go to Barbara Scott for her saintly support, encouragement and tireless work in transcribing tapes and typing and retyping manuscripts.

We salute patient partners: John McCormick, Roger Walters, Michael Graubart, Hilary Fisher and, in particular, Philippa Vick for extraordinary patience in the face of severe provocation by Nigel Wellings who took the major editorial role during the illness and death of John McCormick.

Our appreciation goes to Hazel Marshall who edited with thorough devotion papers and a taped interview between Barbara Somers and Elizabeth Wilde McCormick for Chapter 8.

Profound thanks to Namkhai Norbu Rimpoche for lighting the original Buddhist spark that has lain almost dormant for too many years and to Hilmar Schonauer who showed how to make it legitimately flame once more. Their depth of understanding has acted as the inspiration within Chapter 9.

We are grateful to Frances Baruch for permission to use a photograph of her beautiful sculpture on the cover.

Finally, thanks to Ruth McCurry for commissioning the book prior to her retirement and to Karen Haynes for taking it forward.

Notes on Contributors

Claire Chappell is a UKCP-registered transpersonal psychotherapist and an educational therapist. She is a member of the core training group as well as teaching, supervising and running workshops. In addition to her private practice with adults she also works with children and adolescents and with their families and schools.

Valerie Coumont Graubart has been practising as a psychotherapist since 1986. She is a supervisor and trainer at Guy's Hospital, London and Hellesdon Hospital, Norwich as well as at the Centre for Transpersonal Psychology where she is also a member of the core training group. Her inner-city NHS work has added to her awareness of the impact of social, political and historical forces on the development of the individual.

Valerie Harding Davies is director of counselling and psychotherapy at Keele University. She is a practising psychotherapist and works from a transpersonal perspective. She has been associated with the Centre for Transpersonal Psychology since the mid-1970s. She has run workshops and given papers on transpersonal psychology throughout the UK and at international conferences. She is a consultant, trainer and supervisor of counsellors and psychotherapists within the private sector, the NHS and in the field of education.

Stephen Friedrich was born in Germany before the Second World War, came to England after it and then received a thoroughly British education. After university and National Service he worked in industry for thirty years and then entered on a new career when he started training to be a psychotherapist with the Association of Independent Psychotherapists. He is now in private practice in London.

Elizabeth Wilde McCormick is a psychotherapist, writer and teacher. She has been involved with transpersonal psychology in London since 1974 and is currently a workshop leader, a director of the CTP psychotherapy training programme and a consultant. Her background is in humanistic psychology, social psychiatry and cognitive analytic therapy. She is the author of five books, including *Change for the Better* (1990, 1996), *Surviving Breakdown* (1988, 1993, 1997) and *Living on the Edge* (1997).

Ann Shearer is an analytical psychologist in private practice in London. She is a member and former convener of the Independent Group of Analytical Psychologists.

Her books include *Disability: Who's Handicap?* (1981), *Woman: Her Changing Image* (1987) and *Athene: Image and Energy* (1996). Before training she worked as a freelance journalist and for the *Guardian*.

Barbara Somers is a psychotherapist with a comprehensive background in Jungian psychology, Zen and Taoism. In 1973 she co-founded, with Ian Gordon Brown, the Centre for Transpersonal Psychology, to which she remains a consultant. In 1995 she founded the Centre for Transpersonal Perspectives, London. She has a private practice in Chichester, Sussex.

Philippa Vick is a UKCP-registered transpersonal psychotherapist in private practice in London. She teaches her special interest in the energetic inter-relationship of psyche and soma on the CTP professional preparation. Her background is in Hakomi therapy, the work of Bob Moore and body/mind energetics therapy. Before and during training she practised traditional Chinese acupuncture.

Nigel Wellings is a UKCP-registered psychoanalytic psychotherapist and transpersonal psychotherapist in private practice in London. He is a director of the CTP psychotherapy training programme and a consultant, where he also teaches, supervises and runs workshops. Before training he painted Tibetan Buddhist icons, principally completing commissions for the books of Namkhai Norbu Rimpoche and members of the Dzogchen Community.

CHAPTER 1

Beginning the Work

Nigel Wellings and Elizabeth Wilde McCormick

This book offers an introduction to the theory and practice of transpersonal psychotherapy as it is currently being taught and explored at the Centre for Transpersonal Psychology in the United Kingdom. Bringing their own philosophical attitudes and clinical understanding, the authors of the nine chapters all contribute to the preparation of transpersonal psychotherapy practitioners. The book, reflecting the curriculum, is designed to be read as a process, taking students of psychotherapy through stages of awareness, awakening and understanding of the central principles of clinical practice. We begin with an understanding of the therapeutic relationship, seen as the vessel in which the transformative experience of therapy takes place. This is followed by an exploration of early childhood and the later presence of the child within the adult. Next, how life inevitably psychologically wounds us and the various patterns of adaption to the wound which gives rise to 'character styles'. Then to the initiations and demands of the adult life of men and women and a consideration of gender. Following this, a visit to the wisdom of the dreamworld and a challenging look at the connections, profundities and dangers of psychotherapy and spiritual practice. Finally we describe some techniques that may be used as an adjunct to the principle work.

To this work each contributor brings their own voice, expressing their own understanding of transpersonal psychotherapy and so readers are exposed to many different approaches to clinical practice, use of language and what is meant by the umbrella term 'transpersonal'. We believe that this celebration of difference and even discord creates a rich and honest soil from which, however difficult, inclusive of paradox, argument, and dissension, something interesting, heartfelt and vigorously growing will emerge.

A BRIEF HISTORY OF TRANSPERSONAL PSYCHOLOGY

The word 'transpersonal' was first used by William James in 1906, in his book *The Varieties of Religious Experience*. Dr Mark Epstein (1995) remarks that at this time James fully expected a psychology, which placed transpersonal experience at its centre, to have an influential voice during the next century, not knowing that Freud's psychoanalysis was to take this place. This voice took slightly more than sixty years to speak and finally came in 1969 with the American publication of the *Journal of*

Transpersonal Psychology edited by Anthony Sutich. The Editorial Board at this time included the well-known names of Roberto Assagioli, Stanislav Grof, Arthur Koestler, Abraham Maslow and Ira Progoff. The conceptual developments which preceded this were concerned with honouring the experience of states of being not recognized by other approaches to psychological thinking. Naming a psychology 'transpersonal' acknowledged these states of being in their own right, rather than their being reduced by interpretations from psychologies with a different philosophical outlook. Since this time the understanding of transpersonal experience has differentiated and evolved. This book continues, reflecting the process of development where every person who is drawn to the work must further explore and redefine their understanding, avoiding dogmatism and keeping the process of forging a relationship with the spirit of the work alive.

THE DEVELOPMENT OF TRANSPERSONAL PSYCHOLOGY IN BRITAIN

Drawn to this exploration, Ian Gordon Brown, Joan Evans and Diana Whitmore worked together with the Italian psychologist Roberto Assagioli, the father of psychosynthesis and one of the original pioneers in transpersonal psychology. Later they each returned to Britain and became the founders of three important Centres representing transpersonal psychology here. Whitmore founded the Psychosynthesis and Education Trust; Evans the Institute of Psychosynthesis and during 1973, Ian Gordon Brown, together with Barbara Somers, founded in London, the Centre for Transpersonal Psychology.

As well as his work with Roberto Assagioli, Ian was deeply involved with the Alice Bayley work and was also an industrial psychologist and founder of the Industrial Participation Association. Barbara brought twenty years' experience in Jungian psychotherapy and an interest in Tibetan meditation and Zen martial arts. Together they began the work of the Centre with a series of workshops reflecting these interests and drawing from their own creative understanding. In 1977 they began an informal training for professionals in transpersonal skills in counselling and psychotherapy, from which, eventually, over 500 people graduated. In 1997, after the unexpected and sad death of Ian Gordon Brown, the Centre's work was reconstructed upon the foundations Ian and Barbara had laid and these most recent developments in thinking and practices are contained within the chapters of this book.

TRANSPERSONAL PSYCHOLOGY AND PSYCHOTHERAPY

'Transpersonal' has become an umbrella term for naming those experiences where consciousness extends beyond (trans) the individual or personal. These experiences are filtered through the individual person, hence the word trans-personal rather than post-personal or non-personal. The wide range of human experience covered by the umbrella term 'transpersonal' and enquired about by transpersonal psychology includes the nature of the ego, spiritual emergency revealed in crises, illness and breaking down to breakthrough; in near death experiences and states of mind beyond 'normal' perception, as in the experience of aesthetic rapture, bliss, awe, ecstasy, wonder and reverence; in altered states of consciousness, such as pre-cognition, depth intuitions and transcendence; various states of consciousness generated by drugs, movement and breathing and finally meditative and contemplative practices. Transpersonal experience also includes states of enlightenment generated by these, experience of emptiness, of being at one with the universe, the giving and receiving of unconditional love and compassion for others and for life itself.

While transpersonal psychotherapy's theoretical basis stems from transpersonal psychology, transpersonal psychotherapists may also be influenced by any school of psychotherapy. It is equally possible to practise transpersonal psychotherapy from a psychoanalytic ground as it is from an existential or Jungian ground. It was for this reason that the original training was called a *perspective* that could be added to and would enrich any pre-existing theoretical orientation. However, at the Centre for Transpersonal Psychology a Jungian orientation has been largely dominant, though not exclusively, and now is beginning to open out with the presence of Buddhist psychology finding a greater voice. From this it will be clear that transpersonal psychology draws upon and uses what is really good and solid from a variety of philosophical approaches and it is because of this the contradictory ideas within Jung and Object Relations, Developmental Psychology and Archetypal Psychology, will all be found together. However, at its core is the understanding that human beings are capable of making a living and meaningful relationship with suffering, a process James Hillman calls soul making, and also have the capacity to step into states of 'spiritual' awareness that move beyond the ordinary everyday consciousness of personality. Because these states have been explored so fully and are usually the domain of religion, this may lead some to spiritual practices of prayer, meditation and contemplation outside and beyond therapy. This core belief means that a transpersonal psychotherapy practitioner, as well as sharing common psychotherapeutic aims, will also be open to the possibility of a patient awakening to, and inhabiting the wider transpersonal spaces within their being. For some people this alone brings about a state of healing, whether the outside circumstances are changed or not, because their fundamental attitude has shifted from unconscious victim to their own fears and desires into having an open and accepting relationship with all of life. Thus we become more than the sum of our problems. Furthermore, this can and does occur whether or not the idea 'transpersonal' is named, because the possibility for this sphere of experience is already within the psyche, ready to be recognized. This however is not to say that transpersonal psychotherapy encourages or approves of misusing spirituality to avoid the more prosaic but essential tasks of appropriate ego formation. It is fully cognizant of ego defences and therapeutic collusions representing themselves as spirituality.

DISCRIMINATING AWARENESS

The understanding and language of the transpersonal aspects of human experience has traditionally been carried by those most committed to the artistic and contemplative life, the poets, artists, visionaries and mystics, those who have honoured a creative and religious life. However, since these transpersonal aspects are part of the human psyche it is also appropriate for the more scientific approach of psychology to make them its proper business. The great test, for our current age of debate, and for the training of therapists, is to be able to objectively consider and subjectively enter the experiences under the transpersonal umbrella, thereby bringing science and art together. If we are to be able to speak authentically about the value (or not) of contemplation we must first explore it for ourselves, and then be objective about our experience. Perhaps the example of C. G. Jung is pertinent here. During his well recorded breakdown he became traveller, artist, observer and scientist. He was within the actual experiences of his breakdown descent, observing the pattern of his experience and recording images and dialogues in his notebooks. He later said that it was from this period of encounter with the unconscious that all his later (and greatest) work grew.

It is vital to become discriminating in our approach to transpersonal experience because these experiences are so often open to misinterpretation and self delusion. There is a great need for any enquiry to distinguish between pseudo spirituality, spiritual 'escapism' or 'tourism', and profound and authentic spiritual experiences. It is important too that spirituality and spiritual practice do not become psychologized because this gives too often a reductionist, pathologized view of what is a common and profound experience for many millions of human beings. Spiritual discipline, not unlike scientific research, demands rigour and attention, self-awareness and continual self-renewal. It demands that the ego personality ultimately enters into the service of the process of that which is trans-personal. Then the engagement of the two becomes the fulcrum for discovering what is real.

Transpersonal psychotherapists need to distinguish, in themselves and their patients, transpersonal or spiritual experience which has emerged from mature con-sciousness, the result of a stable ego system, and the longing of a fragile ego system to merge back or regress into an infantile state of fusion and bliss. The latter can lead someone to search for the all embracing, all loving, magical encounter with a perfect other where they feel special and saved. Serious psychological wounding and many addictions are the source of such longing and many psychological, religious and spiritual groups can be seen as the haven or heaven so desired. The test, to bring the longing inside, to withdraw the idealizing projections, to arrive at a more mature spirituality, occurs when the person questions the idealized other and begins to feel restless. Their struggle with their perceived 'saviour', sometimes a therapist, some-times an organization, sometimes a teacher, needs to become a heroic quest leading to separation and the maturity to stand alone and thereby relate more fully. If unrecog-nized and unconsciously acted out, this necessary challenge can result in expulsion from the chosen group and may cause personal alienation. As therapist, we need to understand this powerful regressive pull back into preconscious bliss, knowing it often has a fixated, urgent, unrelated quality because of its infantile nature, and help to both name the illusion of 'magical' holding and help build a strong enough ego within which the voice of the mature self may be heard.

MISUSE OF POWER

The therapist is a professional person designated by their training body as fit and qualified to share intimately the psychic world of another. To stand in the place of the Witness, Healer, Priest, Doctor, Father, Mother, and the energies constellated around these archetypes, both positive and negative. The practice of our craft, a curious mixture of art and science, rests more upon the nature of the person we are than any other profession. Our ability to sit 'well enough' with authority and power and have absolute integrity is a crucial matter because the power projected by the patient onto the therapist is so easily open to abuse. This abuse of power may take the form of over rigid adherence to some school or technique which creates the idea of the 'all knowing therapist', an expert treating the patient who knows nothing. Furthermore, practitioners who are not self aware, not mindful, not in self questioning dialogue with themselves and others, can so easily be seduced into identifying with the projections of another. This abuse of power may take the form of identifying with the idealized projections of the patient for the therapist's self gratification or by abandoning an angry, hating patient before these experiences have been worked through which then leaves that person with an even greater sense of worthlessness than they came with. Another is by responding to seductive overtures leaving no safe place for a patient to have their powerful erotic feelings respected, in their own right, without being taken advantage of. The same for 'falling in love', where the therapist is merely an 'agent' enabling the patient's capacity to be awakened into an experience of love that is a crucial part of coming home to themselves and to what for them is of the inner Beloved. Abusing power over these poignant and demanding feelings means that the patient remains stuck, or, worse, thrown back again into and compounding experiences of abuse.

Equally, and very much a danger for therapists who have gone into the profession to 'do good' is feeding upon another's need of one thus maintaining a state of dependency. Being drawn into the powerful web of a therapist for the therapist's own needs is the antithesis of relationship. The therapeutic relationship rests upon its boundaries and limitations and sees itself primarily as a vessel through which another person may pass into the love, inspiration and freedom of their own separate life. Appropriate separation is the goal of therapy – the one profession that works hard to make itself redundant! Since most of us have unfinished business with separation, whether from those who cared or did not care for us as infants, or from psychological structures that no longer serve us, the fact that therapeutic work must end and the relationship share a goodbye, offers an important 'model' for future relationships, whether with others or within oneself.

Particularly for us, in a therapy based upon a psychology which includes the possibility of spiritual awareness, this process of separation is crucial. To identify with the archetypes of the Priest and the Healer, the Wise Man or Woman, the Shaman and

Magician, is to lose touch with our humanity, and any ability we may have to be in relationship with another in such a way that healing takes place spontaneously will be lost or distorted. To avoid this we must be able to separate ourselves from the temptations of such inflation and the invitations to assume these inflated persona offered by some patients. Here, the practice of mindfulness, meditation and contemplation allows us to see clearly and sit back from archetypal inflammations of the ego and to behave in a rightful way towards others who approach us for help. The role of a transpersonal psychotherapist is to inhabit a mindful space in themselves first which will enable them to be able to be in this place with another, and to act as a sane midwife for the process in the other to unfold. Once born, the patient and their own unique attitude to spiritual awareness and practice, may (or may not) then take root in the world, and not at the feet of the therapist, in whatever system they find appropriate.

Power can also be used positively, but it is usually the kind of power that emerges from true compassion and is related to the power of mindfulness, clarity and love. If love is the main motivating factor behind the work of the therapeutic relationship, it is the love inspired by the process of the work itself. Such love is not to do with attachment but to the process of separation in order for there to be a coming together. Helen Luke observes: 'It is possible to glimpse for a moment that love which is personal involvement *and* impersonal detachment, each discriminated with the utmost exactitude and at the same time indissolubly one.' (1992, p. 170).

BEING PRESENT IN SUFFERING

At the heart of all psychotherapy is human suffering and an understanding of how this might be best helped. Throughout this book we will return to the belief that pain which becomes meaningful is more easily borne and may in time even open us to a greater sense of who we are. For this reason psychotherapy often seems a process of 'endarkenment' as we enter the underworld of our own shadow and confront the hidden fears that lurk within. It is important not to romanticize this. The fear can be so great that it is easily capable of keeping us frozen in a half existence for the rest of our lives. Frequently one may sit with someone who plainly understands how they have arrived at an untenable place in their life, who wants to move on and yet is utterly incapable of doing so until they find a way of being with their fear. Different methods offer different options here. It is not enough to simply intellectually understand our wounds and how they affect our lives. Rationality has little to no effect upon the unconscious. Nor is it the emotional expression of wounds that *finally* heals them (though it certainly gives some immediate relief). We all know of someone who has become an expert at catharsis and screams and shouts prodigiously but with no apparent change. This is because both the intellectual and the emotional methods take us away from the actual feeling and prevent us from being present with it. To be present with it means allowing the feeling to be felt fully, both as a feeling and as a sensation within the body; to feel its texture, its energy, its colour and shape, its sound and its movement and yet not to fall into it, to identify or act out of it. Discovering this method, one may be amazed at how an ill-defined sense of discord and irritation, once sat with, remaining present, opens out into a big spacious feeling that has complicated emotional currents running through it. Continuing to stay with these feelings, they began to spontaneously, without intention, dissolve and move on. This happens, not because of a desire for change, in itself a new source of conflict, but simply because emotions (and thoughts) stayed with in this way automatically move on, or 'self release'. By neither repressing emotion nor by unconsciously acting out emotion we make our own vessel of transformation where it is not the will of the ego that creates change but the greater nature that runs through us all. This method is a direct extension of the practice of mindfulness, seamlessly grafted onto psychotherapy, and as such promises to go further than just exchanging one set of emotions for another, but more profoundly, to reach to the heart of suffering and bring its release.

THEORETICAL AND PHILOSOPHICAL IDEAS

Transpersonal psychology draws from a variety of theoretical perspectives. Here we will look at some of the central ideas that occur in the subsequent chapters.

EGO

Ego means 'I'. As such it is the most familiar of psychological terms. Conventional psychotherapeutic wisdom has it that we must form a healthy ego during infancy and childhood if as adults we are happily to take our place in the world of work, relationships and family. This ego ideally should be a balance of openness and sensitivity to the unconscious while at the same time having sufficient robustness that it is neither distructively overwhelmed by either the world or its own shadow. Fundamentally a healthy ego is one that can be in the world and allow its boundaries to expand and dissolve at will and will not experience this as a psychotic breakdown. This understanding of ego will run throughout this book. Though perhaps not very deep, it is exceedingly useful and practical because the majority of people who come into therapy have either an ill formed ego or an ego that needs to be more open to its unconscious ground. It is perhaps because of this clinical reality that psychoanalysis has concentrated on the formation of ego at great depth and in great detail but has not gone much further than this. However transpersonal psychology, while freely using analytic ideas, also acknowledges and appreciates trans-egoic states of consciousness and additional ways of understanding the ego.

Mark Epstein (1998), expanding the conventional view, observes that our egos are actually made out of a complex set of self representations. He suggests that the ego is built up over a long period of time out of our interactions with others, the world and our own already existing self images. From these interactions we take away a self representation which is an image surrounded with value-laden emotions of who we are. If we consider for a moment we will see how we have an internal list of roles, characteristics, beliefs and values that we identify with (including identity based on spiritual beliefs and membership of 'spiritual' groups). Usually most of these are unconscious and remain so until some event occurs, and they become conscious through loss. Just imagine having to spend a cold and hungry night out on the streets alone and you will probably come up against many that otherwise would remain unchallenged. A patient once spoke of a decision he had made to leave his family and home abroad and return to England. Once he arrived he was utterly without any of the components of his life; no work, no partner, no child, no home, no recognition of role by a community. He said that he felt as if his life had suddenly become like the inside of a stainless steel drum, perfectly polished with no hand or foot holds and he was suspended within it without any connection. The feeling of this was terrifying, all his identity was stripped away and this was so unbearably painful that he very soon returned grateful and chastened to his original existence. We can understand this experience as one where the man's self representations, created by the relationship to the various parts of his life, were wiped out and the fear generated by being himself without them so great that it was unbearable.

Next, Epstein asks if the self representations, the flesh and bones of the ego, this sense of I, are in fact real. My patient very much believed that he had lost himself as he wandered disorientated and in emotional shock as a result of the sudden and total truncation of his familiar life, but actually he was not dead nor was he in limbo and he did have feelings, indeed a great deal of feelings. The problem was not that he had become a nothing, but that he did not know how to be with the new feeling of emptiness and this is what then caused fear and a regressive defence of returning to the familiar. This experience of the self representations, the components of self image, dropping away is not only a typical experience of loss and breakdown but also something actively pursued in insight meditation practice. Descriptions of this (Engler 1984) describe how under meditative analysis the self representations are seen to break down as the illusion of a self continuing in time melts away to reveal a space between the self representations (experienced as thoughts, emotions and fantasies about ourselves and our lives), that is full of consciousness, yet empty of self.

At this point transpersonal psychology may point beyond conventional psychotherapeutic understanding of ego and say that there are many different descriptions of states of consciousness that remain cognizant but free of self representations. That these states are generated by psycho/physical disciplines and they represent themselves generally as the real or natural nature of the mind. That in effect the self representations are a delusion and that the state of underlying clarity is who we *actually* are. This idea will be followed up in Chapter 9 where we will also see how this understanding may be transferred into the practice of psychotherapy. If many of us enter psychotherapy because either our self representations have not properly or fully formed or that formed they have been disrupted, then perhaps a transpersonal approach not only includes establishing realistic self representations, thus creating a healthy ego, but more than this, also enables the patient to at least glimpse the transpersonal state 'beneath' the self representations so that we may know that this is not annihilation but actually a momentary connection to the ground of being. As we will see, techniques such as unconditional presence may facilitate this as does the Buddhist method of insight meditation mentioned above.

THE SHADOW

The shadow, a term coined by C. G. Jung, is used in several different ways. Sometimes it signifies those experiences and feelings that are inconsistent with the adaptions that the conscious personality, the ego, has to make on the path of individuation. As we will see later, some frustration is actually desirable and we are entirely capable of receiving it and using it for our own good. Indeed, we can only have an ego in direct proportion to the material we repress in the shadow. However too much frustration, not being nourished, not being allowed to assert and separate, not receiving the right messages about our place in the family, all cause parts of ourselves either not to form or, once formed, be lost. These experiences occasionally are emotionally traumatic but more frequently come as a more subtle and all pervasive 'atmosphere' of fear. The ego, to defend its sense of invulnerability, must repress such feelings into the shadow. As such the shadow is partially synonymous with the personal unconscious and is the repository of the autonomous complex structures that are built up around experiences (each having an archetypal core) and the feelings (good and bad) that are associated with them; some are accessible to consciousness, some not. It is this notion of the unconscious that psychoanalytic understanding accepts.

A second use of the term shadow not only includes the personal unconscious but the collective unconscious as well. While the personal unconscious comprises personal experiences the collective unconscious contains the archetypes. I will explore these more fully below but what is important here is to say that the shadow in this way also includes the anima and animus, the Self and also other images of the universal experiences we may all be touched by. Thus the shadow does not only contain repressed material but also material *in potentia* and as such, the ego's anxiety about the shadow may not just be a fear of overwhelming painful feelings but also of a fuller self it has yet to become. Indeed, in practice, these two may actually be the same thing. For example, the redemption of a powerful sense of self assertion from within a self punishing personality is both claiming something repressed in the personal unconscious and also expanding into a potential, contained within the archetype of the Self, yet to be realized. This broader understanding of personal and collective levels of the unconscious is entirely Jungian.

ARCHETYPES

Over many millions of years universal experiences such as birth, pairing and mating, survival and death have in turn become an integral part of human nature. These universal dispositions are innate and structure the pattern of our lives and may be called archetypes. Though we cannot see an archetype, because it is not a 'thing' but a function, we can know of its existence by deduction as it is evident through its manifestation. This patterning function we call the *archetype per se* and its two areas of manifestation are as *instinct* and *archetypal image*. Thus we can say that the aims of the instincts are evoked and represented by the archetypal images. For example, the universal *instinct* to find another and continue the species is reflected in universal *images* of the Beloved Other. The universal *instinct* to mother is reflected in the universal *image* of Mother and Child. The image speaks in the language of symbol and so we can say that there are archetypal symbols or that symbol is the language of the archetype. As such, gods and goddesses become metaphors for our human behaviour and myths are archetypal enactments. Furthermore, C. G. Jung believed that the structure and dynamics of the psyche are governed archetypally and this is reflected in the inner images of the persona, the shadow, anima and animus and the Self in all their varied symbolic representations.

Archetypes may not be experienced directly. As the skeletal form of experience they are clothed in our individual experiences which gives the universal pattern personal form. Indeed the very process of psychological maturation is defined by the extent that the ego has differentiated itself from the collective pattern, through the process of individuation, and has the ability consciously to choose how much and which archetypes will influence it. An example of this would be the conscious choice made by a woman not to have children, thus largely disidentifying with the archetype of the mother, and perhaps instead, under the aegis of Athene, a symbolic representation of feminine analytical intelligence and competitiveness, perfect her professional life. Or again, a man recognizing a mass rally becoming archetypally possessed and choosing to walk away alone. Having said this it is also impossible ever to be free from archetypal influence and all personal material will have an archetypal core which will continue to exert powers of fascination and will sometimes overwhelm the will and the emotions, causing an inflation of the ego (think here of falling in love). This is most likely at times when the ego is particularly fragile, times of stress, of inner and outer crisis, or times of rapture and delight, naturally or artificially induced. Fundamentally a balance is needed, too much identification with archetypal material will create an inflated personality that has little personal expression or experience, a state associated with immaturity and madness. Too little connection to archetypal material will create a lifeless personality that will feel estranged from its source and may be plagued with a longing for renewal.

Ken Wilber has expanded these Jungian ideas and suggests that there are 'true archetypes'. He argues, drawing on mystical philosophy, that out of Emptiness, the fundamental state of reality, emerge the first forms which all subsequent and lower forms reflect and upon which their existence is dependent. He says:

> Those forms are the actual archetypes, a term which means 'original pattern' or 'primary mold'. There is a Light of which all lesser lights are pale shadows, there is a Bliss of which all lesser joys are anaemic copies, there is a Consciousness of which all lesser cognitions are mere reflections, there is a primordial Sound of which all lesser sounds are thin echoes. These are the real archetypes. (1996, pp. 217–18)

This more ancient view is placed within Wilber's notion of the 'Spectrum of Consciousness' that will be touched upon in Chapter 9. Here he suggests that there exist various bands of manifestation that become progressively more concrete as they *appear* to devolve from pure consciousness. The first wave of manifestation he calls the Transpersonal Band and the content of this band are the 'true archetypes' mentioned above. Unlike Jung, he believes that these archetypes may be experienced directly, not simply through their manifestation, and that this may be achieved within the deepest and most sublime states of contemplation. He says:

> These archetypes, the true archetypes, are a meditative experience, and you cannot understand these archetypes without performing the [meditative] experiment. They are not images existing in mythic worldspace, they are not philosophical concepts existing in rational worldspace; they are meditative phenomena existing in subtle worldspace. (1996, pp. 217–18).

For us this is an interesting emphasis. Although, remembering Jung's original definition, that archetypal activity revolves largely around collective yet personal instinctual drives and their symbolic representation, it is also true that within these simple biological imperatives exist intimations of something more. Perhaps this is alluded to in the alchemical symbolism that takes the common stone and finds within it the philosophic healing stone, the lapis. So although the archetypes are wedded to the instinctual demands of nature, they also carry the possibility that this instinctual life may be made sublime. Certainly this is true of the archetypes of the anima and animus and the Self, all of which not only govern the outer reality of biological pairing and copulation but also, as an inner reality, a longing for and experience of union with the Other that, if realized, creates spiritual wholeness. Perhaps this is where the link to Wilber's understanding may be made. Not sharing Jung's anxieties about practising meditation he is able to recognize that entering the contemplative state gives experiencial access to the 'true' archetypes. This process demands a dissolution of ego boundaries and the entering into non-dual consciousness and so represents going much further than simply realizing the biological potential of the archetype through developing a healthy instinctual ego. Consequently, we may think of the archetypes not just as a common soil from which we all grow in individual ways but also as common seeds that may be cultivated into something divine. As such archetypes are not just prepersonal, blueprints of universal activities, but also transpersonal, essential symbolic potencies that trans-egoic states of consciousness give access to and which, metaphorically, call from our deepest selves. Thus we may conclude that there are in fact two levels or experiences of archetypes, those that are the first spiritual forms and those that, further down the chain, are collective nodal points that human 'non-spiritual' experience gathers around; one perspective is transpersonal and one prepersonal.

THE SELF

We will see a variety of meanings clustered around the word 'self'. The first is designated by a small 's' and means the total person, including persona, ego and the unconscious. This self is not a static entity but develops and evolves through the individuation process. Establishing this self initially through ego formation and finally through ego expansion and dissolution may be considered the ideal goal of life. It is this usage of self, inclusive of ego and the unconscious, that psychoanalytic literature is usually referring to though without including the idea of its final dissolution.

The second meaning is designated with a large 'S'. Here Self is understood as the archetype that provides the foundation of the ego complex and as such is the 'blueprint' for the personal self referred to above. This archetype reveals itself in our need and ability to find and make meaning from the chaos of our lives and the world around us. This includes the ability to perceive and experience the numinous, the felt presence of divinity and spirituality, and for this reason Jung has called the Self, the God image in the psyche. Finally as the God image it must by definition be greater than the ego and so descriptions of it become paradoxical as they approach its ineffability. Hence it is both the centre and the periphery of the psyche simultaneously. This concept is Jungian and has been largely absorbed by transpersonal psychology at the Centre for Transpersonal Psychology as a synonym for 'The Transpersonal'.

The third use is 'no-self'. When this is referred to (principally in Chapter 9), what is meant is that when ultimately viewed there is nothing within us that can be seen as some essential personal part that has an ultimate, real or unchanging nature. That notions of a soul, a spirit or a Self do not under contemplative investigation reveal some part of us that is eternal and divine. This of course is the Buddhist doctrine of *anatta*, no soul or self, and it finds a place here because transpersonal psychology in America has been greatly influenced by Buddhist psychology which has, following Wilber, placed archetypes and transpersonal experience as penultimate to a final state of (no-self) spiritual realization.

AN ALTERNATIVE MAP OF UNCONSCIOUS PROCESS

John Welwood (1977) refines our understanding of the ego's relationship to unconscious processes. He distinguishes between 'focal attention' which rests upon a never ending series of subjects (as you read you are using this focal, or focused attention on the ideas in this sentence), and 'diffuse attention' which perceives experiences as a whole. His example is listening to music. Focal attention pulls out one part by concentrating on it. Diffuse attention simply takes in the whole. However, we are doing this all the time: as we focus we are also, via diffuse consciousness, receiving vast amounts of information. He imagines this diffuse attention in layers and calls these a series of 'grounds', each contained within a larger one beneath and around it.

The first level he names the *Situational Ground* which carries what Gendlin calls the 'felt sense' (see Chapters 9 and 10). The felt sense is the sum of all the unspecific understanding and feeling we have around that which we focus on and which gives it a 'felt meaning'. Think here of your response to reading this book again. Behind what you specifically think and feel about it exists a whole 'fuzzy feel' that makes it different from other books you have previously read. A more usual name for this ground is the concept of the preconscious.

Beneath this and wider is the *Personal Ground* which is a little less accessible. Here all the events that have shaped our personal self, influence our experience in a background way. Conventionally this would be called the personal unconscious but here we want to get away from the image of a hidden box full of complexes and rather emphasize the dynamic and momentary interaction of this ground as an active participant in perception, interpretation and understanding of the world and experience. Furthermore, this ground has the ability to correct focal attention by adding to it unnoticed information. This is the 'holistic tendency' that Jung attributed to the Self and which is demonstrated in the compensation of dreams and other personal ground activity.

Beneath this the widest level and more inaccessible still is the *Transpersonal Ground* which has two aspects, one corresponding to our 'bodily orientation to the world' and the other 'the forward impetus of the organism'. This transpersonal ground is the place where we are embedded as an organism in the environment and are archetypally organized. The first aspect is simply that our human body influences how we experience and the significance we attach to this. In that our bodies are universally found they are archetypal and as archetypes they organize perceptions into patterns that accrue personal experience around them. For instance, the physical fact that our head is above our torso gives rise to images of up and down and then to all the collective and personal associations that go with these two words.

The second aspect, 'the forward impetus of the organism', is that which 'continually functions as a background guide and inspiration for the individual's growth'. This is not to be thought of here as some sort of intention that emanates from the Self but rather as a relationship with the broadest and deepest spectrum of perception that makes available to consciousness 'sudden insights, inventions, creative inspirations, dream visions, [and] inspirations'. Again this is not something hidden in our depth but the very broadest ground of diffuse attention at work. Direct experience of this may be obtained through contemplative practice where it is found as a unitary state with oneself and the world. Buddhist psychology has described this as the first stage of manifestation, the *alayavijnana*, the realm of the true archetypes Wilber describes above and experientially it may be felt as 'the sheer vividness of being-here that underlies and surrounds . . . experience'. Conceiving of this as a usually unconscious experience of *relationship* takes us away from the idea of archetypes as inborn structures or contents of the collective unconscious.

Finally we come to the *Basic Open Ground*. This is defined as 'pure immediate presence before it becomes differentiated into any form of subject–object duality'. Reading this I am reminded of the Tibetan notion of *hedewa* which observes that for a split second after a shock, in the disorientated state, we have direct access to the pure nature of the mind, here called basic open ground. Have someone shout at you unexpectedly and you will directly understand this. This experience, not particularly esoteric, is going on all the time but we simply do not notice it. This is because in every moment this naked state is continuously and instantly clothed in thoughts and feelings as it arises. It is the fabric of this that we come to believe is ourselves (self representations) and in this way we keep the illusion of ourselves going. However meditation practice finally leads into direct knowledge of this state by creating a gap in the stream of contents and then contemplation enables us to remain in pure presence effortlessly.

One importance of this alternative map is that it represents transpersonal and enlightened states, not as numinous contents rising out of the collective unconscious, which would imply that they are somehow contained and latent within it. But more

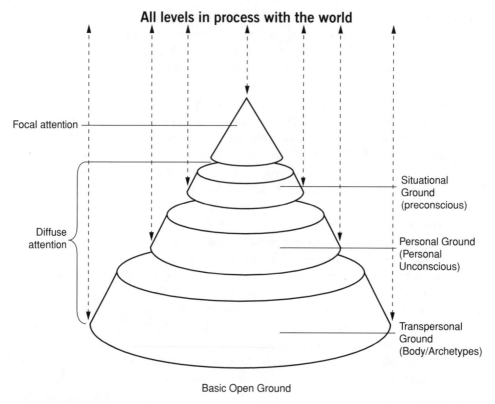

Figure 1 Welwood's model of unconscious process

accurately as the basic 'stuff' that underlies the progressive levels of manifestation that we believe to be ourselves. Thus Welwood can summarize by saying 'Awareness begins with openness, becomes humanized at the transpersonal level, individualized at the personal level and particularizes at the situational level'. Furthermore, this has clinical implications, the least not being that fear of the unconscious here becomes fear of the egolessness of the basic open ground. Something the man who returned to England and mentioned above knew all too painfully.

THE EDINGER MAP

Edward Edinger (1992, p. 5) reminds us of the classical Jungian theory that the first half of life is primarily concerned with the emergence of the ego from the Self while the second half concerns the ego returning to the Self, but on return, ideally conscious of its union.

In this process we see at the first stages the ego moving from a total identification with the Self to a point at midlife where ego and self are most estranged. At this point necessity creates an opportunity for ego and the feelings of alienation may spur the ego to try to reclaim some of its lost energy. If this is so a reconnection with the Self, obtained via many means, therapy among them, may begin to establish a ego/Self axis that acts as a connecting dialogue between the two. This creates an ongoing homeo-stasis, a self regulating psychological balance, that evolves, by the end of life, as a spiritual experience of universality as ego and Self unite consciously.

Edinger, acknowledging the work of Michael Fordham (1957), also notices that within each lifetime the ego repeatedly disintegrates and reintegrates with the Self as a source of psychological nourishment. Here we need to think of going to sleep, of mental breakdowns that become breakthroughs, of meditative practices that dissolve ego boundaries, of any event that transforms the ego by enlarging it with the potential held within the Self. As such we need an image that is more than a linear journey through life but one that is a continual alternation between Self and ego and which spirals along.

Looking at this map critically we can see that it offers some useful ways of thinking about common experience. It is certainly true that we are renewed by relaxing our self image and allowing something new in and that the middle of life may become a wasteland for some which is cured by creative work, paying attention to dreams and other unconscious expressions and practising some form of religious or spiritual discipline. However, against this is the empirical observation by psychologists of infant development which has challenged the belief that the ego is identified with the Self as this idea suggests. This question comes up in several later chapters, either explicitly or implicitly, and on balance remains unanswered because while it is true that a tiny infant does reach out immediately in such a way that suggests she is already a separate being, to what extent this demonstrates her own experience of herself as separate must remain unknown.

A second line of criticism, this time philosophic, would also question the mythic assumption in this idea which is entirely based upon the belief that life is a journey. While this is obviously true in a biological sense it may not be so true in a spiritual sense. The Zen understanding of the Gateless Gate tells us that while we remain unconscious of our already existing pure nature we imagine that it is somewhere other than where we are and so continue to search in the hope of finding it. However, once found by entering the state of non-dual consciousness, we look back and see that the gate we passed through, on the enlightened side does not exist. In this way the idea is a product of unenlightened mind and may also do a disservice by adding weight to the delusion that what we search for is somewhere else.

GOING SOMEWHERE AND BEING ALREADY THERE

The idea above leads us to touch upon the two great mythic rivers that have flowed down through the religious systems of East and West. We in the West have come to be identified with the heroic archetype that quests for a longed for other. Plato's story of an original being with four arms and four legs split asunder by the gods and doomed ever to wander in search of its other half speaks of this. This has given rise to the notions of a journey leading to the Beloved, the Supreme God, and that a relationship coloured with longing for this god, perhaps reflected in a far country, a mythic city or a Lady, gives meaning and purpose to the hero's challenging journey. Many personal journeys mirror this archetypal journey and in the traditions of Judaism, Christianity and Islam we find saints and sinners struggling to come to their own relationship with God. From this it is also clear that modern psychotherapy continues within this mythic constellation.

Against this, a far older tradition, primarily expressed by Hinduism and Buddhism, speaks of divinity as ultimately an abstract state that is never anywhere other than where we are now. What prevents us from recognizing it is our own blindness and both systems have devised methods of spiritual discipline to help us see, to help us Awake. As the famous Zen saying has it, 'If you see Buddha on the road, kill him'. Not only does this tell us that all conceptions of the awakened state are false but perhaps also that that found on paths is of no worth and even may be a danger if it takes us out of the eternal present.

In this book these two myths duck and dive through each other. Mainly the Western myth of journey will be most visible, perhaps because psychology as a Western animal is so shot through with the heroic that it is difficult to conceive of anything without it. However, as the book progresses the second myth becomes more apparent until finally, following some American transpersonal psychologists, it provides a profound understanding of dualism and the path out of suffering. Wherever we speak of emptiness, no-self, mindfulness, presence, bare attention, meditation and contemplation, all of these are drawn from and reflect the Eastern, and particularly the Buddhist, traditions.

THE JOURNEY OF THE SEED

This is a poetic image and as such is a description of feeling. Many of us entering therapy will complain of feeling that we are somehow not in the right place or have come out of familial circumstances that feel they have nothing to do with us. Perhaps the frequent fantasy of children and adolescents that their parents are not their own is more than a struggle to accept reality beyond narcissistic grandiosity and truly tells of feelings of personal estrangement. The metaphor of the journey of the seed addresses this.

In this we assume that at birth there was a seed that contained our 'true nature' and that given the right environment it would grow and flourish as a realization of the potential within it. Here we are not talking of the seed as the universal potential of our species that each of us all carry but more personally, *my* seed holding *my own* unique potential. Let us say that this seed was of an orange tree, something a little exotic that needs warmth to grow. However, landing in a cold and inhospitable place, unsuitable for its nature, it suffers a series of frustrations that distort its natural growth and turn it into a stunted and sick plant instead. A mere shadow of what it could be. Examples of this may be a scientifically inclined child landing in a family of artists who are anti-science or a very tactile child born into a physically reserved family.

In this way many of us have not had the nourishment to become what we have the ability to be. In many of the chapters these developmental arrests are described in different ways and all share the basic belief that it is possible to return to the seed, the undeveloped possibilities of the unrealized child, and restart or catch up with the process of healthy expression. Initially this may be very painful because it will mean cutting back the straggly growth, a process frequently started by loss or breakdown, but once the space is made new growth may then appear.

What is also particularly interesting in this is the idea of a 'true self' that is in some way personal and present at birth. This goes beyond conventional psychotherapeutic understanding because it is saying more than we have an individual character already in the womb or that we carry familial dispositions genetically. Rather it suggests the idea of reincarnation and the karmic creation of personal characteristics from one life to the next. Jung himself dabbled with this idea in his introduction to the Tibetan Book of the Great Liberation (CW 11 para. 759–858) but was fearful of the accusation of holding the then unfashionable belief of Lamarckianism which held that personal qualities could be inherited. More recently Roger Woolger (1994) has explored the possibility of past life regressions that among other explanations leaves open the door to reincarnation as an actuality. Others, often influenced by Buddhism and Hinduism, as an article of faith, will have no trouble with this and will happily embrace the theory of reincarnation as an obvious truth. However, even if we accept reincarnation, and consequently personal characteristics appearing at the beginning of one life as a result of the last, this does not answer *what or who is reincarnating*. Hinduism offers the view that there is a personal self, the *atman*, that continues through many, many incarnations moving ever towards the light as wisdom is accrued. For many Westerners, harbouring unconsciously the Christian promise of heaven and perhaps Western Spiritualist beliefs, this is familiar and answers the question with the reply that the true self is the soul and it is this which is reincarnating. However Mark Epstein, a Buddhist psychotherapist who has contributed extensively to the field of transpersonal psychology, offers another reply when he writes:

> When asked by one of his Western students puzzling over the Buddhist teaching of egolessness [no-self], 'Well if there is no [true] self, what is it that then reincarnates?', the Tibetan lama Chogyam Trungpa laughed and answered without hesitation. 'Neurosis' he replied. (1998, p. 86)

Perhaps what finally matters, whether we call that which we arrive with a personal divine spark or a bundle of karmic traces or indeed a combination of both, is that there is something quite unique about all forms of life. As psychotherapists we honour this, knowing whatever the nature of the seed, that as a poetic entity it speaks of a promise that is also a wound, that seems lost and yet may be found again.

MYSTERY

However, finally not all things can be understood, which is possibly a relief, and what remains unknown remains a mystery. There is *mystery* in the exchange within the therapeutic relationship. We can never know how far or where a client may take us.

Therapists work with the unknown; they have to be prepared to be surprised. Sometimes, soon after therapists find themselves wondering: 'Has this person moved as far as they need to do for now?' or, 'I wonder if they are getting ready to finish?', they have a dream, a revelation, or meet a new person and this brings them into another understanding. The mystery is in how these two parts, the therapist's thought and the unfolding synchronous events of the client are related. We don't have to have an answer but be mindful and happy in our not knowing. Buddha himself refused to be drawn on the origins of the universe; perhaps he was happy to leave this as a mystery?

One story is of a woman who came with 'post traumatic stress' after a serious accident into therapy. She began to talk about ending therapy when she was feeling better after eighteen months. She felt she had been 'indulgent' enough. Then she had a dream about young children playing in a back garden who became separated from her, suggesting that she had become estranged from the playful and creative forces of renewal and growth within her own psyche. The quality and meaning of the dream offered her an awakening experience that changed her attitude to herself. From the symptomatic relief of 'getting over a past serious situation' she moved into reverential exploration.

A different story is of a young nurse who had been severely depressed for a long time and was on heavy medication. During her therapy she went into deep descent and did not move beyond the process of living in a very dark place during her five years of therapy. Her survival through the most annihilating inner experience is one mystery, and in this case the therapeutic relationship was a vital, but mysterious link with an 'unconditional life' as she was exploring it for herself. It is hard to name accurately the process that differentiates these two different experiences. All people use therapy in their own way and we must make no value judgement about it.

Another mystery is the issue of timing. A therapist may say the same thing to a client on many occasions and it seems to go unnoticed. Then one day the person comes in all excited, having read something similar, or the very thing itself, in a book or being told it by an enlightened other, and it's as if they have stumbled upon it for the first time. These mysteries demonstrate that the person is truly getting engaged in their own life and responses and not stuck in having to take the therapist's word for it.

Therapy needs not to make its users feel inferior because they have not become enlightened or got angry enough, nor its therapists fall into dismay for lack of 'change'. There is an alarming and persistent myth about therapy that if you have had enough and with the right person you will be all sorted out. Failure to do so can feel like an attack upon one's experience and also leave one endlessly looking for 'perfect care' and for what is designated 'enough'. While it is fundamental for therapists to try and receive the best training we can, it seems equally important to enter into the mystery of the therapeutic exchange and allow the mystery itself to be a body of knowledge. Therapists learn far more from their own scientific enquiry and research as they are working and questioning each exchange with another than they do from textbooks or seminars. Their own commitment to the process of engagement, their curiosity and hunger to understand can be the mysterious 'x' factor that ignites the relationship into something nearer to healing than any formalized learning can teach.

REFERENCES

Edinger, E. F. (1992). *Ego and Archetype*. Boston and London: Shambhala.

Engler, J. (1984) 'Therapeutic Aims in Psychotherapy and Meditation: Developmental Stages of Representation of the Self', *Journal of Transpersonal Psychology*, **16**(1), p. 25.

Epstein, M. (1995). *Thoughts Without A Thinker*. New York: Basic Books.

Epstein, M. (1998). *Going To Pieces Without Falling Apart*. New York: Thorsons.

Fordham, M. (1957). *New Developments in Analytical Psychology*. London: Routledge and Kegan Paul.

Jung, C. G. (1969). *Psychology and Religion: West and East*. vol. 11 of *Collected Works*. London: Routledge and Kegan Paul.

Luke, H. (1992). *The Way of Discrimination in Kaleidoscope*. New York: Parabola Books.

Welwood, J. (1977). 'Meditation and the Unconscious, A New Perspective', *Journal of Transpersonal Psychology*, **9**(1).

Wilber, K. (1996). *A Brief History of Everything*. Boston: Shambhala.

Wilber, K., Engler, J. and Brown, D. P. (1986). *Transformations of Consciousness*. Boston and London: Shambhala.

Woolger, R. J. (1994). *Other Lives, Other Selves*. London: Aquarian.

CHAPTER 2

The Therapeutic Relationship

Elizabeth Wilde McCormick

Analysis/therapy is a process whereby a space is made in man/woman from whence God may speak. (Hermann Hesse)

Editor's note: When most people think back on a sustained period of psychotherapy it is their relationship with their therapist that remains most memorable. Within this complex, rich and sometimes troubling relationship is contained the whole of the therapeutic work and as a mirror it reflects the process of knowledge, transformation and healing. It is not insignificant nor exaggerated that C. G. Jung likened it to an alchemical process wherein that which is dark and poisonous is made sublime and cures all ills. In this chapter, Elizabeth McCormick takes us into this rare and precious exploration with another, showing something of its interior, its deeply personal, soulful quality and also the transpersonal, spiritual moments when presence lifts both therapist and patient into a place where striving to be other falls away. For the Transpersonal Psychotherapist and others sharing this perspective, the marriage of soul and spirit, bridged by image and contemplative silence and held within the vessel of the therapist's awareness, is the heart of the work.

N.W.

INTRODUCTION

What does it mean to sit in a room with another person where one of the chairs is assigned 'client' or 'patient' and the other 'therapist'?

The nature of the therapeutic relationship is a curiosity of our time. In the public arena it is increasingly the focus of litigation, of 'therapy junkies', of story, joke, and Hollywood movies. It is the one aspect of all approaches to therapy (currently in Britain there are 450 different kinds of therapy!) that research has shown is the determining factor in the process of change. It is unlike any other human relationship, intensely intimate, client revealing all to therapist who reveals little or nothing, and contained by professional boundaries. It can become a unique friendship within which the growth and exchange of love is possible.

The practice emerges historically from and shares elements of the confessional. The telling of secrets, the revelation and purgation of 'sin', the sharing of wounding and pain which is met by a trusted person in an 'officially' designated safe and sacred space. Being listened to and being heard, means being able to listen to oneself, and holds the potential to experience healing. Freud perhaps recognizing this said: 'I bind the wounds, God heals'. In terms of the secular therapeutic relationship the healing experience can come from the disappearance of one's presenting symptoms and from being offered a place where one may begin to be in alignment with one's 'self'. This 'knowing and accepting oneself as one truly is', is the foundation for moving into life differently from a life dominated by reactions to external problems.

Transpersonal psychotherapy recognizes the potential of the therapeutic relationship as it works towards making itself redundant as what transpires within the body of the work is internalized by the patient into a relationship with psyche, with spirit, soul and Self, and with life itself. The primary *use* of the human relationship is for the experience and integration of wholeness. This wholeness, projected onto the therapist and carried by the mysteriousness of the therapeutic relationship, is experienced and taken in by the patient in the service of their own individuation process. It is the passage to the glimpses of wholeness that transpersonal psychotherapy considers crucial. Healing is then composed of moments of reflection, an awareness of what we feel and think, focusing and imaging, a deepening of understanding by way of a 'felt sense' leading to a 'felt shift' (see Chapter 9) and beyond this moments of being non-identified with the personal contents of consciousness. Transpersonal experience at its most profound is where the subject/object division ends.

THE THERAPEUTIC RELATIONSHIP IN HISTORICAL CONTEXT

Towards the end of the last century, Freud made his extraordinary conceptual leap from a study of the human mind as a neurologist into a study of the unconscious. The mysterious and sometimes 'mystical' 'art' of the therapeutic relationship met the scientific medical model approach to human exchange. Freud seems to have been motivated by art and religion as well as by science and he possibly oscillated between their effects throughout his lifetime. In a 1934 interview with Giovani Papini he said that 'I am really an artist, a man of letters, though still in appearance a doctor'. He felt that his case histories should read like novels, and he was a good writer, drawing on the world of literature as well as science to give an accurate picture of a person's life. Contrary to the five times a week psychoanalytic model that has been strictly adopted by his followers, in early practice Freud was an advocate of brief therapy. Six or seven sessions were the norm in the early days, and he would walk about with his patients.

At first he regarded what he called transference as an obstacle to therapy and would have preferred to be regarded as a scientist or surgeon. He had been witness to the frightening effect of an eroticized transference onto his friend Breuer from Anna O. He later changed his view, but only went as far as developing his idea of the 'blank screen' approach onto which transference was projected – still avoiding the more intense intimate emotional contact with patients.

In 1907 when Jung first visited Freud in Vienna, Freud asked him what he thought of transference and Jung replied: 'it is the alpha and omega of treatment', to which Freud replied: 'then you have grasped the main thing' (Jung 1945). But they thought of it and developed it quite differently. For Jung, who drew his understanding of exchanges between human beings from a much wider symbolic realm than Freud –

from the collective, from archetypal structure, from religion and alchemy as well as medicine and story – the transference was only of value when it was spontaneous. He felt that it could not be contrived by 'blank screen' settings, nor could it be demanded. Such an enforced demand was akin to enforced faith – nothing but 'spiritual cramp' (Jung 1945, para. 359). Jung became more interested in the links between processes revealed by his alchemical studies, and the union of opposites within psychic life, in particular the union of masculine and feminine, of Eros and Psyche, in the coniunctio, or hieros gamos, the Divine Wedding.

Now, in classical psychoanalysis and therapies based only upon object relations theory, the main relationship is the transference relationship. The analyst or psychoanalytic therapist interprets all the material the patient brings as being to do with the therapeutic relationship. Any 'chance' remark, or 'ordinary' exchange – the 'hello' or 'goodbye' – is interpreted, or not engaged with except by silence.

At the most rigid end of the spectrum is the story of a practitioner who said that she was pleased to have got her work down to as little as three grunts per fifty minutes; and the analyst whose patient arrived having been in a car accident with his head bandaged which was not referred to at all. These experiences can be limiting, frightening, infuriating and disempowering and, as Jeffrey Masson (1988) writes in *Against Therapy*, 'deflect a person from deep reflection on the sources of human misery'.

Conversely, the silence and freedom from having to engage in any way can have a deepening and liberating effect. Marie Cardinale (1975) observes in *The Words to Say It*, 'That the least important symptom had meaning – for example, during this period of total silence, if I breathed a sigh, even a very little one, the doctor would say "Yes? . . . Yes?" as if to make me understand that there was perhaps an opening there, at the precise moment when I had uttered the sigh'.

Therapies that do not observe an opening silence so that the patient can move into their inner landscape directly without being deflected by 'social' exchange, run the risk of working only on a superficial level. If therapy becomes too 'chatty' it loses its professional edge and leaves the client feeling obliged, unable to get really cross or challenge or say what they really feel.

Since the 1960s we have seen the growth of humanistic, existential and transpersonal psychotherapeutic theories. All of these are based on a model that works largely in the present and assume an inherent move towards wholeness. Here the relationship between therapist and client is one of equality. Eugene Gendlin (1981) writes, 'The essence of working with another person is to be present as a living being. And that is lucky, because if we had to be smart, or good, or mature, or wise, then we would probably be in trouble'.

For the transpersonal psychotherapist the ultimate authority is the Self and it is the energy of the Self that guides where the healing needs to take place, which may be quite outside ideas of healing presented by the ego. In *Healing into Life and Death*, Stephen Levene (1989) writes about the ever present possibility for connecting to the energy we call transpersonal right up to and beyond the moment of death. His question, 'where does the healing need to take place?', is an important question for transpersonal therapists because it removes the focus of control from any social, medical, or therapist agenda for change and healing and allows for the Self to be honoured. In this way the therapist becomes an ambassador for the soul. Recognition of the hidden language behind presenting symptoms, seen and dignified (rather than reduced) as the artistry of survival helps to create the golden thread that leads the patient back to re-find their sense of self. When this is shared with another, in the intimacy of the exchange, in the privacy and freedom of the consulting room, the relationship moves from its professional and personal enclosure, into something limitless. When this is experienced by and owned by a patient, they have begun their own relationship with the intimate, private and individual world of spiritual connection. If transpersonal psychotherapy can be the bridge, then their own choice of spiritual practice will take their development further across the bridge between the two worlds.

Different again, yet in continuum, in therapies influenced by Buddhist psychology, the therapist's own mindfulness and compassion are essential. These qualities enable something of the 'ground of being' – the ultimate transpersonal state – to be present in the therapy, as well as a full sense of humanity. Buddhist psychology, unlike most Western psychology, contains a vision of complete healing. (Buddha-hood, to be fully awakened), that goes far beyond simply establishing a place in the world where one can satisfactorily function at work and within relationships. A therapist who shares this view will hold two levels of understanding. The first level is the conventional understanding that recognizes that some experiences, beliefs, feelings and thoughts cause less pain than others. At this level we then try to exchange the painful for the less painful, the destructive with the constructive, neurosis with individuation. By this means we embrace fully the complexity and richness of our individual lives by moving through fear. The second level is unique to the Buddhist and transpersonal perspective. It recognizes that the attempt to constantly exchange 'bad' experiences for 'good' is *ultimately* unsuccessful because continually trying to keep suffering at bay is simply impossible. To end suffering we must relinquish the drive for 'self-improvement' and instead remain mindfully with our experience *as it is*. The therapist who holds both these levels of understanding supports the development of a whole and healthy ego (level one) and also, when clinically appropriate, recognizes that ego dissolution (final goal of level two) is the deeper solution. In practice this will mean not only being mindfully present within the session but also facilitating methods (see Chapter 9), that increase the presence of the patient.

> The present moment is where life can be found, and if you don't arrive there, you miss your appointment with life. You don't have to run any more.
> Breathing in we say 'I have arrived'.
> Breathing out we say 'I am home'.
> (Hahn, 1991)

THE VESSEL OF THE THERAPEUTIC RELATIONSHIP

If the therapeutic relationship is to serve as an initiatory process for the ego it needs a vessel that will withstand the struggles and fragmentations of personality and difficult transferences, will be able to bear the chill winds or suffocating cloaks of the past, and the fiery rages when the heat is on. This vessel holds the potential for fantasy – how it might have been, how it could be; for illumination, change, for healing, for transformation and for the growth of love; for the ever present possibility of coming home to one's self and recognizing it as such.

An image for the vessel is important to us as therapists because when the heat is on it also contains us as well as our clients. One image for this is The T'ing, the Chinese cooking pot (*I Ching* hexagram 50) which invites us further into the imaginative process and tells us that 'Nothing transforms things as much as the T'ing'. This is because the process of 'removal of stagnating stuff' – the old habits and complexes by which we have survived but which now threaten or limit us – allows a space for a new sense of self to emerge. It also suggests a transpersonal element, 'All that is visible must grow beyond itself, extend into the realms of the invisible'. Here we see links between the T'ing and the alchemical flask where processes of change and transformation move base metal into gold. The different stages of the alchemical processes – calcinatio, solutio, coagulatio, sublimatio, morificatio, separatio and coniunctio, offer images of the different processes within a long therapy that help both client and therapist stay with the process as a whole (Edinger 1985). These include the initial strangeness, even alienation, the fears, the old patterns; the times of feeling stuck, trapped, or dissolved, lost, failing: wanting to give up and leave, acting out, the trying out of something new, feeling fragile, unprepared, the emergence of different attitudes.

The Vessel as Guardian of Boundaries

When men and women become medical practitioners they adhere to a principle going back to Hippocrates 'first, do no harm'. They are also influenced by the image of Aescelepius, the wounded healer whose own bleeding wound keeps him connected to the nature of woundedness, enabling him to offer healing to others and the Caduceus, carrying the two serpents of healing and poison, opposites in dualism, ultimately to be united. Therapists also serve professional statements of intent, a code of ethics and practice, which is built in to every professional training organization and can be seen as one of the guards to protect patients and therapists from harm. The *I Ching*, quoting Confucius, offers us an image for what happens when the contents of the vessel are spilled and the work is spoiled. This can be seen in therapeutic terms as a break in the therapeutic relationship due to the breaking of boundaries, misuse of power, or inappropriate behaviour by therapists. Confucius says about the spilling and breaking of the vessel 'Weak character coupled with honoured place, meagre knowledge with large plans, limited powers with heavy responsibility, will seldom escape disaster' (Hex. 50 Line 4 commentary).

Another guard comes from what we bring of ourselves to the therapeutic encounter. Being able to maintain appropriate 'inner' boundaries will be dependent upon our ability to know ourselves and acknowledge our own shadow. This will include the use of theory as a defence against the insecurity of not knowing. If therapists hold a rigid view about 'wellness' or 'cure' they come from a position of having a defensive agenda rather than being open to where the patient might take them. If we view the process of therapy as being that of the emergence of an unknown self we might liken the work to that of the midwife waiting upon the birth of an the unborn child. Other images are of the night watch, the witness, the guide.

Making Good Boundaries

The therapeutic relationship is *externally* guarded by standards of professional training, by adherence to a training body with a code of ethics, by the rules and structure of therapy, and by good supervision. The consulting room itself, the time and place of appointments, agreements over money, the working contract in terms of time, negotiations over cancellations, holidays and endings are also external guards. Guardianship and structure create an edge, something to rub up against, to protest against as well as to be held by. Unconscious life so often emerges in the cracks and divisions created by the agreed structure of the professional work. The challenges to structure by not turning up, by coming late, by not paying, all become an integral part of the work and need to be held by the structure that is being challenged. The structure allows for the rebel to emerge: 'the proof of my existence is my resistance'; for the hungry needy child to wail at an impending separation; for the neglected soul craving perfect care to be presented in non-payment of fees: 'If you really loved me you wouldn't expect me to pay'. And so often, the hidden agenda: 'If I'm late will you notice? will you punish me? will you allow me to be angry with you because of your demands?'

The therapeutic relationship is guarded *internally* by the therapist's ongoing self-regulatory systems of listening to themselves, meditative and contemplative practice and by drawing on the relationships with teachers, elders, and the ancestors, the wisdom of all those who have gone before us and whose teaching guides us. In practice this will include the therapist's own experience of therapy and its integration into their daily life and also use of discussion with colleagues and in supervision. Finally guardianship of the vessel of therapy comes down to our own integrity and honesty and the quality of awareness and presence that we bring to the work. These are the stepping stones of good practice for becoming a therapist.

The Vessel as Facilitating Environment

For the therapeutic relationship to flourish, the vessel needs to be what D. W. Winnicott calls 'the facilitating environment'. It is a place where we are held safe, protected, where past hurts and woundings are accepted and contained. We need a place where, if needed, we may safely regress in order for early wounds to be witnessed by an other, the therapist, who can be alongside them, is not afraid of them or sits in judgement of them. In reconnecting safely with images and energies of early life we, as patient, may also begin being alongside our own wounds, and know that they are not the lethal, desperate, rejectable demons we have believed them to be, that in the process of befriending them they become less absolute, less demonic.

Recognizing the need for holding – as if the person in the room were indeed a very small infant, taking the small faltering steps of an infant learning to walk, talk, smile, is the business of the relationship. The therapist's language, posture, tone of voice all need to reflect this understanding of the moments when these aspects of the patient are manifest. The vessel becomes a place to speak the unspeakable and be believed, to be heard, a place to experiment, play, redress a balance. In this 'facilitating environment' we may experience the unspoken developmental process of becoming. Through being seen and accepted we move into being safe enough to grow into who we really are, and then are able to leave the therapeutic vessel of relationship behind, because we hold it in ourselves.

Creating the Vessel of the Facilitating Environment

Therapists draw upon their professional training and personal experience of therapy and ordinary life when creating the facilitating environment. Before any relationship of any kind can get under way, a comprehensive understanding of the internal structures which dominate early patterns of relating need to be understood. The training's theoretical content helps to name the wounds which underlie suffering involved in relationship, and offers an understanding of the nature of these wounds in order to create the continuity of being needed for healing. A person who has experienced a highly critical early life, who sees their life always through the lens of the criticizing other and carries the wound of the crushed criticized child will need an experience of an unconditional environment in order to be safe enough to relax. Transference invitations for the therapist to embody the critical other will need to be recognized so that this too can be named and the patient begin to understand their involvement in maintaining the dynamic of criticism. In this way therapists bring into the vessel what Petruska Clarkson (1995) refers to as the 'developmentally needed relationship'.

Winnicott's transitional object – the infant's first creative act of individuality and separation – may emerge within the relationship by using the therapist's voice, their sayings, or actual objects in the therapist's room that are taken into the patient's psyche and pondered on between sessions. My own experience of this came when I became aware of carrying the image of the coloured pencils that stood in a jar on the table between the analyst and myself. At first I just knew that I liked them, and that they carried a certain energy. One day as I sat in the room and during a fairly long silence (something quite painful for me which I then associated with disapproval) I looked at the pencils and realized, excitingly, that they were for my own use. I could, if I wished, take hold of them and draw something. I made a transition from the position of the frozen-out disapproved of child waiting to be told off to an act of spontaneous freedom. Soon after this time I began painting again in my own time after an absence of five years.

Patients need to know their therapist is there for them, in that room at the appointed hour, regularly in the same rhythm and continuum as if at their birth. Therapists stand in for the good enough other not experienced in early life. The experience of a containing other comes either through individual therapy (or through another form of relationship), and helps develop the ability to be able to hold the thread for another and rejoice in their unfoldment.

An example of the effect of simply being there every week in therapy was a young man who came to see me about his cleaning phobia. He had to get up in the night to clean the bath several times. Also, an issue for him was not knowing whether he wanted a homosexual or heterosexual relationship. He had married young 'on automatic', and worked in design. When he arrived for his first session he was wearing a lemon cat suit and ballet shoes. He had long flowing hair. He was extremely nervous and moved a lot as if trying to avoid being trapped, or some kind of target. I felt a bit like an attacker but had no way of speaking of this to him at first. He settled down into 'becoming' after we had our first important connection. I had asked him to draw the image of the corn bin he referred to a lot. As he drew the crayon over the paper he said 'oh, I know, it's all this stuff here inside me I'm afraid of isn't it?' Our eyes met, and in the silence we shared his movement into being alongside his own inner reality, his own pain, with his friend the crayon as the initiator.

Part of the story he brought was being abused by a scoutmaster over a period of six years. He carried shame and guilt from that time, fear of attack from others to whom he might get close. He felt he had taken flight into an early marriage to hide away from his male abuser. We worked to put together the scattered jigsaw puzzle of his early life. He wrote, brought in photographs, we checked dates by tracing people, the clothes he was wearing at the time, pop music in the charts, his parents' various moves, his father's death. At the end of the eighteen months we worked together, the realization was that the abuse had in fact taken place over a period of summer camp and during six weeks of one particular summer. But the space it took up in his psyche was much vaster and dominant. His relief at this reality was profound, as was the choice he now felt he had about his sexuality.

The Vessel as Transformational Space

For John Welwood (1994) emotions begin to flow as blood shed by the ego, whenever the shell around the heart is punctured. Our suffering, maintained by the defences, our earliest protections, opens to give access to levels of feeling and struggle that have hitherto been masked by attitudes, behaviours or symptoms. Symbolically these break us open in order to have the possibility for spaciousness around the heart. The return to the heart, to an experience of self that has always been present can feel like a transformation. This transformation is to do with the ordinary, to coming home to who we really are, and part of this may be the potential to connect to something beyond the everyday.

Throughout his work Abraham Maslow writes about making the growth choice towards self actualization. 'In letting go, all that is sacrificed is the attachment to the situation'. Christopher Bollas (1989) speaks of the transformational 'object', as an existential rather than representational knowing. That is, mother, or whoever was mother, is experienced as a continual process of transformation, before she is perceived as a provider of nourishment and frustration. It is as if the infant has at her core the ability and yearning for transformation that is brought into being by relationship.

Making Space for Transformational Potential

The *way* therapists move through the space of the vessel, mirroring the self, mirroring the everyday being, that the person is more than the sum of the many parts, or many symptoms, holds the potential for awakening that transformational object that as adults we search and yearn for. This way holds open possibilities for meaning that are the patient's own meaning, to which they make their own connection. A Transpersonal Psychotherapist has within their theory and practice the intention of including and moving beyond the limits of the ego boundaries into the spaces within that allow for reflection upon the experience and the boundlessness of the numinous. This may be a soulful experience of being held in the dark moisture of the depths of suffering and finding something in that darkness that calls to us of its essence, its meaning. It may be in the rising of the spirit, something I experienced early on after an analytic session when I found myself driving away from the session listening intently to a Puccini aria I knew well but it was as if I had never heard it so vividly. It seemed to enter into my being so that I and it were one. I had to stop the car on the side of the road and just listen. The experience lasted perhaps four minutes. I spoke of it the following week in therapy and my experience lived again, between us.

Returning to the image presented by the I Ching, the vessel may be experienced as having 'golden handles and being carried'. Perhaps this suggests that when the therapeutic vessel feels more portable, there is a sense of it being internalized within the patient, becoming the patient's own safe place for alignment with the Self and with the presence of the therapist internalized as part of their own compassionate observer. In the hexagram's last line it mentions jade, the most durable substance which has a beautiful colour and lustre. This could be likened to an experience of that which is most precious, the jewel, the pearl of great price, that the transformational space of the vessel reveals when it has completed its work.

What do we Bring to the Vessel of Ourselves?

The therapeutic vessel created by each encounter will be unique. It will be forged by what the therapist brings to it – from training, from supervision, their own therapy and from all the aspects of life as human beings; and by what each patient brings into it, from their own history, life drama, personality, self and unconscious.

Here are some of the qualities and capacities that I think are important for a therapist to develop, and which assist in the process of forging the vessel of relationship:

Respect for the outer and inner life of the individual, in whatever way this is presented. The seed of the individual may throw up peculiar fruits as its growth twists and turns around its environmental experience. Everything that happens to us, and everything that is communicated within the therapeutic vessel, offers vital information about the person. Respecting the entire canvas of a life means that we are open to see more than the sum of the parts. This may contribute to the process of stepping from being identified only by the wound.

Belief. Our patients need us to believe them, that we are taking their inner world and feelings, their stories seriously, even when their stories inspire disbelief. In my twenty years' experience as a practising therapist I have heard things that would not be believed in any novel or horror movie. The process of standing aside helps us to ponder reflectively on 'whose voice is this?'; 'whose story is this?'; 'where is this coming from?';

'what part of the person is telling me this?'. We stand in the position of supporting advocate, described by Alice Miller as empowering the individual to be heard in their own right and thus to be able to hear themselves. Our task is to listen fully and allow the fabric of the whole to be manifest. Once we can bear it and carry the whole, there is more likelihood our patients will be able to find a place where they can be in relationship with their own story.

An open, non-judgemental approach. Our questions are open questions such as: 'what is it like? How does that feel?' Even when we think we know the answers, they will be our therapist's answers, not those of our patient. Once someone told me he had been to Rome for the weekend and my images were of art and sculpture. I waited for the person to tell me about it as the atmosphere got colder: 'my brother was murdered there in 1963'.

Empathic resonance. As therapists we are on the side of the patient. Empathic resonance helps to establish trust in the telling of the story and in the therapeutic process itself. Only when there is trust is the space wide enough for us to challenge. We need to be able to stand up to the dark forces as they manifest through our patients and we can only do this if we have established an empathic resonance first. Statements such as 'It is not in the best interests of this work for me to be bullied by your sour old man subpersonality' would seem bleak without the context of established empathy.

Developing empathy is not some loose minded simplistic 'being there for you' or 'coming from a caring place'. It is in parallel with the process of keeping one's heart open to another as in true, rather than 'idiot' compassion.

Daring. Do we ask regularly: 'Am I prepared to be surprised by this person, by the journey we will make together? Am I prepared to be stretched, to go into dark places, to go where this person will take me?' What is it that draws us into accepting someone into the process of therapy, beyond the obvious first understanding? Daring can lead to 'mistakes', from which we learn, and also to stretch ourselves into wider understandings.

Curiosity and passion. It helps if we are genuinely curious about people and their stories. Without curiosity we may become complacent, bound by theory and pathology, pathologizing our patients as 'narcissist', 'borderline', 'passive/aggressive', instead of people struggling with life. This means that we fail to liberate our imagination or unconscious in the quality or content of our responses. We need to marvel at the lengths people have to go to manage and to communicate their suffering, the diversions people create for fear of a worse fate. A sense of wonder at the colour of the human drama frees us from old judgements. It can help us to be more ready to develop compassion for human life.

Foolishness. Are we prepared to appear an idiot who takes time to understand? To offer responses such as 'I don't quite understand'. Or, 'are you saying . . .?' and 'do you mean . . .?' 'Have I got this right? Tell me again. I'm sorry if I have forgotten that.' Our ability not to know and allow the response from the patient helps to draw us into a deeper level of communication. We are equal, we can check things out, get things wrong, make a 'mistake' and be alongside it with our patient in relationship.

Humility. Leaving ourselves on one side and yet bringing ourselves into the room as and when appropriate is an art we learn from experience; to never know better, and to never know first and to know when we think we know.

Attention and the act of faith. This emerges from experience, from sticking with difficult times, and from really listening to oneself and one's patient. This particular 'act of faith' is nothing to do with religion or psychological theory in itself, but emerges organically from our relationship with the work inside the vessel. It is attained by devotion to the process of the work itself. It is not lazily following a belief handed down by someone else, but is related to the act of mindful attention to the processes that are unfolding and speaking of them from that place. In 'Slouching Toward Bethlehem' (1982), Dr Nina Coltart writes of the time in a therapy when darkness begins to close in, 'but it is a darkness having that special quality of the unknown which is moving towards being known'. She writes that it is possible 'in fifth gear, when the act of faith is most fully deployed, when our listening ear seems to be directly connected with our tongue and speech', to speak out forcefully as advocate of the life trying to be born.

The Dynamics of the Vessel

No-one is neutral in the meeting with another. Humans do not live in a vacuum, we are all affected by the presence of another person. Contents of the shadow get projected onto others and onto us as we too project onto others also. The quality of a person may remind us of someone else, may stir in us feelings we do not understand. These conscious and unconscious aspects, that emerge when we sit as therapists in the forging vessel of the relationship, are of extreme value. They help us to understand the story of the patient's emotional life, both in terms of his relationship with others and with himself. And we, as therapists, are drawn into this because of the intimacy of the space, and because frequently there are wounds to inter and intra relationships that need healing. In outlining the principles of transference and counter-transference, the way they relate together, we begin to have a working understanding of the multifaceted, mysterious and complex ideas that make the dynamics within the vessel.

The Contribution of Object Relations Theory

To understand this inner world we need to return to our first relationship with mother or who was mother for us. Opinion is divided over to what extent the infant's identity is fused with mother and to what extent signs of individuality are immediately present. However, what does seem true is that not only is the infant utterly reliant on her mother but that also the mother's internal and external world impact on the infant's experience and to that extent, what mother experiences so does her baby. Initially the baby experiences this world as either 'all good' (warm, feeding, held, loved) or 'all bad' (hungry, cold, frightened, angry, lonely). This is simply because the baby's memory is growing and until it is more developed she lives in the eternal moment. During this early phase her own needs are naturally paramount and she relates to her mother as an object that either serves or frustrates these needs. Object relations theory describes this as the mother being experienced as a *part object.* That is, she is an entity that the baby is attracted to and which (sometimes) satisfies the baby's needs. When needs are satisfied mother is a *good object* and when they are not she is a *bad object*. Furthermore, these experiences of mother move from being *external objects* to *internal objects* as the baby internalizes them as part of her inner world, her imagination, from where they may either comfort her or scare her (because they carry her own projected rage). Hence we can say a *good internal object* or a *bad* or *persecutory internal object*.

As time goes on (Melanie Klein thinks by about the sixth month, Winnicott later and perhaps not even until adulthood), if the infant's frustrated needs and resulting anger have been accepted without punishment or fear she will come to realize that the good mother who cuddles, cradles, feeds and loves is also the bad mother who is absent, cold, hurtful and frightening and that this is a person separate from herself. This is a difficult time for the baby because mother must now become a *whole object*, a person separate from the baby and the baby's control, towards whom ambivalent feelings of love and hate are felt. Bringing these two together happens when gradually the baby feels guilty and sad, fearful of hurting her mother and losing mother's love, and so makes reparation in order to be comforted; she is still loved and her anger has done no harm. Winnicott calls this *the stage of concern* (1979).

However, sometimes this process goes wrong or is damaged because the infant does not feel securely attached to her mother. The reasons for this may be either an emotional problem, perhaps a post-natal depression or some external danger that threatens both mother and her child. When this occurs it is more difficult for the infant to express her rage and make reparation when her needs are frustrated or unmet, perhaps in the pre-verbal and early belief that the expression of anger and protest will further distance a mother she is already unsure of. Left with these painful and frightening emotions, with no way to name, understand or manage them, she may resort to the primitive defence of *splitting* whereby one part of her experience is retained and identified with and another part is denied and projected onto her mother or someone or something else in her environment. Here there are a number of possibilities. The child may either project and retain either the good or bad parts of her experience, each unconscious choice leading to a lifetime of consequences. In the next section we will see how these choices have more or less constant patterns and how once identified, they may be used to help the patient, once the child, to understand the choice their child self made and may be make another one.

Dr Anthony Ryle's cognitive reappraisal of the Object Relations School Theorists, in particular Ogden, Fairbairn and Kohut, has helped me to move from dense and complex theory, dominated by malevolent and beneficent objects, namely breasts and penises in various stages of unwanted tumescence, into charting clearly the language of the two-way process that the term object relating implies. This two-way process is named by Ryle as 'reciprocal role procedure', and is seen as a learned response to, and activity for, survival (Ryle 1995). Role procedures are based upon our early management of emotional pain and are a learned attempt to survive what at the time are intolerable feelings. They help to name both the damaged and damage maintaining aspects of the core wound and their reciprocal nature. Thus, if our early experience is of a rejecting other, we will carry the wound of the rejected inner child and perhaps feel unworthy and useless. We will also carry the image and experience of a rejecting other.

In relationships the rejected aspect will anticipate and expect the rejecting other because of the unhealed wound. This may be played out either in the rejection of oneself or of unconsciously anticipating and seeking others who are actually rejecting and so confirm the core wound. The more severe early life, the more restricting are the roles learned, the less secure the ego structure, the more limited space for experience of self, and the more extreme behaviours are needed to survive and call for help.

'Role' can be described in Transpersonal psychotherapy in terms of sub-personality – the symbolic representations of the 'demanding judge' to the 'crushed little girl'. Until recognized, dialogued with, and their position revised and allowed to grow and change, the learned 'roles', the sub-personalities, limit our experience of relationship.

Understanding how patients are invited into transference because of their learned role experience, means that therapists are freed to 'use' the human relationship as the modelling clay for awareness, change, and frequently, transformation. This is important for every relationship encounter, and particularly important in patients whose early life has been emotionally destructive.

When we enter therapy, naturally we bring these early infant and child experiences with us and usually they are unconscious. As contents of the shadow they are projected into the relationship with the therapist and so the therapist is experienced in the same way as the parents were. I remember believing that my analysts were either not understanding me or that having understood, they were disapproving. These very painful feelings were actually being transferred from my experience of my parents who I had come to feel were disinterested and critical. When this occurs it is called transference, the unconscious transference of earlier experience into the present relationship with the therapist so that our own emotional history appears repeated. In this way the abandoned, abused or maltreated child in the adult may be re-experienced in the vessel of the therapy in relationship to the imagined person of the therapist.

An important variation on this is called *projective identification*. This is experienced when the therapist is 'invited' to carry the patient's *own* feelings that she has been unable to tolerate consciously and thus they have been denied, repressed and then projected. These may include rage, hatred, disintegration or fragmentation and so therapists find themselves embodying, actually feeling, something painful, terrifying or very fragile, that belongs to the patient but which the patient is not conscious of. This process may be actually felt through the body in the form of blanking off, intense drowsiness, nausea, or via the senses, such as smell, feel or sound. The process may also be carried through a prevailing image the therapist is unable to make sense of, an attacker for instance, a wooden repetitive toy, a screaming infant. From the patient's perspective, perceiving what is unacceptable in themselves in their therapist provides a means to control it and in this way the ego defends itself against that which is dreaded.

In the example above, if in fact it was my own unconscious disinterest and disapproval of myself, perhaps internalized from my parents, then the therapist may well have felt those qualities in himself and I, feeling his disinterest and disapproval, could be tempted to leave. However, in leaving the therapist I would be repeating a defensive closure and the feelings, being my own, would come with me. From the therapist's perspective it is important to allow such manifestations (which can appear quite magical) to be pondered on before speaking of them to the patient, *if at all*. Supervision, reading and one's own process of digestion are all vital before such presentations can be shared in a way that is useful and allow for integration in the work.

Table 2.1 Patterns of care that can dominate our relationships until we revise them

The way we experienced early care	What we are left feeling inside (core wound)	Ways we cope (survival)
Absent:		
Rejecting	Rejected	Placating
Abandoning	Abandoned	Parental child (look after others)
Conditional:		
Judging	Judged	Striving
Belittling	Humiliated	Hypervigilant
Demanding	Crushed	Admired-or-rubbished split
Too tight:		
Overcontrolling	Restricted	Avoiding or rebelling
Fused dependency	Fearful	Flight into fantasy/wrapped in bliss
Too loose:		
Anxious	Fearful	Avoiding
Depressed	Fragile	Placating
Abandoning	Left	Depression
	'Nowhere world'	'False self'
Envious	Fearful	'Magical guilt'
	Hated	Self-sabotage
Neglecting:		
Physical	Neglected	Cannot take care
Emotional	Hurt	Mood swings
Emotional	Angry	Feel in bits
Mental	Fragmented	Self-neglect
Abusive:		
Violent	Abused	Victim/bully swings
	Hurt	Hits out to self or others
	Rage unexpressed	Fantasy of 'perfect care'
Good enough:		
Not 'too good'	Loveable	Good enough
Not 'too bad'	Responsive	Sense of self
Loving	Secure	Trusting
Caring	Cared for	Loving
		Healthy

Counter-transference

As is apparent from above, the therapist must feel something too and frequently will have powerful emotional responses. This is called counter-transference. There may be two sources for these. The first includes the human responses to some element of the patient's story, perhaps empathy or anger. More profoundly we have also seen above that counter-transference feelings may be the registering of projective identification. These come via the unconscious and are often felt in our body. They are crucial sources of information that enable us to understand something of our patient's inner world and the emotional forces that have made it. Winnicott says of this: 'the analyst does not waste the valuable material that comes in terms of the emotional relationship between patient and analyst. Here, in the unconscious transference appear samples of the personal pattern of the patient's emotional life or psychic reality' (1965 p. 117). Often this category of experience is frightening to the therapist who is made anxious, feeling perhaps intense destructive feelings towards a patient she believes she should care for. If she can step back from a personal identification with these feelings she may well discover that she is in fact picking up the patient's own destructiveness or a destructiveness directed towards the patient at an earlier phase in their life. The second source is what the therapist herself brings and which the patient touches or constellates, bringing material to the surface that is the therapist's alone. What is essential here is the therapist's ability to distinguish what belongs to her and what belongs to the patient. It is for this reason that deep and prolonged personal therapy is an essential requirement of any good psychotherapeutic training.

A simple check-list for these counter-transference experiences is as follows:

- 'In what way is what I am feeling to do with my patient?'
- 'Can I identify myself at one end of their reciprocal role?'
- 'Is what I feel *their* anger, *their* pain?'
- 'Am I feeling confused because my patient is confused but unable to name it and thus do those feelings belong to him/her?'

Check out these questions with what you know of the patient's material, their history and what has been happening in the sessions:

- How much of what I am feeling actually belongs to *me*, to my material, my unconscious?
- Am I identifying with my patient?
- Am I tired, too close to the material being presented?

Use supervision to go on checking these things. Check the feeling quality of thoughts we have about patients between sessions. Most importantly, check those feelings you have when you see their name in the diary or just before they are due to come for a session. Are you pleased, excited, anxious, afraid, does your heart sink? All these feelings offer information about the patient's inner world and its impact upon us and the vessel.

Also, we as therapists need to understand our own learned 'reciprocal role procedures' and be mindful of them, as well as being aware of those brought by the patient. The clarity of this cognitive reappraisal is extremely helpful for both understanding the more complex and hidden aspects of potential transference and counter-transference. It also models a more democratic, collaborative approach, inviting the patient to be observer to their own processes, and to be mindful of their charge. Knowing which roles are likely to be enacted in a therapy helps us to meet them with all our understanding and compassion rather than be lost within them.

The chart (Table 2.1) helps to outline some of the ways in which these roles may be enacted. It is intended as a guide only. Each therapy will reveal different language for those 'roles' and feelings which have been absorbed within one life.

DIFFICULT TRANSFERENCES

Most of us naturally prefer a nice light transference where there is sufficient Eros to make the therapeutic alliance a pleasurable and rewarding experience. However, this does not always happen and then we have difficult transferences.

Negative Transference

Strong feelings of all kinds are part of therapy and experienced by both patient and therapist. They may include confusion, sleepiness, fear, feeling lost, stuck, seduction, as well as active dislike, disdain, rage, anger, contempt. These negative feelings are brought into the vessel to be dared, spoken of and for the patient to begin a relationship with what has been a negative presence within their psyche. If a negative transference goes on for a long time and seems unspeakable, it can feel very heavy, suffocating, even maddening. It can bring the work to a standstill, especially if the negative feelings transferred come from a time which is pre-verbal. The work demands a two-way process – of sitting it out, making sure our responses maintain openness and acceptance for the process regardless of what we are being made to feel; and really understanding what is behind the negativity. The angry infant may also be the hurt infant.

Someone who has been constantly disliked may invite the therapist into that arena to also experience it. Many new therapists take a negative transference personally and even experienced therapists get thrown when accused or made to feel bad. All of us need to use supervision as a 'debriefing' and sounding board. Sometimes, negative transference gets dumped back onto the patient in a punishing way, compounding the problems. The process needs proper digestion as a whole. There are always two people in the room. The reciprocal role chart on page 33 helps us understand the two-way process involved in transference/counter-transference. If we are receiving a bullying note from a patient, somewhere in there is a bullied other – usually the child. The therapist might carry the feeling of the bullied child for a while, while the patient gets the energy of the bully into the room. At some point both aspects will need to be understood as belonging inextricably to each other so that they may be disentangled, and a third way envisioned and practised.

The Erotic Transference

Eros brings the soul into immediate contact with another, eliminating the distance between subject and object. This allows for the opening flow of energy between two souls. Eros is also a 'mighty Demon' (Stein 1973) and the danger is of falling into a destructive compulsiveness. In therapy this paradox prevails. The experience of 'falling in love' with the therapist ideally offers the opportunity to experience the nature of one's own Eros, the capacity of one's ability to love another and to have one's love received. This can be the coniunctio, the inner marriage of opposites that begins to end the tyranny of duality and polarization within the psyche. A transpersonal therapist needs to be mindful of the power of this experience and to receive it tenderly, allowing its faltering steps as well as its mighty rush, and to be mindful of the desire embedded within the theory itself, of the ultimate human relationship with the Beloved.

If Eros has claimed a more fixated, sexualized grip upon the person, this grip will be felt also by the therapist. The sexual temperature will rise, narrowing the thinking process, pull at all the senses, and feel extremely uncomfortable. The patient may begin to dress provocatively, speak explicitly about their sexual needs and dreams, act in sexually suggestive ways, sitting with legs apart, rubbing their hands over their body or mouth, narrowing their eyes, or actually make a pass at the therapist. It is challenging to work with. One does not want to be rejecting of the energy that is being awakened and one does not want to act upon it. Handling an erotic transference takes skill, patience and the ability to stand in a firm and compassionate place.

Hatred in the Transference

Hatred, the co-partner with love, can also emerge head on, but, more often is often hard to recognize, because it is well hidden, and comes disguised as everything but. It surprised me one day when working with a very mild, pleasing young woman with a soft quiet little voice who sat very still and looked like a startled rabbit at any intervention. I found myself reducing my interaction with her to very little, keeping careful note of my tone of voice, lest anything too direct shatter her – like walking on eggshells. One day, when this little pantomime of numbing counter-transference was about to send me off to sleep I caught a look. It was electrifying. It was a look from the corner of her eye and it was as if a great sea monster from the bottom of the ocean had stretched out its claw, then winged it in again, quick. I woke up in sheer terror.

The moment hung between us menacingly. I decided to plunge in – months of sitting drowning in bad feeling and reducing the energy of the vessel to a turgid nothing had had their day. 'What was that?' I asked. She looked startled. 'Did you just give me a filthy look?' She looked horrified, shaking her head. I continued on, determined to let this sea monster know I had seen it. 'Just out of the corner of your eye – it was as if some part of you was very, very angry indeed. Hating this whole process of sitting with me in this room.' She looked very frightened. A bit later I said 'It wouldn't be surprising would it, if you did feel hateful towards being vulnerable. You've often said how you hate your depression for what it has exposed you to, and being here reminds you of it, all the time. But it's very hard for you to bear it.'

In speaking of this, I felt like a sadist to her masochist. She began a series of very angry dreams where small people were being run down by horses; taunted by monsters; in threat of being annihilated by a huge ball rolling down a hill. We were able to speak truly about the terrors of her early teasing and humiliation. She had turned inwardly to a passive grandiose suffering to gain any sense of self. Hatred of self and others and the paradoxical gratification through illness maintained her depression with which no-one could help her.

Working with the Transference and Counter-transference

The therapist's task is to:

(a) recognize and take the heat and the cold of these three-way processes;
(b) to embody the unspoken core wounds in the counter-transference and in projective identification; and
(c) to offer the process of 'usage' of self as 'object' – allowing the 'as if' experience in order for the process of wound reparation to ego identity to begin, and the wider potential space for experience of selfhood to be born.

'When there is a shift from the use of others to perpetuate the false self to the use of others to discover real self the individual has begun the journey home' (Johnson 1994).

Transference and counter-transference feelings may be immediate, or they may need time to build up in the forging vessel. They need to be referred to naturally, as part of the continuum of the work, not aggressively such as 'I can see you're cutting off from me today as if I were your father'. Rather, we note and digest the feeling in the room and those we are receiving from the patient. We allow the felt sense of these experiences to inform us and guide our tone and timing. We might say, 'when you spoke just now I had a sense that you were scared – something about the way you held your breath. Can you say more about this?' In following the feeling down we may well come into contact with father and our part in offering it a hook. Alternatively, we can ask: 'I wondered just then if you found my silence a bit like your father's coldness you've told me about.'

Use of transference understanding helps loosen the grip of old 'roles' and widen the space for self. For Wilfred Bion (1965), when a clinician puts a new idea to a patient based upon the way he/she feels usage has been made, the idea, or mental object may open inner spaces for experiencing and knowing. For example, 'when we last spoke of my own illness it made you feel afraid, a bit like the abandonment you felt when your mother was ill, but today you seem to experience it as a kind of sharing.'

Actively Naming Transference

We may be active in working with roles as embodied in the transference, by using *images, diagrams, drawings*, that name the roles as subpersonalities and allows for an *observer* self to be created. One young man, who had learned to charm and please to the point of obliterating himself seemed to reach a standstill in therapy, and I felt as if I was in the place of the obliterating 'other'. We worked with a pile of saucers to try and experience what he was feeling. When asked to choose an object to represent himself he chose a very small egg. When asked to show where he felt he was right now, he slowly, placed one saucer after another over this tiny egg and burst into uncontrollable tears. He saw, immediately, how this feeling originated in his family where he had felt overwhelmed to the point of being snuffed out. He had been fighting the power of women ever since, falling into deep withdrawals and then secretly planning revenge. The work following the saucer experience took the form of vivid painting of his rage and terror of being possessed – red vaginas with huge teeth that he had to knock out with his violence. The active work in making these 'roles' explicit helped to give a language to what had been impossible, to clear the space between us for him to find himself.

What we bring to the vessel of ourselves – our ideas about what kind of therapist we are, what we are working for and in what light and dark we are holding the person before us is already counter-transference. In this way, as James Hillman writes in *The Myth of Analysis*, the therapist starts from 'a well conceived position given to him by the daimon of his desire both to bring the health of awareness, imagination and beauty to life in the soul and to constellate with his psyche the Eros of the other. It is no longer the analyst upon whom projections are transferred, rather, through the (therapist) the intentions of the coniunctio myth are transferred upon the (patient) who counters these effects from the start' (1972, p. 107).

Two particular transferences, from those who suffer borderline and narcissistic wounds, test this daimon to the full.

Borderline and Narcissistic Presentations

In these cases no relationship is possible until the therapist understands how to respond to and work with the limitations posed by the polarization of 'good' and 'bad'. The patient, as a compensation for neglect or abuse, may have created internally a fantasy of perfect care, and an idealization of others who are in a caring position. This projection is powerful and may invite therapists to play saviour, or fall for being special, adored and admired. However, it only takes one small disagreement or perceived slight for the patient to experience the therapy as abusive (the opposite pole), and the roller coaster of swings from one extreme to the other has begun. While these swings may be clear and able to be named, the more difficult counter-transference feelings of confusion, helplessness, persecution, indeterminate rage, and a strong desire to abandon the therapy and the patient are harder to handle and need a sound clinical understanding and supervision. Healing begins to take place when the swings are able to be tolerated within the therapeutic relationship and they become less dominating and all consuming.

Types of Narcissistic Transference

Kohut (1977) has described three levels of narcissistic wounding that are reflected in three levels of transference relationship and Jocoby (1989) has some valuable therapeutic insights to add.

The Merging Transference

In this most severe expression of the wound we merge our sense of self with that of an idealized significant other. Typically this happens in a relationship with someone whom we revere and we then bathe in the light that our idealization bestows upon them. We think of the other as *my* beautiful partner or *my* brilliant therapist and in so doing defend ourselves from the underlying anxieties about our own denied feelings of worthlessness. In this relationship the other is only there to serve us and we feel entitled to use them as an object for our needs. When, as therapist we resist this, narcissistic rage ensues and from being idealized we are scorned and denigrated. Being therapist with such a person leaves us feeling that we are only valued for what we give and should we fail in any way that we are then valueless; all feelings that the narcissistically wounded patient unconsciously feels about themselves. Because of this it is extremely difficult to form a transference relationship and it is this that forms the greatest barrier to a successful outcome within the therapy. Opinions are divided as to whether a successful therapy is even possible. While this is the wound's most profound presentation, those of us with wounds of a similar but lesser degree may be aware of the presence of this within us and at times of stress may regress back to this level.

The Twinship Transference

In this intermediary wound we recognize that we and the other are separate but unconsciously assume that we and they are more or less identical. Here it is the alter ego who is idealized and this wound is most often seen in adolescent psychology that yearns for and believes in 'soul mates' where there is a fantasy of joining with a perfect other. I remember some years ago being astonished by a portrait of a spiritual teacher drawn by one of his students. The portrait was obviously of the teacher but also uncannily of the student as well. The student had drawn her experience of the teacher as her twin, or perhaps more seriously, as one merged identity. This wound defends against further separation which is felt as a threat. However, therapeutic work is appropriate and separation anxiety in therapy reveals itself as the patient identifying with the therapist and of being unable to tolerate differences between them. Perhaps the immature desire to become a therapist too, often a phase of the work, comes from this wound.

The Mirror Transference

This is the most mature expression because it is directed at becoming a separate self. Here the other is used to reflect back recognition of accomplishments. In itself this is not unhealthy since we all come to know ourselves through reflection in another. However, here what the therapist is invited to mirror back is not the real self which is based on reality but the false self and so mirroring this would be to fall into collusion with a defensive structure. Here the therapist causes upset once he fails to acknowledge some attribute that the false self is using to buttress itself against the equally inflated sense of inferiority hidden in the shadow. It is not that the therapist should withhold praise, indeed this would be to re-wound, but that the praise should be directed at the real self for real accomplishments in the real world, however small.

Looking at these three wounds it is apparent that the narcissistically wounded are entirely defined by their relationship to others while at the same time having either no or little relationship with this other. While it is natural to seek ourselves through another we must also allow the other to be separate and to separate from them. The nature of infantile narcissistic relationships prevents this until such a time that the separation is not felt as destructive. At all levels the absolute character of the idealization must change into a relationship that can contain both good and bad experiences.

Borderline Personality Disorder

The word 'borderline' is frequently misunderstood to mean a state of mind that is on the border between psychotic and neurotic personality structures. However, it would be better to conceive of it as a separate state, not within a continuum, that has characteristics that are both psychotic, in that they appear unconnected to reality and also neurotic, in that they represent places of developmental arrest. Symptoms frequently include impulsive and self-destructive behaviour, anger and depression, brief psychotic losses of reality and either dependent or superficial and transient relationships. When we have a borderline personality disorder we are suffering the most severe expression of a wounding that originates from the failure to successfully separate from mother, or whoever is mother for us, during the first two years of life. Identity is found in our fused or merged state with another which makes us clinging, controlling, needy and manipulative. However, this fusion alienates us from the real self and in the shadow the repressed desire for independence and its generation of a real self elicits guilt and rage. The rage is an important dynamic because it is protest, anger and rage that have never been allowed expression or, having expression, have instantly been met with rejection. In all cases the borderline rage, projected onto the therapist, is defended against, as a source of terror, unconsciously identified within passive aggression, and yet constantly constellated in the world as the field of the complex confirms its original making. Thus all relationships confirm the belief that to be separate equals abandonment and to be in relationship equals annihilation. However, positively, it is the same rage, constructively used, that can become the engine of the stalled individuation.

In therapy the borderline and merged narcissistic presentations share the same problem of the transference being unconsciously resisted and this partly is what makes working with this wound so difficult. However, while the narcissistic presentation revolves around issues of worth, the borderline revolves around issues of existence. Schwartz-Salant (1989) gives a graphic description of working with this wound. On the surface the patient may seem extremely demanding and compliant and yet they also control the therapy so that any effect is nullified. Here we see 'the characteristic borderline quality of simultaneous drives towards fusion and separation' (Schwartz-Salant 1989, p. 163). At the heart of the work is the patient's fear that to form a therapeutic alliance with the therapist is to once more become subsumed by another's needs. The therapist, receiving these unconscious feelings, via their own unconscious, may feel frustration, failure, anger and despair and they too do not want to be with this difficult and painfully troublesome patient. Together they may deny the underlying reality that what is really wanted is that no relationship should happen. Thus they act out the original wounding in which the child had no life of their own and the therapist/parent confirms the child's belief that they are not wanted for themselves. And beneath this the desire in the shadow to destroy relationship acts as a distorted forerunner to form a separate, independent existence. Until this truth is acknowledged as the reality of what the patient deeply needs and the therapist can contain and not act out the uncomfortable reality of their own needs (that the patient should be well), it will not be possible for a wholesome relationship to develop in which the patient and therapist can both be in relationship with each other and not find this destructive. The active naming of the different states of raw being, in a diagrammatic form, each of them rigidly boxed in with their own reciprocal role structures, that maintain a sense of fragmentation and alienation, helps the process of developing an observer: the 'I' who sees 'me'. This, hopefully, creates the possibility of a safe enough space for the liberation of the patient's rage, which unless skilfully received (not managed) may be violently self-destructive as it emerges raw from the unconscious. However, the inner image of the abandoned or dead child, the representation of the true self, may not be resurrected until this violence is accepted into the personality as a whole as a force for change. The difficulty of this therapeutic relationship should not be underestimated and expert supervision and the abandonment of heroic intent will be necessary for any therapist attempting it.

PHASES OF THE WORK: IMPLICATIONS FOR THE THERAPEUTIC RELATIONSHIP

The Initial Contact

Everything that has gone before the first session has something to contribute to the potential therapeutic relationship. Appointment making via letter, telephone or personal request enables us to ask ourselves what is the attitude within these exchanges, what does this tell us about the person and their needs and expectations of therapy? Even though these exchanges should remain brief and practical, to a keen ear, much may be immediately clear.

The First Session and Assessment

There are two functions to a psychotherapeutic assessment. One is to assess whether psychotherapy might be useful to the person in terms of their presenting 'problem' or issue; the second is to assess the kind of therapy most appropriate and with whom. The public sector usually has guidelines for assessment and number of sessions to be offered. Also, with the formalized 'purchasing' of services now current in the British Health Service, the kind and length of therapy will be set in advance. In the private sector the field is more open, more variable and the need for vigilance greater.

Sometimes a patient is referred from another agency with a referral letter indicating that some form of assessment has already taken place, and that the therapist has been selected for a particular reason. In situations where patients are referred 'out of the blue' or self-referred the main issue for therapists is to be able to know with whom they can work therapeutically, and which patients are best referred elsewhere.

For therapists in private practice the assessment often amounts to the first session although it is very important for the therapist not to assume it is simply a first session and fail to make an assessment. Different therapists do this in different ways and these ways are always in development: however, there are some general principles to remember. Basically the therapist must come to some understanding of the potential patient's presenting and underlying problems, self assess their own use, offer an opportunity for the patient to ask questions and also describe the therapeutic contract. Once this is done the person can then either decide on the spot to continue or (my preference) go home and think on it. My own method revolves around the fundamental questions 'why has this person come and why now' and devotes approximately half the time to the answer. In addition to this, I will also be considering the questions listed below. Next, perhaps ten minutes for any clarifications and questions and then ten for the contract and ending. Finishing on the contract is important because not only does a clear contract prevent confusion later, it also begins to build the therapeutic vessel and, by its brutal practicality, in effect disengages the transference that many patients instantly attach to the therapist as potential saviour. This is a transference that it is not appropriate to receive until both parties have decided to work with each other. Of course all good plans go astray and such a plan in the face of a sea of tears must dissolve. However, here still the contract must be agreed before starting even if it means a second assessment meeting. For a new therapist, the content of the contract is best designed with the help of the supervisor and is important as an essential part of the vessel.

Observing and Keeping an Open Mind: Considerations During the First Session

1. What presence does this person bring with them? How might I describe it for myself? (May only find an answer afterwards.) Image, feeling, note.
2. Body language – how does the person carry themselves, sit, hold their various body parts – head, arms, legs, torso. For example: open/closed/challenging/demure/hostile/seductive.
3. Eye contact – expression in the eyes; eye movements; direct look; closed eyes; changes in expression.
4. Dress – appropriately for climate, status, age, etc., or, unusual, inappropriate (bathing suit in the middle of winter), or poorly put together expressing confusion, depression, at odds with themselves. (Need to watch our own fantasies about dress here. Someone may be an eccentric artist who greatly enjoys and is in relationship with their costumes!)
5. General health – does this person look well? – skin tone, colour, body size, odour, teeth, etc.

For Pondering Afterwards

What do my answers to the above tell me about the person?

6. How can I gauge the strength and robustness of their ego personality – in the history, e.g. their commitments, relationships, ways of looking after themselves, completing tasks.
7. What is being communicated to me on a level of (a) feeling; (b) thinking; (c) body; (d) intuition; (e) spirit? Which function is dominant? Which is hidden or poorly integrated?
8. What story do they bring and what is its central theme? – e.g. rejection; loss; abandonment; emotional hurt and pain; confusion.
9. What sense do I have of their 'seed' and how it has manifest during their life? – e.g. what makes the heart sing? when have they been happy? what has helped them through the bad times?
10. What sense do we get of the frustration of archetypal intent presented as 'pathology' or 'wounding' and the corresponding 'learning' they are struggling with? – to separate; to let go of anger; to stand alone; to be brave enough to love; to allow themselves to 'be' real.
11. How does this person make me feel? What happens in my body, feeling, thinking, what is my intuitive hunch about them? What are silences like with them?
12. What transference invitations can I sense, or predict I might have to encounter?
13. Are there any issues that might get in the way of the work?
14. How can I begin to reflect on their story now? Supervision questions.
15. Do I feel I can work with them? – (a) can I meet professionally what they have brought? (b) can I put myself into the vessel with them and go to the unknown with them?

Referring On

Sometimes we cannot work with someone and we must refer on. Dr Nina Coltart said to me once that she felt choosing a therapist for a patient was akin to marriage guidance, the mix of gender, race, education, age, social class and intelligence, the use of language all contributed to the success of the work. The art is not to achieve sameness, but compatibility. An older woman might have a very successful therapy with a younger man; a black man a successful therapy with a white man or woman. The important initial factors are attunement, trust, with a general feeling of good chemistry and liking. Therapy is not possible if there is dislike on either side or if there is too much negative transference at the very first meeting. Human beings' prime need in relationship is attachment. We need to attach, to feel safe, to let go, before we can move away again. This personal aspect allows for the projection of other figures – mother, father, sister, brother, teacher, friend, to be embodied for the purpose of change in perception and for reparation.

It is also important as a therapist to ask ourselves whether we feel able to go where the patient may take us, knowing that we cannot go very much further in life experience than where we have gone within ourselves. Also that we know when we have not the right skills and sufficient experience to meet difficult presentations.

Referring Difficult Presentations

Recognition of difficult presentations such as severe narcissistic and borderline problems means therapists have the choice to refer to others more experienced in working in this area. In private practice this is essential. In other settings such as GP surgeries, day centres, drop in centres where time limited therapy is the model and supervision is efficient and plentiful it may be necessary to get used to working with 'difficult' patients, and, if possible, limit their number in one's caseload to only two. Many trainee therapists do not have the luxury to choose and, sadly, too often difficult patients are given to trainees to struggle with which can often be alarming and discouraging, as well as potentially rewarding and heartening.

How to Recognize Difficult Presentations

1. Disturbed personal history; sometimes previous psychiatric admissions; history of self-harm, violence, suicidality.
2. Extreme responses such as sudden flights into mood change, shifts in feeling in the room, shifts in word usage. Therapists easily feel confused and as if they are handling water running through their fingers.

In order for *any* communication to occur, these shifting states need to be named first and the act of naming them forms the first building block of the relationship.

Dissociative Disorder and Multiple Personality

Patients with a history of fragmentation and multiple selves need the care of those who specialize in this work. It often happens however, that awareness of the results of a violent and abusive early history is deeply buried under presenting problems and may emerge when a long-standing trust has developed within the therapeutic relationship. In my experience, if this occurs the best person to stay with this difficult material is the therapist who is engaged in the work, and already has a trusted relationship. Pulling someone out of therapy for referral to an 'expert' can be extremely damaging to the relationship established and may repeat early patterns of abuse; yet, if the therapist truly cannot manage, it is still better to do this than continue to fail entirely.

Memory

Patients who have been severely traumatized may experience flashbacks and images that at first are incomprehensible. The current debate within psychotherapy on the nature of memory – true or false – has fuelled a great tension for therapists and their clients and the issue of trust is challenged. Therapists need now to learn about the nature of memory, and the nature and effect of trauma. They need a clearly defined way of working with highly charged images from early life, particularly those images that would appear to be related to the trauma of childhood sexual abuse. Believing in the reported experience, as it is witnessed within the vessel, helps responses and questions to emerge naturally.

Research into the nature of memory reveals that while ordinary memory is dynamic and both changes and decreases over time, traumatic memory has been described as 'indelible'. We watch the breath and the body as it holds trauma, we listen to the felt life, the note, the atmosphere of the silences and energy of the images. Our work then is to unravel the agony that lives on in the psyche of our patient. Then, through the vessel of belief and the safety of being heard and not judged and sentenced, what has been scripted as indelible and held in place by vigilance may begin to sit side by side with other experiences. Only after this therapeutic experience within the vessel can steps at reality testing have any meaning. If the images as felt become memories as reported and are subject to literalization, both therapist and patient suffer from the invasion of an outside dynamic which does no service to the healing process needed. 'One has to know one's buried truth in order to be able to live one's life. The "not telling" of the story serves as a perpetuation of its tyranny. When one's history is abolished one's identity ceases to exist as well' (Laub and Averhahn 1998).

Keeping Records

After we have agreed to take someone on we need to make sure we keep accurate records of their personal details to refer to. These are ideally kept on a small card in a card index box which is separate to the file in which you write session notes.

The card index should include: Full name; Address and home, work and mobile telephone numbers; Date of birth; Name of referral agent; GP's name and address (I usually explain that I will not write to any other professional person without their permission first, but that I need to have the GP's number in case of the need for medical support during the therapy); Date of assessment; Date of first session; Whether the therapy is long or short term.

Session Notes and Note-taking – Confidentiality is Crucial

Notes need to be kept in a locked filing cabinet. The content of the notes needs to include: Date of session; Number of sessions, supervision notes, reading; Focus of the session; Any additional information (dreams, drawings – either originals if you have been asked to look after them or sketches you make after the session).

Notes can be subpoenaed in a court of law. They need to be kept for five years after the end of therapy and then shredded. A 'buddy system' where another therapist keeps a list of current patient caseload in case of emergency maintains confidentiality and acts as a support for the therapist. Therapists need to leave in their will instructions for the burning of case material in the event of their death.

THE MIDDLE PHASE

The middle phase of work begins once the 'novelty' factor of therapy has dissolved. In a brief therapy this may be after the first third of the number of sessions, in a longer therapy it may be after the first eighteen months.

Here the magical 'in loveness' of the new has worn off. There may be disillusionment as well as a general feeling of letting go. I always feel a relief as therapist when this begins to happen because I feel that now the real relationship can develop.

The therapeutic issues for the middle phase are to do with the subtleties of the timing of interventions. This will be directed by the patient's need for development and reparation. A careful note of dreams, use of language and image, a watchful eye on body language, dress and changing mood are all part of the growing of the therapeutic relationship. As the transference relationship lessens, so the 'person to person' relationship grows, and the space for other, wider experiences of consciousness and sense of self widens.

Therapist Interventions

For the periods of long 'plateau' or feeling 'stuck', interventions which are to do with building a stronger sense of self will be directed at carefully mirroring that self back in whatever minute form it emerges. If the 'stuckness' seems to do with hanging on to past fear that has been explored and named, the interventions will be to create both a safe space for the new experience and a challenge to the part that is holding on out of fear.

Subtle interventions are learned from practice, from supervision and from one's own therapy. It is always helpful to tape a session (with permission) and look in detail at one's responses as therapist. This helps us to keep asking:

- What I am about to say ... who does this serve? Me, or the patient?
- Which part of the person am I speaking to when I ask this?
- What am I reflecting back to the person when I say this?
- What new space do I wish to open up for this person?
- How shall I leave this? As it is, raw ragged, hurting, in order to allow the person to go away with the feeling as if trusted to hold it? Or, do I need to tie up these ragged pieces for the person, as they would be more confused if I don't try?

There are times when it appears we are inactive. We should never underestimate the value of our presence. Feeling into the felt sense or getting an image for where you feel you are together helps. Images might be 'stuck', 'bogged down', skimming on the surface. Sometimes periods of apparent inertness are because some new material is about to appear.

Self Disclosure

As the relationship moves towards a real meeting, and much less of a transference relationship, it is necessary to be careful about the amount of self disclosure. To say 'I remember struggling with this one when . . .' may be just the kind of sharing needed to encourage someone to brave the new and contribute to the development of an equal relationship. Or, the person may feel overwhelmed or competitive. Or again, knowing more of the therapist may bring more reality into the relationship and encourage a withdrawal of projections. These subtle judgements are important. We are simply mindful of the difference.

Timing of Intuition

Many therapists have an intuitive knowing about their patient. While this is valuable, intuitive insights need to be digested and pondered on for their accuracy and appropriateness to be usefully shared. Mostly we need to keep our intuitive flashes to ourselves or we 'burden' the patient and appear too magical.

Dark Night of the Soul

Sometimes therapy is the permissible container for depression and breakdown which needs to happen because the adapted self has been too narrow, too brittle, thwarting the soul life. The middle phase may reflect this process by a retreat into a long drawn out period of feeling little, and lost. The therapist is witness to the process as well as wise midwife to the self waiting for the time to be born. Support for therapists and patients comes from the poetry of T. S. Eliot when he writes: 'the faith, the hope and the love are all in the waiting'. A wise midwife knows when to call in other experts, such as when a prolonged depression seems to deepen and the person becomes in need of the support of medication; or when someone actually needs the containment of a hospital for the processes they are undergoing. Mostly though, therapists learn to endure the long dark night alongside their patients, in anticipation of dawn and a new sense of self born of the true surrender of the carapace in which they were held.

Are Therapists allowed to Laugh?

Humour is now recognized as good medicine and workshops on laughter help sick children and ageing rheumatics. Therapy has been notoriously a humour-free zone, frowned upon in traditional analysis and psychotherapy as inappropriate, childish, taking away from the inner truth of the concern. Certainly if we use humour as a defence against our own fear or not knowing; if we laugh because we are embarrassed or do not know what to do we lose contact with our patient and the relationship struggles. If we collude with laughter or humour at the expense of meeting the emotional need to have us enter the feeling behind the act, we do them a disservice. Simple questions that do not puncture but attempt to hold the moment such as: 'Was it *really* funny?', or 'I notice you are making light of this, is that what you *really* feel?' help to leaven the contact. Laughter itself can also be extremely powerful as a shared contact of equality, when it is spontaneous, impeccably timed and completely genuine.

Complications and threats to the Therapeutic Relationship

Acting Out

Coming late repeatedly to sessions, missing sessions, coming on the wrong day, 'forgetting' to pay bills, are all normal and usual aspects of mild acting out in therapy and always related to some unconscious expression that needs to be named. This may be to do with ambivalence about getting close; anger at having to come because of need, envy of therapists' 'better' position; or fear of disclosure. But there are no generalizations. Also, buses do go slow and accidents happen! Therapists are human first and professionals alert to repeated patterns second. These patterns need to be explored and brought into the work as a whole.

More serious levels of acting out would include telephoning at all hours, demanding behaviour towards a therapist or their family, threats of violence, stalking, writing angry or threatening letters, even standing in the garden of the therapist or ringing their doorbell repeatedly. These are serious challenges to the stability of the relationship. While all therapists in their lifetime's practice would experience some of this, the issues need to be discussed fully in supervision and the support of supervision and colleagues is vitally important.

Suicidal Intent

Thoughts such as 'I can't go on'; ' I just want out'; 'what's the point'; fantasies such as driving into a tree, going to sleep forever, a growing cynicism, 'who cares anyway', may indicate suicidality. These times are always trying and worrying for therapists.

While as Transpersonal therapists we recognize that the soul needs the depth experience to usher in change, acknowledgement of the seriousness of suicidal thinking or intent opens the potential for new thinking and rethinking. The ability to really speak of the burden that wants to be put down and have it heard, sows seeds of trust within the relationship. The potential suicide is believed, their pain taken seriously. In Schneidman's studies (1987) the most important offering is the recognition of the unbearable psychological pain and the space of time to re-think. For it is the thinking process that, if too narrowed and distorted, can direct the last impulsive act.

Listening for the Note of the Suicide Within

1. Name the subpersonality or part courting death, using straightforward language. 'It feels as if this is the one who thinks it's a good idea to kill yourself' is more direct than: 'I wonder if you fantasize about passing away?'
2. Explore what it is that wants to die or be killed off. What *kind* of death?

3. Explore revenge fantasies '. . . I'll die and then they'll see . . .'. Anger and hate turned against the self as object will need a wider canvas for expression.
4. Allow space for the quality and depth of despair.

Patients may feel more vulnerable to suicidal thoughts during depression, or as they are beginning to recover and have more energy. The experience of loss, failure, while being 'juicy' for the process of individuation is always a defeat for the ego. If the ego is brittle, built upon the shifting sands of others' admiration and approval, there may be a process where the idea of self-annihilation offers the only comfort.

Some therapists, working with actively suicidal patients ask for a suicide contract. This may be a contact to *not* attempt suicide during the course of the therapy, or the therapy ends immediately. Or, it is an agreement to explore the suicidal thoughts, but not actualization. The agreement needs to describe what the patient can do if the desire to act upon the thought becomes urgent, such as using the telephone support of Samaritans, or telephoning their GP, or you as therapist if this is appropriate to the nature of the intent. The issue for the therapeutic relationship is hugely challenging and not insignificant, for once we are part of the shared inner landscape we are no longer uninvolved and we may have an important role to play. Clearly defining what that role is will be a matter for individual psyches and discussion in supervision. Sometimes it is a surprise for patients to find that there is someone who will be affected by their death, and this may be the first time that the nature of the therapeutic relationship has been acknowledged.

ENDINGS AND IMPLICATIONS FOR THE THERAPEUTIC RELATIONSHIP

Endings may be planned with a date set for ending, or they may become a natural conclusion to the completion of the work. Endings begin with the final phase of the work, when someone has begun their journey home to themselves and the therapy delights in seeing this new life in action – in easy challenges, in assertions, in the forthright nature of a self that shines right through. There may be external changes manifested such as change of job, dress, relationship, belief system; and internal changes such as lessening of original symptoms, a greater kindness and acceptance; even the preparation for continuing the nurturance of the inner life after therapy ends through dream and journal recording. Part of the final phase is also to look at what has *not* changed, what is still around like an old callous, likely to rub now and again but hopefully not the gaping wound it once was. Sometimes the most significant issue for a therapy is having survived it; having survived a close relationship we are less fearful of getting close to others.

There is always sadness and loss when a therapy ends, a little death, which is an appropriate feeling and this needs to be reflected in the work. Sometimes loss is depicted in dreams of missing someone or something, moving house, travelling on a new road, being given a jewel with which to go alone into a dark wood. Sometimes there is a return to the fears and symptoms – as if the psyche is making a last ditch attempt to make sure the old wounds are not dominant. These times allow the old wounding to be experienced differently and the ending of an important relationship managed, in reality, through to its complete end.

FINALLY

Transference, like all human relationships evokes extreme responses. For some therapists it is the heart of the work and for others a problematical intrusion. In *The Myth of Analysis*, Hillman (1972, p. 107) celebrates it: 'We are in transference wherever we go, whenever a connection means something to the soul'. Transference modelled on soul making, upon individuation, means that an impulse must be ignited through one's attraction (transference) to another. Where there is no transference, nothing much happens, the energy has not been ignited. The 'spark' ignited by the intensity of relationship in its hothouse weekly meeting can be seen as psyche's demand for the forging of change through the love offered by the nature of the work. In this sense, transference can be seen as a demand or invitation for love. Biological survival need for attachment to another human is basic and vital; to move into the image of 'wholeness' we need a way of recognizing the meaning to the soul in the patterns of erotic love and to come to love, the call of the self, as it moves us in psyche. Love for Psyche and soul for Eros. If we only see transference as a 'limitation', as something 'wrong' or 'bad', or as being limited to early life figures, we miss the point of its energetic thrust. Jungian analyst and art therapist Joy Schaverien writes that there is nothing 'wrong' with psyche: 'Psyche (rather), seeks initiation through the process of soul making, for which a specific type of relationship with another human being is required' (1992).

REFERENCES

Bacal, H. and Newman, K. (1990). *Theories of Object Relations: Bridges to Self Psychology*. New York: Colombia University Press.

Bion, W. R. (1965). *Transformations*. London: Karnac (1984).

Bollas, C. (1989). *Forces of Destiny*. London: Free Association Books.

Chu, Frey, Ganzel and Matthews (1999). 'Memories of childhood abuse: Dissociation, amnesia and corroboration', *American Journal of Psychiatry*, 156, 749–55.

Clarkson, P. (1995). *The Therapeutic Relationship*. London: Whurr.

Coltart, N. (1982). *'Slouching Toward Bethlehem'*, printed in The British School of Psychoanalysis, independent edition, ed. G. Kohon. London: Free Association Books.

Coltart, N. (1996). *The Baby and the Bathwater*. London: Karnac.

Cardinale, M. (1975). *The Words to Say It*. London: The Women's Press Ltd (1993).

Eliot, T. S. (1936). *Collected Poems 1909–1962*. London: Faber & Faber (1963).

Freud, S. (1985). *Studies On Hysteria*, vol. 3. Pelican Freud Library London: (1965).

Gendlin, E. T. (1978). *Focusing*. New York: Bantam Books (1981).

Gendlin, E. T. (1981). *The Primacy of Human Presence*.

Hahn, Thich Nhat (1975). *The Miracle of Mindfulness*. London: Rider (1991).

Hillman, J. (1964). *Suicide And The Soul.* Zurich: Spring Publications.

Hillman, J. (1972). *The Myth of Analysis*, p. 107. New York: Harper (1978).

Jacoby, M. (1989). 'Reflections On Heinz Kohut's Concept Of Narcissism'. In A. Samuels (ed.), *Psychopathology: Contemporary Jungian Perspectives*, pp. 139–56. London: Karnac.

Johnson, R. (1994). *Character Styles.* New York: Norton.

Jung, C. G. (1945). *The Psychology of the Transference*, vol. 16 of *Collected Works*, para. 357 and para. 359. London: Routledge and Kegan Paul.

Klein, M. (1969). *Envy and Gratitude.* London: Hogarth Press (1984).

Kohut, H. (1977). *The Restoration Of The Self.* New York: International Universities Press.

Laub, Dori and Averhahn, Nanette (1998). *Accuracy About Abuse.*

Levene, S. (1987). *Healing into Life and Death.* New York: Doubleday/Anchor.

Maslow, A. (1965). *The Farther Reaches of Human Nature.* New York: Viking (1971).

Masson, J. (1988). *Against Therapy.* London: Fontana (1990).

Papini, G. (1969). 'A Visit to Freud', reprinted in the *Review of Existential Psychology and Psychiatry* 9(2), pp. 130–34.

Ryle, A. (1990, 1995). *Cognitive Analytic Therapy.* London: Wiley (1995).

Ryle, A. (1997). *Cognitive Analytic Therapy and Borderline Personality Disorder.* London: Wiley.

Schaverien, J. (1992). *The Revealing Image.* London: Routledge.

Schneidman, E. (1985). *Definition of Suicide.* London: Wiley.

Schwartz-Salant, N. (1989). 'The Borderline Personality: Vision & Healing'. In A. Samuels (ed.), *Psychopathology Contemporary Jungian Perspectives*, pp. 157–204. London: Karnac.

Stein, Robert (1973). *Incest and Human Love.* Dallas: Spring Publications (1984).

Suttie, I. (1935) *The Origins of Love and Hate.* London: Penguin.

Walsh, R. and Vaughan F. (1993). *Paths Beyond Ego.* Tarcher/Perigree: Jeremy Racher.

Welwood, J. (1994). *Awakening The Heart.* Boston and London: Shambhala.

Wilber, K. (1995). *Sex, Ecology, Spirituality: The Spirit of Evolution.* Boston: Shambhala.

Wilhelm, R. (1951). *I Ching. Book of Changes.* London: Routledge.

Winnicott, D. W. (1979). *The Maturational Processes and the Facilitating Environment.* London: Hogarth Press (1979).

Yallom, I. (1989). *Love's Executioner, and other tales of psychotherapy.* London: Penguin.

CHAPTER 3

Once Upon a Time ... Stories, Beliefs and Myths

Claire Chappell

Editor's note: Our lives start with a mystery. While careful and precise scientific observation has revealed archetypal patterns of psychological development, what remains is the unfathomable truth that each of us arrives different into the world and lives a unique version of human life. In this chapter Claire Chappell holds the two poles of this mystery together. In her first section the timeless and collective patterns of the soul's incarnation are set down and seen through various psychological theories drawn from different schools of psychotherapy and also through the older and more poetic lens of fairy tale and myth. Understanding these patterns enables us to have hold of the big picture of which each of us is an expression. Her second section demonstrates how understanding this is then used in clinical practice. C. G. Jung said that we should learn all the theory we can and then forget it as we sit with another. This is here illustrated beautifully and we see how the vessel of the work, the quality of bare attention, a compassionately spacious non-judgemental presence, effects spontaneous transformation. Transpersonal Psychology here is not something other or transcendent away from ourselves in some other place or time but rather an immanent quality that is found by resting mindfully within the therapeutic relationship.

N.W.

INTRODUCTION

As psychotherapists we have a choice of psychological theories to guide our practice with children, adolescents and adults. Our choice of theory will be governed by our personal beliefs and values and, beneath these, the collective myths that inform the culture in which we live. Before looking at some of the psychological theories available and their application in clinical practice, let us briefly explore the nature of beliefs and myths.

BELIEFS

Beliefs are experienced as true or self-evident. They may be both conscious and unconscious. As transpersonal psychotherapists we may consciously hold beliefs that reflect values that are associated with the transpersonal perspective, beliefs about the purpose and meaning of life. Other beliefs, however, remain unconscious until situations or events challenge our sense of who we are. On these occasions, we may be surprised, horrified or shamed as we discover beliefs which we would consciously disavow. This chapter explores and demonstrates how the tensions, between the consciously held beliefs and the powerful unconscious ones that remain active within the shadow, play a major part in our life story. Each family and each individual within that family holds both. From the perspective of the growing child, new to the world, we learn the beliefs we need in order to be loved, cared for and to survive. We learn these beliefs from the adults through the way that we are treated, and through what the adults do rather than from what is said. These beliefs become our truth.

This is not to say, of course, that therapists should not have beliefs; that is impossible. Nor that our belief systems need to coincide with those of our clients. Sometimes the understanding that we and the client are holding very different beliefs can be stimulating and even fun! However, we do need to know that our beliefs are there, both conscious and unconscious, and how they may influence the therapeutic process. Once we have this awareness we can then compassionately witness the life stories our clients bring us and help them to understand the beliefs that, consciously and unconsciously, may have come to rule their lives.

MYTHS

Myths illustrate archetypal themes that are ever present, again consciously and unconsciously, throughout our lives. They contain stories of heroic adventures, quests and journeys: Odysseus and his return to Penelope; Dorothy and her search for the Wizard of Oz. Some myths are love stories: Tristan and Isolde; Rama and Sita; Guinevere and Launcelot. Some contain war stories: the battling Titans; the Trojan Wars. They may also encapsulate the lives and actions of the animal powers, spirits, angels, gods and goddesses that we evoke, placate, implore and worship. Joseph Campbell has called these manifestations of the deep archetypal waters the 'Masks of God', and suggests that 'Shakespeare's definition of his art, "to hold, as 'twere, the mirror up to nature" is equally a definition of mythology' (Campbell 1987, p. 9). Mythology is as a mirror to the soul and so it reconciles the conscious ego with its shadowy roots.

As psychotherapists, deeply involved in this reconciliation, these mythological tales help us to think about the big archetypal themes that operate in our own and our clients' small individual stories. There are themes of miraculous births and childhoods which herald the coming of the solar hero. There are quests; the dying of old life patterns; the initiations to undergo and the return with new understandings, the treasure of the search. We find the mythical struggles and the ecstasy of war and love echoed in the experiences of the shadow and in the animus and anima. The presence of the Self, the god image within the psyche, may be glimpsed in those chaotic and terrifying moments when somehow, out of great suffering, something meaningful emerges and lifts the person beyond him or herself. We move from Gethsemane, through death and the underworld, to the Resurrection.

In the first part of this chapter I explore the value for psychotherapists, of understanding the impact of these beliefs and myths, both individual and collective, on the growing child. I link this with some theories of psychological development. In part two, 'The Child in the Adult', through three case examples drawn from my therapeutic practice, I explore how woundings during the developmental phases of childhood and adolescence can manifest later and how we might work with these in therapy. In doing this I have drawn from various psychological theories as they all have different strengths to offer. I do not believe it is a matter of an either/or approach but rather the more inclusive understanding of and/and. Finally, rather than write s/he or adopt the plural, I sometimes use 'she' to refer to the child and sometimes 'he'.

MOTHER AND BABY: 0–2 YEARS

The myths of pregnancy

I am not yet born, O hear me! (Louis MacNeice)

Pregnancy is a time of not knowing, of expectation, wonder, uncertainty. As soon as a woman tells the world she is pregnant, myths and old wives' tales come to the surface. There are myths about every stage of pregnancy. For example, the way a woman 'carries' the baby and the severity of morning sickness both purport to tell the gender of the baby. Even in these days of amniocentesis, antenatal clinics and scans, the process of pregnancy is one of waiting, of wondrous mystery.

In early religious beliefs, the wind, rivers and the serpent were thought to be responsible for impregnating women. Robert Graves (1992) writes that the oldest religions were based on the 'worship of the many-titled Mother-Goddess'. He says that 'Ancient Europe had no gods. The Great Goddess was regarded as immortal, changeless and omnipotent; and the concept of fatherhood had not been introduced into religious thought' (Graves 1992, p. 13). Early Greek mythology was about matriarchal societies, where the queen took lovers for fun, not for procreation. But 'once the relevance of coition to child-bearing had been officially admitted' says Graves, 'man's religious and political status improved' (p. 14).

Christianity's story of the immaculate conception and virgin birth can be seen as a tenet of faith or a myth, depending upon our own personal belief system. Marion Woodman (1985) comments that 'the word "virgin" does not mean "chaste" in either its Greek or Hebrew origins but rather "being full of nature, free, uncontrolled". The virgin archetype, Artemis in Greek mythology, is also about "becoming" and "being full of potential".' And Barbara Walker (1996) says, 'The title, virgin, didn't mean physical virginity, it meant simply – unmarried' (Walker 1996, p. 1048).

In my work with families, I ask parents to tell me the stories around their pregnancies and their children's births. Frequently I find that the way the pregnant mother feels about her pregnancy influences her perceptions of the baby, sometimes consciously and sometimes unconsciously. If the pregnancy and the birth were 'normal' then often her expectations of the baby are that 'all will be well'. Equally if the pregnancy has been difficult then the mother's anxiety about the baby is often higher. This is the start of our journey and the myths around our life in the womb are important for our own personal mythical journey.

The myths of birth

Our birth is but a sleep and a forgetting. (William Wordsworth)

Birth is associated with newness, with the beginning of something different. A baby may be devoutly wished for or it may be felt as a threat to the status quo. It is an opportunity to start again, to welcome in fresh energy, as in the birth of each New Year. The Christian birth of Jesus is such a myth. It symbolizes the renewing of energy, the starting of a new time cycle with all the attendant hopes and anticipation.

The births of the Gods in many myths have often been momentous events. Graves (1992) gives several variations of the birth of Aphrodite. Either she is rising naked from the foam of the sea riding on a scallop shell; or she 'sprang from the foam which gathered about the genitals of Uranus, when Cronus threw them into the sea; or that Zeus begot her on Dione, daughter either of Oceanus and Tetys the sea-nymph, or of Air and Earth. But all agree that she takes the air accompanied by doves and sparrows' (Graves 1992, p. 49). What an entrance into life! Michael Jordan (1995) says that the birth of a deity in many cultures does not occur by natural human means, it has to be superhuman.

> Thus the goddess Athena springs, fully armed, from the forehead of Zeus, while the divine super-hero of Nkundo myth, Lianja, emerges in like manner from his mother's thigh ... The birth process also tends to be cathartic and violent. The implication is that deities cannot be born by the same process as that which allows a mortal child into the world. Were such beings to be delivered by normal means it would perhaps dilute their numinous character. (Jordan 1995, p. xi)

Though the birth of a human child carries the archetypal elements of newness and anticipation, often the reality of the human birth is pain and suffering. Germaine Greer writes that, 'giving birth is the hardest physical task that is asked of any human, yet it happens daily under both luxurious and horrendous situations, and we barely notice' (Greer 1999, p. 106). The pains of labour, although soon forgotten as an experience, become part of a woman's psyche. The act of labour may be soon over but the intensity is not forgotten. Women's stories are full of the awesome experience of childbirth, even taking into account the clinical nature of many birth processes. Tales of birth tend to be passed on orally and become part of the family mythology, usually remaining with female members.

The nature of the individual birth and the way it is recorded takes its place in our own psyche. We hear we were 'untimely ripped' from our mother's womb, or that we 'nearly killed our mother' or 'we slid out perfectly formed and wide-eyed.' Elizabeth McCormick cites work done by a psychotherapist, Angela Wilton, into birth stories. 'She noticed how the atmosphere around the birth stories was often mirrored in the person's ways of relating to others' (McCormick 1996, p. 129). For example a client, with whom I worked for several years, said she spent her life 'in a hurry'. She gave the impression of staying for only a second or two before she had to rush on to the next activity. She spoke quickly, left sentences half finished and gasped for breath. Her birth had been premature and her mother said that she arrived 'in a great hurry', that the doctors and nurses had been 'in a panic' and that 'everyone knew about Anne's fast arrival'.

There are, of course, many different theories about the effect that these birth stories, or of women's perceptions of the unborn child, have upon the psyche of baby. The whole area of intra-uterine and birth experiences is now a very rich field of research. Freud and later Winnicott (1958a) wrote about the effect of anxiety and birth trauma upon the baby. Since then Stanislav Grof (1975, 1990) has developed theories about perinatal experiences. He also strongly supports the theory that babies have both positive and negative experiences in the environment of the womb which affect their psychological development. He maintains that our first transpersonal experiences are experiences in the womb.

Infancy and the loss of eden: 0–6 months

The infant,
Mewling and puking in the nurse's arms. (Shakespeare, *As You Like It*)

As infants we are totally dependent upon adult systems of love and care in order to survive and so it is essential that we are welcomed into a safe world. The mother (carer) – baby relationship is paramount and life is precarious and precious. The quality of holding between the mother/carer and baby will influence us in all subsequent close and intimate relationships. Those who shape our physical world will leave their print on our hearts and souls. Commenting on this point, Dr Anthony Stevens says 'the most wonderful feature of the primal relationship between infant and mother [is] that it is ruled by Eros. It is perfused with love. The moment the mother–child dyad is formed Eros is constellated; and it is out of love that ego–consciousness, selfhood and personal identity grow' (Stevens 1982, p. 13). We are vulnerable, helpless and a wondrous miracle.

However not all babies are greeted with unqualified love and safety. Myths and fairy tales acknowledge this. In many myths, soon after birth, the baby is abandoned or persecuted as were Romulus and Remus, or abandoned for their protection and raised by lowly foster parents like Oedipus, Moses, or Perdita (meaning lost) in Shakespeare's *The Winter's Tale*. The infant is often rendered helpless by the death of one parent and the abandonment by the other, as in the fairy tales of Cinderella and Rapunzel. When an infant is vulnerable it is a potential victim to adults' mistreatment and cruelty. In literature, as well as in fairy stories the abuse of children is a constant theme. Charles Dickens spent many years of his life, writing books to highlight the harsh world of the child in, for instance *Oliver Twist*, *Nicholas Nickleby*, *Bleak House* and *David Copperfield*. Roald Dahl and Rosemary Sutcliffe, the modern equivalents, show the harsh reality in which some children now exist.

Although our evolutionary progress has not yet allowed us to be born fully independent, once born the human baby is no longer part of the mother. No matter how physically close the two may be, separation has begun. Most theories (Mahler 1975, Bowlby 1953, Kohut 1971) agree about the importance of the early stages of the symbiotic relationship between mother and infant. The conflict arises about the conception of the self and the coming of individual consciousness. Does the presence of primitive communication/language, for instance, represent the presence of a separate ego at near birth? Or are these examples part of what Jung called 'the coalescing of islands of experience' which eventually lead to the formation of a self? The question is at what point does the individual consciousness come into existence? My own perspective is changing. Now I am probably nearer Stanislav Grof's (1990) thinking, as his views resonate with many of the stories I hear from parents about their own experiences of pregnancy and birth. Many of them are convinced that some form of individual consciousness exists in the womb prior to the infant being born.

The nature of attachment and nourishment

What am I?

The quality of the parental attachment is often expressed in the way parents hug, cuddle and touch the baby. We talk of the baby as being 'delicious' and 'she smells good enough to eat'. Parents use all their senses to reinforce the bonding between themselves and the infant. We also use our faces and bodies to mirror and reflect back feelings, sensations and emotions to their child. The mother/carer tries to tune in to the baby's need for food, warmth and comfort. The way parents touch their baby gives a sense of what comes from inside 'me' and what is outside. Through all these methods the baby is learning about boundaries, the differentiation between the 'I' and the 'not-I'. Inside and outside are gradually coming to be sensed as different. Children's literature illustrates this boundary setting with rhymes and stories like the finger game Round and Round the Garden, and This Little Pig Went to Market and *Where the Wild Things Are* by Maurice Sendak. The monsters, enjoying their wild rumpus, say to Max 'Oh please don't go – we'll eat you up – we love you so!'

John Bowlby (1969) looked at this very early stage of life from the perspective of attachment and bonding. He thought that the most significant human quality to be affected by separation and loss was the child's basic ability to trust. If the infant cannot trust in the primal relationship, then all other relationships may be difficult. The baby needs to be able to trust, to be safe while also being very needy and dependent. How we interpret being cared for, getting our basic needs met, will depend on our own individual blueprint and the quality of the attachment between mother/carer and infant (Johnson 1994).

Fairy tales offer another route to understanding this early stage of attachment. Good mothers die young, as in Cinderella and Snow White, and are replaced by wicked step mothers. These stories reflect the child's feelings towards her mother that begin to emerge once she realizes that the mother who answers all her nourishment needs is also the same mother who sometimes frustrates them. At first the baby's emotional experience is total, it is the whole universe. When fed and warm, the baby sleeps soundly and looks in bliss. When hungry or in pain, she screams and shouts with rage. Psychologists describe these experiences as 'good' or 'bad', not implying moral judgement but just simple feelings. The 'good enough mothering' process (Winnicott 1964) helps the baby to begin to define the edges of these emotions. Over the early months the boundaries between mother and child become clearer and by perhaps six months the child begins to suspect that her good, blissful world and her bad, painful world are caused by the same person. Sometimes the bad feelings are overwhelming and the baby cannot deny them. Fearing annihilation she must get rid of them and so projects them into the world of mother. This makes her feel better but makes the world more frightening. Alternatively she may retain all the 'bad' in herself to protect her need for a perfect, nourishing mother and so become identified with the bad. Essentially what is required is a balance. The infant must come to a healthy ambivalence in which the mother who nourishes and also sometimes withholds can be safely loved and hated and loved again without fear of reprisal. If a child receives and senses this emotional acceptance, she will be better able, as an adult, to respond to the complexities of emotional life.

3–12 months

Times They Are A-Changing (Bob Dylan)

Change and movement from one phase and stage of development to another is always a time of upheaval physically and psychologically. From around six months the baby becomes aware of the space between herself and mother. Sometimes you can see it in the baby's eyes. Gone is the immediate delight of seeing a smiling face; instead, there is a more cautious gaze, then perhaps the smile. At this stage the baby is 'playing' with the concept of 'object permanence' which is why games like peek-a-boo are such fun. Mum disappears, so baby feels a slight tension of anxiety. Boo, she appears again, laughter of delight and relief. As she gets older, the child learns to be separate more and more. The distance that she can travel away from mother becomes greater. The child can begin to 'mother' herself, to take care and help herself with small tasks. She is learning mastery over her body, learning to sit up, to walk, to talk.

The child needs the constancy and reassurance of the mother/carer in order to learn all that has to be learnt. The series of films made by James and Joyce Robertson in the late sixties, 'Young Children in Brief Separation', showed the great distress that can be suffered by children through enforced separations when their mothers were in hospital. They concluded that separation for young children, at any age, is always problematic and potentially hazardous. Their work was influential in changing the visiting rules in hospitals for both children and families.

The next momentous step is the acquisition of language. It is one of the most important achievements the infant makes. It becomes the key to more and more communication between the inner and outer worlds. It becomes the medium through which most relationships are conducted. For many it is what gives us our unique humanity (Piaget 1926, Vygotsky 1962). The way that parents respond to all this learning will influence the way that the child learns to learn throughout life. Is learning seen as fun, exciting and wondrous, or is it a matter of rushing on from one stage to the next, a way of competing with others, of proving to the world what good parents we are?

One of the ways that children manage times of change was explored by Winnicott (1958b) in his concept of the 'transitional object.' These objects, like a blanket, or a dummy are what Skynner (Skynner and Cleese 1983) calls 'portable support systems'. Christopher Bollas (1989) talks of the mother as being the transformational object. She helps transform experiences which enable the child to differentiate between what is 'me' and 'not me'.

> The theory of the transitional object has helped us to think about the infant's transition from a partly hallucinated wish world to the creative use of actual objects in the service of the child's desire. (Bollas 1989, p. 117)

I remember listening to baby trying to stand up. There was a running commentary, said in the same tones as mother, 'yes . . . up . . . up . . . 'ngain . . . up . . . up'. The child's ability to mimic mother was like having mother there as part of herself, the internalized good mother, to help and guide her.

WATCH OUT! BADDIES ABOUT: 12 MONTHS–2 YEARS

The emergence of the shadow

I have a little shadow that goes in and out with me. (A. A. Milne)

Toddlers are those clever and fascinating people who suddenly discover that they have power. They are no longer totally dependent upon the adults around them. They are becoming a person with a recognizable ego and personality. They can venture and conquer! They have discovered the word, 'No' and its effect upon adults The myth of the 'terrible twos' is told to worried and anxious parents, when their often soft and loving baby turns into a demanding, strong-willed toddler. The child is learning about will and mastery: physically, with potty training and feeding; and psychologically about things to which he can adapt and about those events that are beyond his control. He begins to anticipate his parents' responses and reactions. The loved child anticipates loving adults; the criticized child anticipates the critical adult. The toddler also begins to recognize complicated and often uncomfortable emotions, like jealousy at a younger sibling's arrival on the scene, or the hurt, and rejection felt when the seemingly loveable adults become, overnight, strict disciplinarians by suggesting that it is bed-time.

Fairy tales are full of giant-sized shadow figures which represent the importance of the feelings that are attached to them. There are the wicked stepmothers, the evil magicians, the wicked witches, the tyrants, the greedy ones and the persecutors. These figures are often 'shadowy'. They do not have a specific personality, they personify one emotion as with the jealousy of Snow White's stepmother. Marie Louise Von Franz (1995) offers a useful description of the shadow: 'we generally define the shadow as the personification of certain aspects of the unconscious personality, which could be added to the ego complex but which, for various reasons, are not'. It reflects the unacceptable feelings that a toddler may have. Everything that is unconscious and/or anything that feels too threatening to our developing ego, makes up our shadow. What we cannot accept we repress or hide in the shadow.

Fairy tales which reflect back to the child unacceptable and unpleasant feelings are useful ways of helping to acknowledge the power of the emotions and to integrate the shadow. However, if the fear is too strong to acknowledge, the child discovers other strategies to help him when he is feeling the pain of the darker side of life. Feelings of abandonment or anxiety, loss, separation, jealousy, envy, can be so powerful that the child has to do something and, being creative, he invents his own defence mechanisms. Early defence structures are to deny the experience and feeling, to repress them, to cut them out of awareness and to split off the feelings. Later more sophisticated defence mechanisms are added to these. Through projection, we place unacceptable emotions onto another. Through projective identification, we project feelings onto another and then identify the other as the feeling. The way we individually react and make up our own mixture of strategies will be unique. It is an interactive process between our archetypal expectations, our personal experience of 'the other', and our personal stories and myths.

I remember one teacher telling me that the problem with defence strategies was that they were formed because they seemed a good idea at the time. The good news was that they worked, the bad news was that they worked. The problem is that later in life when we no longer need to have these strategies, we do not know that they are there or why we invented them, so we keep stubbing our toe on them and wondering why we are stuck. So, to return to the baby, every time the baby starts to feel 'those' feelings again, unconsciously the defence pattern reasserts itself. It is a task of therapy to identify and make conscious these strategies and to try to find the different choices in life that will not simply reconfirm them.

Sibling rivalry: 10 months–3 years

Never mind the ambivalence, what about the hate!

The advent of a sibling can create huge tensions in a family. All parents know about sibling rivalry and the murderous feelings that the older (usually) child can have for the younger. These feelings can be very upsetting for the parents and for the older child who suddenly finds himself in the grip of feelings that he doesn't understand. Or the difficulties may be around a younger sibling, struggling for his place in the family and who needs to be accepted for himself and not continually compared to the older sibling. The position that we had in our family of origin will influence the way we perceive and feel about the space we occupied in that family. Adler (1964) comments that this, in turn, will influence how we relate outside the family, with our peers and later in working and social groups.

Myths and fairy tales abound with stories of the youngest son, the weakest, or the poorest, who triumphs over his brothers and wins the prize; the princess or the kingdom as in, for instance, 'The Three Feathers', 'The Three Brothers' and 'Simeli Mountain' – a variation of Ali Baba. The stories of Cain and Abel and Joseph and the Coat of Many Colours illustrate the overwhelming jealousy and anger that siblings can arouse in each other. The tale of Hansel and Gretel shows how the positive differences between the brother and sister help them to overcome their challenges. Such stories however are relatively few. I wonder if this might be because the brother–sister relationship is thought of as a 'primitive relationship' as in the early creation myths where the gods often married their sisters. Hera was such a sister/wife to Zeus as were

Isis and Osiris. Later, society came to consider this sexual relationship as taboo. Perhaps what we have done is to project the 'taboo' aspects of this relationship into the shadow and then rejected the relationship as an unacceptable part of ourselves. Certainly the way siblings relate to each other is an important part of the developing child's psyche.

MID-CHILDHOOD: 3 YEARS–7 YEARS

The growth of relationship

First we start as a nobody, then we become a somebody, then it's back to being a nobody again. (Ram Dass)

As the external world impinges more and more on the growing child, the individual begins to take steps away from the mothering process and towards the fathering principle, and so out into the world. This is a time of separation and ambivalence. The child realizes that she is a person, that the ego, the 'I' has meaning and power. The child still wants intimacy, caring, loving and also wants independence and challenge. The father becomes the symbol for this independence and striving. Now the child can explore the range of feelings and sensations that are becoming more conscious. Little events can evoke great responses, in the way of temper tantrums, passions for people, food or toys. Dreams often become very vivid with night terrors and the emotional life of the child is full of extremes.

Busy parents are being continually frustrated by their child as she competes for attention, either with the parents or with a sibling. Often the child will show a preference for one parent over the other. The loud screams of jealousy and envy are heard with cries of, 'It's not fair' and 'No, I want Dad to help me'. At the same time the child insists on doing everything for her/himself however long it might take. Mother's stories are full of 'Now it takes me longer to get out of the house than when X was a baby. S/he insists on doing everything "by myself", walking, dressing, going up or down stairs, eating, washing.'

The child is discovering sexuality, gender differences and similarities. The internal conflicting feelings, of rivalry, infant sexuality and the continuing need for care can make this an explosive time for parents. The child needs to be able to explore his/her sexual and psychological differences and similarities within safe adult boundaries.

Myths and stories reflect the themes of this stage. The competition and jealousy between the old Greek gods and goddesses can be found in many of the early stories as told by Graves (1992). The myths of Hera and Zeus reflect the ferocity and pain of feelings, of jealousy and rivalry. Shakespeare's Othello shows the inevitable destruction which follows from acting upon the instinct of jealousy. The Oedipus myth shows the power of the instincts and how difficult it is for consciousness to contain those instincts. Stephen Johnson (1994) says that the reason that this stage in a child's emotional life is difficult, is not only because of the power of the instincts, but also because, 'the issue is triadic, involving a system rather than a dyad. Such complex interactions can occur with other issues as well, but they always occur with the oedipal ones' (Johnson 1994, p. 55).

Most psychological theories say that the child's need for relationships (Johnson 1994, Bowlby 1953), individuation (Mahler 1975) and gradual psychological maturing means that he needs others who are both similar and dissimilar to himself, to love and respect (Kohut 1977). Washburn (1994) says that both girls and boys resolve this difficult time by choosing independence over intimacy, father over mother and in different ways: 'It is a shift that, for boys, is more emphatic and negatively directed against women and that for girls, is more ambivalent and conflictually weighted against themselves.' In taking this view Washburn appears to be indicating a difference between the masculine and feminine journey.

THE LATENCY PERIOD: 7 YEARS–10 YEARS

Enter Star Wars and The Yellow Brick Road

May the Force Be With You (Star Wars)

Now is the time for developing the ego strength, for grounding in the outer world. We need to become rooted in the ego in order to learn the demands of the world we live in. The world of learning and school dominates. Relationships outside the family become important. Gradually the world of monsters and giants, of fairy tales, wonder and magic, recedes and the 'real' world takes over. Archetypically this is the time when powerful collective representations of parental figures are withdrawn and according to Washburn 'these figures are finally seen in their "true" proportions, as human beings rather than gods' (Washburn 1994, p. 105).

Latency is supposed to be a period of calm between the storms of infancy and the turmoil of adolescence. Wilbur (1993) calls this 'membership consciousness' the turning outwards, away from the family. Children now know that adults are not all powerful and all knowing, that they can be judged and found wanting. Adults may be challenged or complained about, not individually, as may happen in adolescence, but in peer groups. These moans and complaints are not always based on personal issues or disagreements. They may occur because the adult has done something that does not conform or is 'unfair'. The concept of fairness is paramount. Both Piaget (1932) and Kohlberg (1976) include this concept as a significant aspect of a child's moral development.

Myths now appear in the guise of films like *Star Wars* and *The Wizard of Oz* TV soaps and cartoon characters. The young hero and heroine are not yet ready to move away from home for good. They are catching glimpses of the challenges to come but must remain in the safety of the home to learn and train. For Dorothy in *The Wizard of Oz*, the aim of her first journey is to seek the wisdom from the wizard and to encounter aspects of her own masculine and feminine before she can return home to her safe place. Luke in *Star Wars* is a lost child who sets out, ill-prepared, to find out about his parents and to help others in distress. But, after his first initiatory adventure, he must become an apprentice and learn his skills as a Jedi knight. The latest *Star Wars* film, *The Phantom Menace* has as the child hero Anakin Skywalker, Luke Skywalker's father. He is born from a virgin, in unusual circumstances, and possesses great powers and potential (reflecting the mythical births of someone superhuman). Only we, the audience, know that Anakin Skywalker goes 'to the dark side' and becomes Darth Vadar, the dark father. This echoes, in part, the puer–senex dynamic, where the ageing puer has refused to transform his energy. The ego remains dominant in the second half of life, becomes inflated and refuses to give up its power. The result is the 'dark side'.

Learned scripts/beliefs

> *Monday's child is fair of face*
> *Tuesday's child is full of grace, etc. (Anon)*

During the ages of six to ten the child is learning the 'scripts' that are around her in addition to those from her very early life. She is not yet questioning those scripts, just taking them in, absorbing them. Scripts are presented by society as 'This Is The Way Life Is'. The child often takes them in and makes them into a belief. Here are a few examples:

The throw-away remark from one six year old to another 'You are too big for that toy': the script taken in is 'My body is unacceptable'.

There is the teacher who says 'Mmm good' in a preoccupied manner in response to a picture painted: the script taken in is 'This is not perfect ... I can't paint'.

'Don't shout at me, you'll give me a headache' by one parent: the script taken in is 'I cause pain. It's all my fault'.

Then when things go wrong, inexplicably wrong, the blame for it is put onto the self: 'Bad things happen to me because ... I'm me and I'm black', or 'because I'm a girl', or 'because I'm a boy and I'm different', or 'because I'm in a wheelchair'.

Alice Miller (1987) quotes the story of the six year old who was told when her mother died, 'You must be brave; don't cry; now go into your room and play nicely' (Miller 1987, p. 41). The child learnt from this that when she becomes moved or upset she must look for a distraction. These scripts are learnt and believed because they are not challenged.

Research has shown that primary school aged children bully others by calling them names which lowers the status of the child in the eyes of others. (DFE 1994). Informal recent research has indicated that names like 'gay', 'homo', are the most powerful and hurtful. For girls the worst taunts are 'slag', or 'gay'. Insults like these show that the charge of homosexuality and promiscuity are still powerful ways of cutting down, excluding and dominating your peers. These scripts are learned early in life.

Racial intolerance is learnt early as is shown clearly in this song from *South Pacific*:

You've got to be taught before it's too late . . . to hate all the people your relatives hate . . . You've got to be carefully taught . . . before you are six or seven or eight . . . to hate everybody whose skin is a different hue . . ., etc.

Is this how the outsider becomes the shadow, the archetypal different one, the enemy?

Finally with the growing awareness we have about child abuse, we need to think about the scripts of the perpetrator of abuse and their effect on the developing child. The 'abuser' often manipulates with honeyed words that have great power, for example, 'You are beautiful and this is our secret'. The script that might be learnt from this is, 'My body is special and I must keep it locked up for you'.

WELCOME TO OUR WORLD: ADOLESCENCE

There's a place for us,
Somewhere a place for us
Time together with time to spare (Leonard Bernstein, *West Side Story*)

When thinking about the themes of adolescence the most important word is change; change that is physical, emotional and psychological. It is an age of discomfort, of not wanting to be wherever you are; of wanting life to be full and empty, both at once. Most adolescents feel they don't fit, whether it is their clothes, their friends or society. Often they feel that nobody has been in this place before, nobody can have felt how they feel now. The stages of adolescence are often an intense reflection of the stages of infancy. There is an emergence from an undefined sexuality into the reality of sexuality. There is movement away from the parents into the outside world. As childhood recedes, the child often becomes lost in the shadow, only to emerge later, demanding to be reclaimed as our 'inner child'. The adolescent's attention is primarily occupied with the relationships in the outer world. Relationships with the family, school and society are all examined, sometimes through drugs, partying, rebellion, violence and gangs. Towards the end of adolescence the theme of 'what is my life about?' appears. The archetypal image of the philosopher often enters into the life of the adolescent. Time is spent thinking about life, death and sex and for thinking beyond themselves, for a quest, a cause, something to live and die for.

Carpe diem – Seize the day

Films like *Dead Poets' Society* and *Trainspotting* show the ambivalence and extremes that are typical of adolescence. The quotation at the beginning of this section is the phrase that starts the fire of creativity burning in *Dead Poets' Society*. It is the inspiration for the vision quest. Richard Frankel (1998) observes that while some other cultures retain adolescent initiation ceremonies and rites ours has no formal marker. He asks,

Is the need for formal markers to acknowledge the passage from childhood to adulthood still alive, albeit unconsciously, in the psyche of modern man and woman? Is the need for initiation archetypal? If the archetype of initiation is a structural component of the psyche, then it is going to occur whether or not a given culture formally invests in such rites. (Frankel 1998, p. 55)

Perhaps we can see this archetypal need searching for expression in same sex gangs. Here initiation is performed by the gangs and gives membership to an exclusive group identity that separates the adolescent from the parents. While this healthy instinct is certainly necessary, the absence of an initiating elder does mean that alienation from the wider society can and does occur.

Another issue which often comes strongly to the surface at this time, although it, too, will have had its precursors in earlier years, is the issue of race.

For all practical purposes 'race' is not so much a biological phenomenon as a social myth (UNESCO). We are all wounded by racism, but for some of us those wounds are anaesthetised. None of us, black or white, wants to feel the pain that racism has caused. But when you feel it, you're awake.' (Toi Derricotte 1997)

Reading statements like this does wake me up. It makes me think about my responsibilities to the individual and to the wider community, something which adolescents do very easily. They constantly make us think about issues that sometimes society would rather ignore, difficult issues like children who are in one-parent families, children in step-families, adopted children, multiple births, disabilities and about us all living in a multiracial, multicultural society. These are all part of the collective myths, the ever increasing circles within which each individual lives and which adolescents question and explore.

Mothers, fathers and daughters

I am all the daughters of my father's house,
And all the brothers too. (Shakespeare, *Twelfth Night*)

The heroine's journey begins to be different from her brother's with the coming of the constellation of the father archetype in childhood. At the stage of moving from the influence of the matriarchal archetype, of caring and nurturing, to the patriarchal archetype of independence, she has different tasks to perform from her brother. She must separate from mother and make a relationship with the world of the masculine and her own inner masculine while still being connected to herself. The goddess Artemis is often seen as the archetypal image behind many adolescent girls. She is fiercely independent, values her freedom and is the icon for all 'tomboys'. Her physical energy is her life force. She has also been recognized as a powerful image behind the feminist movements with her emphasis on 'sisterhood' and self-sufficiency. Artemis symbolizes the need for the adolescent girl to find her relationship with her own inner masculine and feminine before exploring more deeply her own femininity. Marion Woodman believes that, 'Girls can identify with Mother for a much longer period of time, since there is no biological or social imperative for them to separate from her.'

She continues, 'a girl needs to separate out and become her own person. Failure to sever the unconscious bond (between mother and daughter) eventually constellates a negative relationship' (Woodman 1996, p. 25).

At the same time going too far into the world of the father at the expense of her growing feminine can lead to a later necessity to 'reconnect with the femininity source, ground and spirit' (Sylvia Brinton Perera 1981, p. 7). She maintains that this is the path of the feminine journey. She says that young girls, in our society are very good 'daughters of the father' and their path is to break away from father to find their own femininity. Once we have broken away from the outer father, then we can find our own deep femininity and our own internalized father. Thomas Moore believes that both women and men need to find their own deep father figure to provide a sense of authority. 'The feeling that you are the authority of your own life.' He continues, 'We need father figures badly, people who can keep us in touch with or stimulate within us that profound principle in the soul that provides guidance and wisdom' (Moore 1992, p. 37).

The bridge from childhood into womanhood, for daughters, is through menstruation, the rite de passage for girls. Menstruation has always been seen as the Great Female Mystery. The beginning of the ability to recreate is invested with great significance by all cultures. Barbara Walker (1996) takes fourteen pages to detail the many myths, initiation rites and ceremonies that are in the collective consciousness. For a young girl menstruation is the first great surrender to forces beyond her control. The body dictates what happens and the girl can only respond. Physically the body becomes capable of procreation but psychologically she may still be a little girl. As our society has no puberty rites, a lot of splitting and disassociation from the body can and does occur. Often the adolescent girl rejects her body and tries to repress the conflicting feelings she has about herself. Thus the muscle, physicality and sexuality of icons like Madonna and the Spice Girls become important as images of how it may be possible to become a potent and embodied woman.

Female clients frequently remember their first menstruation as a time of confusion and isolation. Many talk of not being able to share their feelings with other female members of their family or close friends. Their experiences were often of being very separate from their mothers at this time. As psychotherapists, we need to understand the importance of puberty and menstruation, the way our clients felt, what was valued and what was devalued.

We also need to explore the individual myths and beliefs that may still be around from this stage and which, consciously or unconsciously, may influence the client's way of being in the world.

THE CHILD IN THE ADULT

In this section I give three examples of how the 'child in the adult' has appeared in some of my therapeutic work with clients. Sometimes represented as 'the inner child', these early feelings can be understood through the beliefs and myths that surrounded these adult clients in childhood.

When we come into therapy, for whatever reason, we come with our own unique case history. We will have our own truths, myths, beliefs and stories. The telling of our tales and having them witnessed by a compassionate 'other' is a powerful and healing experience in itself. Having our stories accepted, perhaps for the first time, is liberating and validating.

In every therapeutic relationship there are several processes going on from the start. One is the telling of the client's material, and another is the context in which the material is presented. The material has its own rhythm and patterns. It will unfold through the stories, dreams, myths and beliefs that the client chooses to tell. It will also evolve through the techniques chosen by the therapist; for example, active imagination, working with dreams and the many different creative techniques.

The context is everything else. It is the 'spaces' between and around the material. When sitting with a client we try to be totally present with whatever happens in the session. As the transpersonal witness we are attentive to the presence of the client, the content of what is being said and the context. By staying with the whole therapeutic process and with ourselves we become, mindful, meditatively reflective, as well as deeply engaged. This mindfulness creates the spaces for change, transformation and healing. It is in these 'spaces' that we can also catch a glimpse of the child in the adult. What can be revealed is the child who has been repressed or rejected; the child who has been put aside for the perceived needs of the adult. Mary was one such client.

Mary

Mary was in her thirties and a single mother of two. Her second child had learning difficulties. She was telling me the story of her pregnancy with her second child. For the last four months of her pregnancy she was in hospital because she had developed difficulties with her womb. Throughout the time in hospital she talked to the baby, laughed and cried to him. She played music and sang to him. She treated the baby as a live presence in the room. She would cry to him of her helplessness, of her anger at the medical profession for not being able to 'do' more. When the boy was eventually born, by caesarean section, he appeared well and healthy for the first few months. Later, he was diagnosed as having learning difficulties and that is when she said 'I knew it all along, they didn't have to tell me. Now I began to know the meaning of suffering but I had prepared him for his trials ahead when he was in my belly. He knew! He was special!'

While listening to her story I was watching her body language, the way she continually clasped her hands round her belly, her hands gently stroking it. Her voice was low, and her facial expression one of wonder and sadness and then anger. Her breathing was shallow and just perceptible. With the words 'he was special', her voice gained strength, she broke into a broad smile, her posture changed. From a collapsed state, she sat up quickly, her back straightened, her head went up, she looked directly at me. There was no doubting the force and power in her face, body and presence. The shift in her energy was dramatic. I felt it in my belly. I mirrored her non–verbal body language, I too sat up straight and immediately felt stronger. She then repeated in a firmer tone, 'Yes, that's right, special' We both stayed silent and straight. I was staying with the feelings that her material was awakening in my body. This empathic connection enabled me to stay present. Seconds before that statement I had been feeling heavy and 'dull', now I was full of energy and alert. There was initially a 'felt sense' connection between us, then a 'felt shift' as the quality of the energy changed. I was wondering what the shift in energy was about, what had happened, what was she feeling and what was the word 'special' about? Mary was now breathing more deeply and I was aware of my breath. I did not ask, aloud, about any of these phenomena, although on another occasion I might have done. I just continued to be as aware as I could of everything that was happening in that moment. By holding the feeling of every energetic change and movement, I felt in tune with her. She then took a deep breath and said 'Special, yes, he is to me. I knew from the moment I was pregnant that this one was different, it wasn't just my womb, I knew before that. I loved him from the start, so I could not get rid of him, I just couldn't'

She then dropped her eyes, her back relaxed, her hands came up to her face and she began to speak slowly and carefully of her own birth and childhood. Her breathing deepened, her face reddened, she had tears in her eyes and she began to talk clearly and with warmth. Her own birth had been difficult, she had been told often 'you nearly caused your mother to die', just as her own second child had threatened her life. She remembered little affection or love from her parents. Hers was a story of pain and neglect and a story she had not told before. Throughout her childhood she had shown great courage and strength to survive both at home and at school. She had been truly 'special' and creative.

In later sessions, we explored her early experiences, through drawings, sandplay and talk. Sandplay therapy enabled her, as it does with many clients, to be both safe and creative and to make a sacred space for healing and transformation. In the sand she was able to manifest physically what she had hidden away from herself. As a child she had been unable to bear the pain of her wounding and had repressed her overwhelming feelings. She had split off from their intensity. This had been a creative way of helping herself to survive and as a strategy it had been very effective. My place in the therapy was to help her re-member the parts of herself that she had split off. I offered her the stillness of my attention, so that our relationship became the vessel for change and transformation. At the level of transference, I became the accepting mother for Mary. I was able to connect with her so that she could re-connect with those neglected parts of herself. The therapeutic sessions were the nurturing space for her to continue towards healing and wholeness. The vessel of the transpersonal therapy is the stillness of the therapist's attention.

Farah

My image of Farah, from her story as a child in her family's flight from the Middle East, is of a small, lonely child in a bleak, mountainous landscape. I met her when she was twenty-eight. She was a successful teacher in an inner city school. Farah came to see me because she felt 'empty, depressed and aimless'. She said that although she never really had time to stop and think because teaching was such a demanding job, underneath all the rushing about she felt really sad. Her relationships with her husband

and child were deteriorating. She loved teaching and although the headteacher was very demanding she respected Farah and gave her positive support. Within minutes of her coming into the room, I felt that Farah was on the verge of crying although she rarely did. When I asked her to stay with the feelings in her body, her felt sense, she would say 'I'm just tired, that's all, it's a relief to sit down'.

Initially Farah, in a flat and expressionless voice, concentrated upon her immediate concerns and worries. She wanted to make things better, and quickly. She thought the problem was that she was trying to do too much. She thought the problems were school based. She told me very little of her early life and said she had no memory of her country of birth or the journey to Europe. She said that she had 'forgotten' that time, and she explained to me 'It was much worse for my parents, had we been found, they would have been shot. We children might have survived, as slaves. We were different from everyone, we had a different religion.'

One day she arrived, very upset and very alive. She was full of anger and energy. She told me that there had been a fight in her class between a girl and boy. The boy had called the girl, among other things 'a cardboard slag' (meaning homeless and worthless) Farah said 'I lost it. I was so angry. I shouted at him. I never shout. I sent him out of the room and then followed him, still shouting. I lost my temper, I never scream. My headteacher was kind but she said I must sort this out. I couldn't go back into class, I was crying so much. I wanted to hit him, call him names, beat him up. I know it was calling her a cardboard slag, that did it, he had such contempt in his voice. How dare anyone do that or say that, it's not right. I know there's more to it than a stupid boy making a remark he doesn't understand, so what is it?'

I asked her how she was feeling, right now, and she said, 'Now, I've stopped being angry I feel shaky, I think I frightened myself.' I asked her to stay with those feelings and to identify where in her body that shaking was. She put her hands, above her breast, by her heart, and said 'Here'. I asked her to keep her hand where it was and see if she remembered having had that feeling before, when she was younger. This helped her to stay with the physical feeling, and let her body speak directly to her. After a silence, she began to tell me bits about the journey across Europe with her parents. She remembered only snippets, the darkness, her feet hurting, being tired, her father carrying her. 'But most of all' she said, beginning almost imperceptibly to shake, 'I was terrified, I didn't know it but I was so frightened. I must have been frightened for years,' she said, 'I was so scared . . . so scared'. She sat with her feelings, feeling the fear in her body, now, mostly in her stomach, still shaking and gradually images came, the landscape, the other families, the children she met, the hunger and then the food.

This very physical link that Farah made between the fear she felt after the confrontation in the classroom and the fear she had felt as a child enabled our work to deepen. Over the next few sessions we looked at her profound feelings of being valueless, of no importance and often an object for contempt. She linked these feelings with the experiences of her journey. She drew her images and sculpted the landscape in the sand. She was very animated, she had reconnected to life. Words and images came pouring out of her. Between sessions she spoke to her parents about their journey and, although initially they had been reluctant, they helped her fill in the details of the story.

After about the third session of being fully engaged in her material she arrived again listless and quiet. It was as if she had 'run out of steam', which Farah knew by now was an indication that she was coming up against another defence strategy, or 'more stuff' as she called it. In the week previously she had created a sandtray and she had chosen two figures to represent her grandparents. She had put them in a far corner of the tray, behind a mound of sand, saying 'they're left at home'. She had not referred back to them. Now she said, 'Last week I didn't say anything about my grandparents. And afterwards I thought . . . and that is just what happened. I didn't say goodbye, I just left. I loved my grandmother and I just left her . . . and she let me go, why did she do that?' The loss of her grandmother, with no explanations, had been the most wounding event of her early years. She had not been able to grieve, she had felt 'silenced' by the events. Her parents, believing that 'forgetting the past' was the best way to be safe and survive, did not attempt to explain to her why they had fled in such fear.

Farah, as a very young child, had been disconnected from her feelings of fear and loss, nor did she have the language to express those feelings. Her parents had been unable to discuss feelings with her. They were not able to provide the space for 'reverie', that dreamlike state where experiences can be told and retold and so made safe and made into family myths (Winnicott 1965). As we continued to work together she was able to get in touch with her deep, hidden anger at her parents and grandparents and to grieve for her grandmother and her abandoned, silenced child- hood. Cut off from her background, Farah had become isolated and depressed. Her defence structures of maintaining her separateness were working well until the moment of crisis when they collapsed. Her crisis was precipitated by a small boy and she was then able to embark on her inner journey into her dark world to reconnect with herself. In the therapy, part of my role was to give space for the reverie that Farah had not had. I was like the parent or grandparent who hears the story being told and retold in an atmosphere of compassion, safety and peace until the child is no longer imprisoned by her past.

Dave

My final example is of Dave who was twenty-two. He was an accountant. He came to me because he was shy and found communicating with people outside work, almost impossible. He had, what he called a 'Prince Charming' personality on the outside, a very pleasant, smiling, friendly man, but he was strictly outside only, inside was a 'lonely bastard'. He wanted to have friends. Although he had a group of acquaintances and would go out with them, he said 'I am always on the edge, on the outside'. He remembered his childhood as 'happy and unexciting'. He thought his difficulties started in adolescence. 'Overnight' he said, 'I became a stroppy teenager, I just wanted to get out. I became bad-tempered and foul.' He disappointed his parents by leaving school early and went travelling for over a year. When he returned he worked in a large departmental store and studied for his accountancy exams. He thought he was popular in the store 'because I was Prince Charming to the customers and worked hard'. He passed his accountancy exams and almost immediately found himself his present job.

He said, 'for the first time in my life, I am earning decent money, living well and I want out, I just want to leave it all, I mean I just want to disappear'. He started keeping a journal and got to know his 'Prince Charming' and 'lonely bastard' through drawing and the sandtray. During this time he experienced great mood swings and was either working hard or sitting at home feeling 'darker and darker'.

One day when he was writing in his journal he said, 'I was sitting there and I realized Prince Charming was really a woman dressed as a man, and it suddenly clicked, that's how I've been feeling, ever since I was a teenager. I've been pretending to be something I'm not. And I think it's around sex. I'm not going to pretend anymore. I think I'm gay and . . . I think . . . I want to do something about it.' As he told me, he was relaxed and calm, his words came out thoughtfully. His body was still and he was breathing deeply. I could 'feel' the space between words as he was saying them, there was truth in each word. His words were very grounded and real. He said that he felt good and strange saying it straight out to me the way he had. 'I feel I'm greeting myself for the first time, hello Dave,' he repeated 'hello Dave.' Then there was silence. A long silence full of space. He continued, 'I think I disappeared when I was thirteen. It was then I silenced myself and decided sex was not for me. At school you had to be either a macho boy or a gay, and I didn't want to be either. Being a macho boy just wasn't me. So I decided to be a nothing.'

I end this example here, as I want only to illustrate how the events in adolescence, for Dave, triggered his ability to receive help. When Dave arrived to see me, he knew that he was not being truly himself. I did not need to point that out to him. The two personas of 'Prince Charming' and 'lonely bastard' had been his creative strategies for feeling 'a nothing' in life. When Dave felt confident that we had both fully accepted the personas of 'Prince Charming' and the 'lonely bastard', then he could begin his journey of integration. He needed open, accepting, friendly space from me in order to trust himself to begin the work he wanted to do. For me this is the essence of my understanding of the transpersonal perspective of psychotherapy. On the surface I try to 'do' very little. I try to listen to, and accept with an open heart, whatever the client brings to the session. I encourage the client to connect thoughts, feelings with their body, now, in the present, and see where those embodied feelings can lead. Then with a sense of mutual musing and wondering we can let the process develop.

CONCLUSION

There are more things . . . (Shakespeare, *Hamlet*)

As adults we have to try to understand what is going on in our unconscious which may be influencing the way we behave, think and feel. In childhood we could safely project our hatred onto wicked stepmothers and our fears onto giants. But adulthood is 'wake-up' time. Our task as adults is to learn to reclaim our projections and understand what is going on in our process. We have to embark on our individual journey to our own underworld to reclaim our own monsters and treasures. We need compassionate and mindful people to travel with us. We want companions who will not leave us at the first danger, who will accompany us, be alongside us, and who, because of their own journey, will be able to empathize with the joy and pain of it all. We need 'unconditional friendliness' (Welwood 1985) from ourselves and from our therapist.

In this chapter I have explored some of the psychological theories, personal and collective myths, and beliefs that accompany the development of a child and adolescent. To include all theories and stories would not be possible in this context. This is but a beginning. These myths, beliefs and stories offer us an understanding of our own human and spiritual development through which the richness of our spirit and soul and those of our clients can be revealed. We need, in our training and practices, to keep developing our compassion and mindfulness so we can learn to look with a friendly eye at the creative, ingenious and extraordinary ways in which we try to find our way through life.

REFERENCES

Adler, A. (1964). *The Individual Psychology of Alfred Adler*. New York: Harper & Row.

Bollas, C. (1989). *Forces of Destiny*. London: Free Assoc. Press.

Bowlby, J. (1953). *Child Care and the Growth of Love*. London: Pelican.

Bowlby, J. (1969). *Attachment and Loss, Volume 1*. London: Hogarth Press.

Bowlby, J. (1973). *Attachment and Loss, Volume 2*. London: Hogarth Press.

Bowlby, J. (1979). *The Making and Breaking of Affectional Bonds*. London: Tavistock Publications.

Campbell, J. (1987). *Creative Mythology*. Dallas: Offset Paperback Manufacturers Inc.

Department for Education (DfE) (1994). *Bullying, don't suffer in silence*. London: HMSO.

Derricotte, T. (1997). *The Black Notebooks*. New York and London: W. W. Norton.

Frankel, R. (1998). *The Adolescent Psyche*. London: Routledge.

Graves, R. (1992). *The Greek Myths*. London: Pelican.

Greer, G. (1999). *The Whole Woman*. London: Doubleday.

Grof, S. (1975). *Realms of the Human Unconscious: observations from LSD research*. New York: Penguin.

Grof, S. (1990). *The Holotropic Mind*. San Francisco: HarperCollins.

Grof, S. (1993). *The Holotrophic Mind*. New York: HarperCollins.

Johnson, S. (1994). *Character Styles*. New York: Norton.

Jordan, M. (1995). *Myths of the World*. London: Kyle Cathie.

Kohlberg, L. (1976). *Moral Development and Behaviour*. New York: Holt, Reinhart and Winston.

Kohut, H. (1971). *The Analysis of the Self*. New York: International Universities Press.

Kohut, H. (1977). *Restoration of the Self*. New York: International Universities Press.

McCormick, E. (1996). *Change for the Better*. New York: Cassell.

Mahler, M. (1975). *The Psychological Birth of the Infant*. London: Hutchinson.

Miller, A. (1987). *The Drama of Being a Child*. London: Virago.

Moore, T. (1992). *Care of the Soul*. London: Piatkus.

Perera, S. Brinton, (1981). *Descent to the Goddess*. Toronto: Inner City Books.

Piaget, J. (1926). *The Language and Thought of the Child*. New York: Harcourt Brace.

Piaget, J. (1932) (1977). *The Moral Judgement of the Child*. New York: Harcourt Brace Jovanovich.

Stevens, A. (1982). *Archetype: a Natural History of the Self*. London: Routledge.

Skynner, R. and Cleese, J. (1983). *Families and how to survive them*. London: Mandarin.

Von Franz, M. (1995). *Shadow and Evil in Fairy Tales*. Boston and London: Shambhala.

Vygotsky, L. (1962). *Language and Thought*. Cambridge, Mass.: MIT Press.

Walker, B. (1996). *The Women's Encyclopedia of Myths and Secrets*. New Jersey: Castle.

Washburn, M. (1994). *Transpersonal Psychology in Psychoanalytic Perspective*. New York: State University of New York Press.

Welwood, J. (1985). *Awakening the Heart*. Boston and London: Shambhala.

Wilbur, K. (1993). *The Spectrum of Consciousness*. New York: Quest Books.

Winnicott, D. W. (1958a). *Birth Memories, Birth Trauma and Anxiety*. In *Collected Papers* (1958). London: Tavistock Publications.

Winnicott, D. W. (1958b). *Transitional Objects and Transitional Phenomena*. In *Collected Papers* (1958). London: Tavistock Publications.

Winnicott, D. W. (1964). *The Child, the Family and the Outside World*. London: Pelican.

Winnicott, D. W. (1965). *The Family and Individual Development*. London: Tavistock Publications.

Woodman, M. (1985). *The Pregnant Virgin*. Toronto: Inner City Books.

Woodman, M. (1996). *Dancing in the Flames*. Dublin: Gill & Macmillan.

CHAPTER 4

The wound

Nigel Wellings

What's love got to do with it? (Tina Turner)

Editor's note: Psychopathology can reduce patterns of human adaptation and suffering into dry terminology, thus limiting our relationship with the many forms of human suffering. While it is necessary to have a firm grasp of developmental processes and a wide understanding of the different responses to environmental hardship and difficulty, it is important to be able to see a patient within their own individual context, with their own unique response and pattern of adjustment. This chapter describes the kinds of woundings to our early development that casts a hold of our personality and shapes character. These woundings can create severe limitations to the flow of human expression, to the development of a strong ego and in particular to the available experience of 'self'. They also create characterological movements that make us who we are, link us to our past and bring us into direct relationship with the frustration of archetypal intent.

Nigel Wellings offers us a creative and compassionate look at patterns of wounding. In bringing us, sometimes painfully, close to those early responses that become shaped into narcissistic or masochistic wounding, he awakens us into complete equality with the patients with whom we work.

Woven into the text is the understanding that the wound also carries the potential for healing. The therapist's understanding and embracing of these potential paths of meeting and healing is at the heart of clinical transpersonal psychotherapeutic practice.

E.W.M.

Each stage of life includes separations and pain. The way we experience and respond to this is influenced by our own inborn dispositions and the culture we are a member of. In the west there is a belief, a prevailing myth, that pain, unhappiness and suffering may be alleviated by psychological health and a sufficiency of material provision. However this is not the only story. Universally there exist different value systems and with these, different understandings of the nature of human suffering. Transpersonal Psychotherapy embraces both occidental and oriental views, combining the perspectives of dynamic psychotherapy, a Western model, and, among others, Buddhist psychology, an Eastern model. In this chapter we will look at human suffering from the Western, psychotherapeutic view and finally consider some spiritual pathologies from the perspectives of both West and East.

A WORD OF CAUTION

Before we start we also need to be aware of the ambivalence that this subject generates among psychotherapists. Samuels (1989) lists in his introduction the objections that are frequently levelled at psychopathologizing. He says descriptive categories become labels that harm the skills of intuition and listening, merely reflect the mind of the categorizer, are relative, reflect ethical prejudices, may be (mis)used politically and fail to reflect the mercurial nature of the psyche. Furthermore a good pathologist is not necessarily a good therapist. To these I would add two more. Firstly, and perhaps most importantly, I have noticed that when we gain an insight into our nature and its suffering through a story, a myth or a fairy tale, then the *feeling* of this insight, makes the person somehow 'bigger' than they were previous to having it. Contrary to this, when an insight is gained via identification with a psychological theory there is often a background 'taste' of somehow being diminished. I am not entirely sure why this should be except to note that the first is an illumination gained by the recognition of oneself through the multidimensional lens of a symbol while the second is through the one-dimensional glass of a theoretical concept. For a simple example compare the *quality* of insight offered by the immediacy of the image of 'Peter Pan' as against 'over prolonged adolescence'. While they mean the same the former carries a wealth of emotional richness while the second does not. The image of Peter Pan does more than say it is time to grow up but adds to this prosaic truth the complex desires and fears that surround this archetypal transition into adult life. As Joseph Campbell has said, the symbol 'opens out behind'. Here it opens the individual to the archetype of youth and the glories and sadnesses that this contains and represents. Because of this seeming truth, all the theoretical concepts that this chapter is constructed from will always be in danger of making their subjects, those so labelled, smaller than they were before they were identified through the glass of whichever description seems to most fit. This is not to say we should not use psychopathological descriptions, but rather every descriptive gain pays the price of limitation.

My second concern is that when we label another with a description of their wound we can obscure the whole person. We may easily do this because many of us deeply fear mental and emotional pain and instinctively seek to protect ourselves by making ourselves different from those that have the 'problem'. Labelling, thus may be used as a distancing defence against our own pain reflected in another's. While this may be understandable for a person who feels vulnerable, for us who practise psychotherapy, it is inexcusable. We need to let the other person in the therapeutic dialogue touch us, sometimes deeply, and know that we and they are both people who are similarly engaged in the difficult and strange event of living. While we can usefully find patterns of experience within people's lives that will enable us to understand their pain better, we must never forget that we also fit these patterns and that, we and our patients, remain individual mysteries which are more then the sum of the wounds. With the analytic insight that this chapter provides it is necessary to mix in equal measure a contemplative attitude of compassionate acceptance that allows the strange other to be. Here clarity of thought needs to be tempered with the sensitivity of the heart.

FROM THE SOWER A SEED

Imagine a seed, perhaps the seed of a tree floating down to earth. Within this seed is the genetic information from which it can potentially reproduce all the characteristics of its species. For this to actually happen two things must also exist, the seed must have access to the environmental factors necessary for growth, the correct soil, space, water and sun. It must also have favourable circumstances, that during its life it is not attacked by anything that would distort or destroy it. Part of the seed's potential is adaptability and it will tolerate a band of less than perfect environmental factors and circumstances. If the shortfall is sustainable the tree will still thrive and since it is rare to have all its needs met perfectly it will, like all trees, bear happily the marks of tough years and the damage of wear and tear. However, as the shortfall increases and the adaptability becomes increasingly stretched, the tree will either fail to grow or will wither and perish. We are just the same. We too have our optimal needs and when they are denied, we also wither and perish. Also, like the tree, we are adaptable and this ability includes being able to find meaning in the frustration of our needs so that circumstances that cause pain may become circumstances that also give us experience that is ultimately viewed as valuable.

SYMPTOM AS SYMBOL

Transpersonal Psychology is primarily interested in the process of our potential finding the maximum expression and the creative adaptions necessary to fit the limits life sets; this is the tension within the individuation process. These areas of frustration are of particular interest because they are frequently the very same areas that, involving struggle, finally bring out the best in us. For this reason the painful distortions that we sometimes have to make to survive, the places of stuckness, the areas of neurosis, are not viewed as a wound to be removed by finding a 'cure' but rather as a gateway into our own unique expression of human possibility. The neurosis, the wound is, in itself, the psyche's attempt to heal itself. The particular qualities or symptoms are simultaneously symbols for what is required for healing. Simplistically, the heart that suffers an attack may also be the same that needs to break open to more intimate relationship. Of course, this is difficult to hear when we want the pain to stop but listening to someone who has found meaning and come to peace with terrible suffering is usually sufficient evidence of how out of pain may come something priceless.

Stories that connect the wound and the healing in the person of the 'wounded healer' are not uncommon. At the beginning of European medicine is found the Greek story of the centaur Chiron who like the Grail King bore an unhealing wound. To Chiron Apollo sent his son Asclepios to be taught the healing arts and from this Asclepios established his sleep cure of purificatory bathing followed by dreaming. This incubation (literally, lying on the ground), a brooding on and heating of the unconscious, would then produce a 'cure'. Again the ancient arts of shamanism seem to have been practised by those who bore physical and psychological wounds, and who, as in the Asclepion cure, would travel from one world to the next in search of the lost soul, the cause of the illness. These original shaman, medicine men and women, the native doctors, seem to have much in common despite the physical distances between them. From them we can see that they formulated a study of the soul's suffering (psychopathology) that has essentially remained intact.

SOUL LOSS, SPIRIT POSSESSION, THE ORIGINAL PSYCHOPATHOLOGY

Forest E. Clements (1932) has distinguished five categories of healing that native doctors use. These include soul restoration, the intrusion of a disease, an (evil) spirit and aggressive sorcery that each require exorcism and lastly, the breaking of a taboo that requires confession and atonement. Dr Antony Stevens (1993) has suggested that these may be further reduced to two 'archetypal' illnesses; soul loss and spirit possession, 'something has got out' and 'something has got in'.

Following Stevens we learn that soul loss most closely resembles what we would call depression. Depression is typified by a loss of the vital spark, the soul. When we suffer this we experience feelings of hopelessness, apathy and agitated anxiety. Our natural appetites for food, sleep and sex are lost and replaced by a sense of alienation from our vital selves. The cure for this is the restoration of the soul and it is interesting that the ancestral methods of shamanism and contemporary psychotherapy still use similar methods to effect this. While the original healers would go on a journey into the underworld on their patients' behalf, there to negotiate or battle for the soul's return, we enter the underworld, the unconscious, with our patients, via the dream, the active imagination and the transference and alongside them make the same struggle. Both methods involve tracking the lost life force and identifying when it was lost and what continues to keep it so.

Spirit possession, something having got in, is more complex. Here it may be an illness, an evil spirit or an antagonistic act of sorcery. In all these events the underlying idea is that there is something out there that causes harm if it gets into our bodies. Put plainly, we can immediately see that this continues as the guiding myth within modern western medicine as well as the universal understanding of healers since earliest times. Apart from the material truth of this, as in bacterial and viral infections, there is also a sense which suggests a world where it is necessary to remain ever vigilant for something beyond our control taking over. What that may be can range from overwhelming others to our own aggressive feelings (placed in others because we dare not recognize them in ourselves), reflected back and then felt as persecutory. That is, we feel threatened by our own projected shadow. The healing for this is traditionally returning the bad thing back to where it belongs. In psychotherapy this means accepting that which is mine as mine and thereby no longer needing the paranoid and obsessional behaviours that were previously used to keep this reality at bay. It is sobering to note that this is an ailment that possesses the entire world, mirrored in the archetypal image of the dangerous outsider and stranger.

The last category, the breaking of taboo which requires confession and atonement is almost in the 'something has got in' group because we are invaded by feelings of guilt and these may only be placed outside ourselves at a cost. The deal includes confession for forgiveness and this still represents an element of therapeutic experience. We put the guilty and shameful parts of ourselves out into the therapeutic vessel where the non-judgemental attitude of the therapist may enable us to find forgiveness for ourselves and others. Catharsis (literally, purification), placing outside by speech, writing, drawing and painting or whatever means, are our modern equivalents of the ancient rituals of purification by water and fire. Is it any surprise that these expressions often come in floods of tears and vicious anger?

THE TOO FRAGILE EGO AND THE TOO RIGID EGO

Following on from here we may begin to look at the soul's suffering from the perspective of contemporary dynamic psychotherapy. Transpersonal Psychotherapy accepts, with other psychotherapeutic schools, the research of developmental psychology that has continued, altered and rejected some of the earlier theoretical models. We can begin to understand this by building upon the two archetypal wounds, soul loss and spirit possession, from the above section. Here they become the patterns of ego wounding that may occur when a combination of inborn disposition, not good enough parenting and external circumstances combine.

To understand this it is first necessary to return to Edinger's idea showing how during the course of a lifetime the personal sense of identity, the ego, emerges out of the totality of the person, the Self, continues in its differentiation until at the midpoint of life ego and Self are at their most separate and then, as life moves to its close, ego is once again slowly subsumed within the Self, but this time, consciously. Of course this is an ideal picture that life usually only approximates at best, however there is enough truth in it to make it useful. It is against this ideal possibility that the wounds to the soul's journey, or more prosaically, the disruption to the ego's development, are set. Ideally, the perfectly healthy ego would be entirely in balance between having sufficient strength so that it contained the shadow and not become identified with its contents on the one hand and sufficient permeability so that the shadow may inform and renew it on the other. And at each stage of the journey that Edinger describes it would be phase appropriate. That is, during the first half of life the ego would become more separate and differentiated from its own unconscious ground and also from other egos and in the latter half it would gradually melt and open as it perceived its archetypal nature, the Self. However, for most, this remains an ideal and we become stuck on one side or the other, in one or another phase. These wounds may be once again placed within two basic categories: too fragile an ego and too rigid an ego.

Too Fragile

If our ego does not properly emerge from the Self, that is the ego is too fragile, then we shall experience a life of being overwhelmed by the contents of the collective and personal unconscious. In an extreme case this may be expressed in a psychotic illness where the ego is incapable of differentiating between the great mythic themes that run through each of us at a collective level and our own individual and human part in them. Having this experience will make functioning in the world very difficult and emotional relationships virtually impossible. At a less severe level a rudimentary ego, sometimes called a weak ego, will be vulnerable to any stress because it is likely to regress under the strain which again is to be overwhelmed by the contents of the unconscious. Living with such an ego needs a lot of defensive structures to keep the danger of fragmentation and annihilation at bay and so will be socially limited. From the shamanic perspective this would come under spirit possession because the rudimentary and vulnerable ego will experience the unconscious as something attacking and invading from outside. Descriptions of typical psychotic delusions repeatedly confirm this.

Too Rigid

If we have too rigid an ego then we will exclude the unconscious and its ability to nourish and renew consciousness. Here the ego may become inflated with its own importance, placing too great a value on rationality and control. Behaving as if there is nothing but ego consciousness will inflame the unconscious and we will develop an unhealthy tension between ego and shadow. This process accelerates itself so that the ego progressively denies more and more of itself and consequently defends less and less space. Emotionally we become brittle, obsessive and incapable of connecting with feeling, the imagination, the unconscious. Indeed all of these may become viewed as the enemy within that must be defended against with rigid structures. Shamanically this is a loss of soul, not necessarily overtly depressed but closed to the anima and vitality of the Self.

Together, these two ways of viewing ego wounds begin to form a method for understanding and responding to the pain others bring us. Those in the fragile ego group need help to form a more secure and confident sense of identity that is robust enough to repress overwhelming feelings that threaten to annihilate it. Typically fragile ego wounds occur at the earliest stages of development. Those with too dense an ego need to find a way to connect with the repressed areas and find the gold within the lead, and so reconnect with a sense of vitality lost on the path to socialization. Typically rigid ego wounds are dealt with later. The next section takes this approach and explores it more fully.

ARCHETYPAL EXPECTATIONS

Here we assume a set of innate unconscious physical and psychological expectations that were evolved over the millions of years as we slowly grew from the most primitive organism to finally emerge as primates. These expectations are of a physical and emotional environment that we inhabited for the majority of our time as nomadic hunter-gatherers before entering settled urban communities. This is something we tend to forget; if a day represented the history of mankind then only in the closing ninety seconds have we stopped being small, cohesive groups moving endlessly across the land. Like all animals we are adapted to fit our ecological niche and any failure in this relationship causes a dysfunction to the entire system. It is only our spectacular adaptability as a species that enables us to continue, and in many ways thrive, under the stress of losing our original Eden.

The expectations are also systems because they express themselves in complex patterns of interaction and also archetypes because they are found universally as innate ordering processes. However the systems of archetypal expectations only become realized if life provides the necessary circumstances for their expression. It is like the seed. It may carry the potential to be a tree but will only realize this if circumstances permit. So what are these archetypal systems?

Dr Antony Stevens (1982), building on the work of C. G. Jung (1936/7, 1954), has suggested the first is care giving and receiving and is represented by the archetypal images of mother and child. The next is competition and dominance represented by archetypal images of the powerful, the heroes and their struggles. To this we may add pair bonding, represented by images of the couple, their copulation and procreation. Next, the understanding of maturity and finally old age and death. It is here that experience generates wisdom and images of the wise man and woman represent this stage symbolically. Lastly, our special ability to create pathways of understanding that lead us beyond the confines of our lives and to have specialist assistance on the path, is represented by the image of the shaman, the magician, the yogi, the seer, the priest and their female counterparts. This is not a complete list. Each of these large systems may be divided into smaller groupings and still remain sufficiently general to remain archetypal, and each of these have vast amounts of symbols representing their complex contents.

Of course we no longer live within our optimal environmental niche and probably most of us would not even survive were we returned to it. Also our adaptability has enabled us to sustain an enormous amount of stress as the environment we have grown to expect is denied. Now in a world that the ancestral self can hardly recognize we still continue with the same archetypal systems: we still grow in families, find partners and have children, grow old and die. We depend upon belonging to a group that has its place and we are suspicious and aggressive to any other that threatens any of these circumstances. We instinctively feel there is more to life than what is visible. In danger we fight, flee or faint. As with the tree though, there comes a point where the stress of these not being met sufficiently begins to cause pain, stasis and finally breakdown that happens on all levels. This is to experience, what Stevens has called, 'frustration of archetypal intent'. This frustration of the expression of our innate possibilities may be seen as a cause for the entire range and depth of psychological problems and adds another level to understanding wounds in addition to them forming around specific and discrete traumas. As such, if we can identify precisely which aspects of our archetypal endowment remain frustrated by denied expression then we have a powerful diagnostic tool by which to understand our suffering.

CHARTING ARCHETYPAL FRUSTRATION FOR CLINICAL USE

One way to apply this practically is to construct a chart that compares what we ideally expected, prompted by our archetypal endowment, and what life actually provided. The time to do this would be perhaps when looking at a life history, alone or with a patient. My preference is with the patient because not only does the patient make connections, when involved, that I usually would not have thought of, but they also frequently come up with improvements and innovations that extend the method. For instance, drawings and quotes in addition to writing events can make the whole thing richer or in the case of twins, both constructing a chart independently and then making a comparison.

As we will see in the next section, the archetypal expectations at the start of life are particularly crowded since it is during this time that massive and condensed learning enables the rapid development of the person. We have an enormous amount of need that must be met sufficiently if we are to grow. To incorporate this in the suggested chart I have included developmental stages, here called instinct, and placed these against general archetypal constellations, here called image. Against these is an illustrative clinical history to demonstrate how the actual deviates from the ideal. To gain a general idea of the areas of the person that remain or have been repressed in the shadow it is only necessary to see what expectations have not been realized in life by comparing the two sides.

Example

In this imaginary example we meet a woman of 32 years of age who has two children and is recently separated from her husband. Both parents are dead, her mother suffering recurring bouts of depression that finally end in her suicide. She is intelligent, imaginative and sensitive but rather shy and has a tendency to withdraw. Her confidence is low and she often makes choices that do not serve her best interest. She is not really sure who she is. Her 'soul' history looks like this:

Archetype		Age	Life events
Image	*Instinct*		
The Self. Images of wholeness. Anima. Images of The Great Mother and Child. The Divine Child. The Hermaphrodite.	Emerge and receive nourishment. Attachment.	**0**	*Post-natal depression. Mother and child alienated.*
		6 months	
The Shadow. Images of threatening other.	Separation continues containing ambivalence.		*Problems with feeding and sleeping. Mother absent with illness.*

Archetype		Age	Life events
Image	*Instinct*		
Brothers and Sisters.		14 months	*Mother returns.*
Hero/heroine. The Animus. Images of The Great Father. The Trickster.	Further differentiation, self-assertion as separate person with own character.	**18 months** 2 years	*Twins arrive.*
		3 years	
Anima/animus. Images of the lovers. Images of taboo and forbidden fruits.	Explore wider range of relationships. Sex, competition and love.		*Brother born. Sent to stay with Grandparents.*
↓		4 years	*Play school. Shy.*
		5 years	*School. Illness. Away for six months. Return out of step with other girls.*
↓			*Father away at work all week.*
	Consolidation period. 'Latency'.	9 years	*Patch, dog, dies. Win prize for piano playing.*
↓			*Grandma dies.*
↓		11 years	*New school, separated from best friend. Wrong uniform detail.*
		Adolescence	
Above continues. Anima/animus re-constellate. Puer/puella. Hero re-constellates. Initiation motifs. Shadow re-constellates. Same-sex groupings.	Further separation. Peer grouping. Enter sexual maturity.		*Start menstruation. Very afraid. Meet Ms. Smith, piano teacher, very kind.*
		14 years	*Father away now returns. Encourages work. Takes me out to visit galleries.*

Archetype		Age	Life events
Image	Instinct		
Shared-sex groupings.			
		15/16 years	*Do well in exams. No boyfriend, but much admired second cousin.*
		17/18 years	*A levels. Do very well in arts subjects. First boyfriend.*
		Adult	
Anima/animus re-constellate. Images of young King & Queen. Mother re-constellates. Father re-constellates. Hero re-constellates.	Pair bonding, children.		*University, split up with first boy friend. Get into drugs. Series of unsatisfactory relationships.*
		22 years	*Father dies of heart failure. Mother in deep depression & drinking. Twins go round the world.*
		25 years	*Settle in new job. Like it, place of belonging. Meet John, husband to be.*
		26 years	*Pregnant & marry John. Mother commits suicide.*
King & Queen. Mother & Father re-constellate.	Establishing place in social hierarchy.		*First child born, move for John's work to America.*
		31 years	*John has an affair during second pregnancy.*
		32 years	*Separate. Left to support myself. Return to work.*
		Mid-life	
Mature King & Queen. Anima/animus, re-constellate. Images of spiritual calling.	Possible opening to transpersonal experience.		*Not applicable in example.*

Archetype		Age	Life events
Image	Instinct		
		Maturity	
Senex, Crone, The Androgyne.	Representative of group memory & wisdom. 'Spiritual life'.		*Not applicable.*
		Old Age	
As above. Images of death similar to birth. Rebirth. The Self.	Separation from the world. Preparation for death.		*Not applicable.*

Note: the archetype *per se* is only known via its image and instinct and the images here are not intended to be a complete list, but rather the 'core' or central images that the multitude of 'secondary' images illustrate.

Constructing the Chart

On the left of the chart we have the core archetypal images that represents each stage of life and the archetypal instinct that governs the typical experiences and actions at that time. It is important to remember that the archetypes are all continuously present throughout an individual's life time and that they are re-activated, or constellate, at each different stage or phase as appropriate. For example, the anima is first felt in the maternal relationship, later with Father, later still with the partner and finally internally in the marriage of opposites. In the centre is age, those figures or periods marked in bold being generally significant times of transition, the others times are of personal importance for the patient. On the right we have the patient's life events, the story of their life. While the archetypal information remains the same, the personal material will obviously differ from person to person. In practice it is only necessary to record the history and in your own mind hold the archetypal phases. However if you find it hard to do this at first and want to write the entire thing out for each person it would be better to do this alone so as not to falsely convey to your patient that there is a way they should be that they have failed.

In our example, comparing the archetypal potential on the left against the actual experience on the right, we will see a number of places where the possibilities are not realized completely. Our patient has made a poor attachment to her mother and has been unable to receive sufficient nourishment from her. At the time when she expects to begin to grow away, eighteen months on, she is unsure of the ill and absent mother and remains anxious and unconfident in her separation. Sibling births and being sent away do nothing to strengthen this. Subsequent steps deepen this underlying anxiety and depression and it is only in adolescence that a positive female image is finally found in the music teacher and with Father's return, as long as it fits his work ethos, she has value also in his eyes. Later relationships, boyfriends and husband, tend to repeat both the experience of emotional deprivation and absence. The final betrayal at the vulnerable period of her pregnancy echoes the abandonment by Mother at birth.

Therapeutically approaching this painful and tragic life story we need to identify those archetypal expectations that remain unrealized or partially met. We can see that her experience of being mothered and fathered are both less than adequate. She has been left insecure in her sense of self and her ability to make strong emotional attachments, that are not conditioned by earlier infantile needs, is poor. Furthermore, these areas of painful complex have repeated themselves in the patterns of her life and so she is in danger of further cementing herself in the unconscious expectations that life can only be the way she already knows it. That she has entered therapy represents an opening in this structure and the hope that she may find a better way of being. In practice we ask ourselves the question 'What has she missed in her life that archetypally she would expect?'. The answer to this then forms the contents of her shadow. Given this example, where so much could be in the shadow, as therapist, we may need to constellate areas of experience that would compensate the schizoid (unsafe to enter the world), oral (undernourished), self disorders (inability to separate), self in relationship (inability to independently relate), wounds that she is likely to carry. (For a fuller description of this approach see the next section on character styles.) Finally, remember that all of this is tentative until the evidence bears it out. While we can get a shrewd idea of how things may have been, people remain different and unexpected and the events that harm one may cause another to thrive.

However, using this model in conjunction with an understanding of the different personality structures, or 'character styles', it is possible to gain a detailed general understanding of the psyche's needs and what to expect when they are not met and also how best to repair therapeutically what has been damaged. There are different arrangements of these which are rewarding to compare (see particularly Kurtz 1970), however these here are based closely on the work of Stephen M. Johnson (1994) and use his descriptive categorizations for the sake of consistency.

CHARACTER STYLES

When considering frustration of archetypal intent we think of human life having typical needs that require fulfilment for optimal health. These include the needs of the infant, the child, the adolescent, the young and mature adult, the old and the dying. Failure to meet these needs contributes to problems ranging from severe deprivation, called personality disorders, to milder suffering, which may be called 'character styles', and depending on the depth and earliness of the wound an individual will be able to manage better or worse with the adversities of life. Because of this, identification of these wounds and finding therapeutic responses that help heal them, is a central concern of all schools of psychotherapy.

Here 'character' is used to mean both conscious and unconscious parts of the entire personality. Persona, ego and shadow. Each character style reflects a typical 'basic existential human issue', or archetypal expectation which starts early in life and continues within different contexts until death. Trauma and frustrations that deny these expectations are met with coping mechanisms, called defences, that are available at the time, thus a toddler meeting frustration of its need for a joyous assertion of 'No!', unable to express itself in the face of subduing parents, may eventually turn to the stubborn defence of masochism. At the time these adaptions make perfect sense and are expressions of the intelligence and adaptability of nature, however in time they become counter-productive and trap their originator in painful and inappropriate ways of being because they tend to be rigid and resistant to change.

It is, however, also important not to imagine that if a perfect mother existed she would be able to rear an 'unfrustrated' child who then would be without problems. The very nature of life makes it impossible to answer every need and so every child does and indeed must experience frustration of its archetypal expectations. It seems that part of our adaption to the emotional environment that we find ourselves inhabiting, is to internalize rapidly the limits this enforces upon us and so limit ourselves. Thus the frustration is not only caused by the environment but also by the rapidly developing ego that immediately starts to construct a shadow by rejecting aspects of the total possibilities available. For instance think of a plains Native American mother who once would have taught her baby not to cry for its own safety. The archetypal disposition includes the instinct to cry, signalling needs, but the baby must quickly adapt to the social/emotional environment if it is to survive by repressing, into the shadow, its desire to cry. Thus our ability to align ourselves with the environment is also the thing that sets us against ourselves. When this is extreme (within the measurement of the individual) it creates psychopathologies that can and do exist for an entire lifetime. It is a tension between, on the one hand, the ultimately irrepressible archetypal expectation, manifest as instinctual needs, and on the other, the internalized blocking that maintains the original frustration.

Let us now look in detail at the character styles that represent the wounds along the path of life. All timings are at best approximate and all phases overlap.

The Schizoid Character

Key theme: Annihilating universe.
Age: Intra-uterine, birth, up to three months.

Imagine entering the world as a new born infant to experience mother as insensitive, cold, distant, possibly abusive. A mother who perhaps is depressed and deeply resents her baby or who is herself desperately frightened and traumatized. We may feel unwelcome and in peril and because our experience in that moment is total and stretches endlessly in time, we may feel in danger of annihilation. Our only defence against this is to withdraw into and relate with our internal imaginal world. However, returning to hide in the womb is not a viable option and we may not avoid, as we continue to grow in years, increasing social interaction. For us this is exceptionally painful, emotions and intimacy have only ever been experienced as life threatening and so all interaction later carries this threat. We may be anxious, avoid attachment, and be out of touch with our feelings and so appear cold and distant. The felt maternal attack is not only internalized, so one attacks oneself and is self destructive, but is also directed at others, so one is likewise disengaged and distantly abusive. In our own mind we continue to live alone absorbed in our own fantasy. Abstraction, imagination and intellectual spirituality are all valued because they are a refuge from the pain of feeling. As such they are defences for a fragile ego that needs to drift off, to withdraw emotionally, to project feelings into others or deny them, to intellectualize, to 'spiritualize', to forget personal history. When we feel in danger we will disappear out of our bodies. Beneath this level, the shadow that must be defended against, whispers of the first experiences of life, the undefined limitless threat, the not knowing if this is outside or perhaps within oneself, that it is we who are wicked and cruel. Here we say to ourselves, 'Everything may kill me, I could destroy others, I have no right to exist, only leaving the world has value'. And those outside view us as hard to approach, possibly cold and sadistic. In extremes there is little human warmth or understanding, no real intimacy that relationship may be built around. Herman Hesse has described this wound in his novel, *Steppenwolf*. Here the character Harry lives an outwardly grey, controlled life, avoiding emotional contact while inwardly his fantasy world contains the terrifying psychodelia of the magic theatre.

When trying to be alongside this profound wound the central issue is safety. With no personal history of containment, security and nurture the baby has only archetypal experience. Initially, the combined experience of mother and child, equalled the entire universe for an eternity of time. Here images of nourishing, fecund goddesses represent our sense of being held within this mothering person's care, while images of her as devouring demoness portray an opposite story. For the schizoid wound it is necessary to evoke an experience of the archetypal goddess who becomes an individual mother, who welcomes the child into the world, within the therapeutic relationship. The therapy must primarily be experienced as safe and supportive. It provides a place where terror does not cause dissociation and it is safe to have a body and be in relationship with another outside of oneself. Once there is something safe and pleasurable to stand in, once we have begun to inhabit our body, it becomes safer to contact feelings. Enjoyment, emotionality, sensuality and physicality are important because they pleasurably define an individual self in relation to another. These will need naming so that they are no longer felt as overwhelming. Also they make way for the more dangerous feelings of terror, rage and grief that have been defended against. Terror may turn eventually to appropriate fear and awe, while the rage must be placed where it belongs in the original circumstances and not displaced inappropriately. Finally the grief of the deep tragedy that not only hurts the child but also the failing mother and all those trapped before her in equally dysfunctional relations, may be felt. Once this begins intimacy is a possibility and we can take our place in the world without fear.

The Oral Character

Key Theme: Nourishment needs unmet.
Age: 0 to approximately $1\frac{1}{2}$ years.

Immediately after birth the newborn infant has need of physical and emotional nourishment. However if the mothering carer is incapable of responding to this need, perhaps because she herself is also very needy, then the baby will give up on its own need before it has been satisfied. Later, once adult, this person will remain either obviously needy and dependent or alternatively will attempt to compensate the need within a persona of caring for others' needs, an attempt that usually fails. In Tibetan Buddhist cosmology there is a hell realm populated by beings called Hungry Ghosts, who have tiny mouths, long, thin necks and vast distended bellies, and are tortured by their inability to satisfy their hunger. This is an accurate image of the feel of this wound. At core we are empty, valueless and desperate. Our own needs never seem to be met because we fail to either recognize them and ask for help or we fail to recognize the nourishment when it is offered. Two possible routes are left to us, we either can remain endearingly clinging and dependent, in the hope of eliciting feeding from someone, or we can compensate and become sweet, kind and helpful and so give to others what we ourselves want. This self denial or identification with other dependent souls typically results in a sort of collapsed personality that is vulnerable to illness and depression. During these frequent periods of collapse, it is at least possible to have legitimately what one deep down longs for, the experience of being central and cared for. However, this is only permissible at the expense of living a life of emotional starvation, and suffering feelings of guilt and worthlessness.

To keep the pain distant we defend ourselves either by pushing away feelings that would tell us how we really feel deep down or by giving to others what we ourselves want. Denial of our need, projecting our need into others, and repeating the experience of the original mothering, by turning against ourselves, are all ways of fending off the fundamental emptiness and rage. To this is added an inflated sense of responsibility for others' needs that makes sure that one's own are seldom noticed. Inside the voice says 'I don't need anyone, I can look after myself', and deeper still, 'I am nothing, I am unlovable, my needs will consume the universe if I let them out'. And to some extent this is true. When we are like this it is common for others to feel that there is nothing they can do to satisfy us, that we never have enough and that they are somehow at fault for not providing. Eventually these others may turn away when they feel the deep fury that rages at the experience of maternal deprivation and the relentless intention to get mother (and her later substitutes) to give the nourishment she was intended for. Sadly, as with most wounds, in their unconscious attempts at healing, they often create the circumstance of their original making.

When we work with this wound in ourselves and others, as with the schizoid wound, it is necessary to establish a more nourishing relationship with our body and feelings. Inhabiting our body and connecting to and strengthening its energy runs parallel to encouraging the expression of the real needs that have remained repressed. Feelings of pain, longing, abandonment despair and rage and also real love for the mother are worked through along with the fear that such expression will be punished by further abandonment. Within ourselves we ultimately must now take responsibility for our own nourishment, whoever was originally at fault, and this means becoming conscious of how we continue, unconsciously, to maintain the starvation (probably in a field of plenty). The compensated persona of 'I am here for you' and 'Mummy's little helper', the looking after of everyone's needs but our own, must be let go of and the deeper feelings of need and resentment beneath released. We need to know that we do have a right to receive love, care and attention without having to entirely sacrifice ourselves and that we can legitimately reach out and ask for it without punishment. We also need to know that now there is no one person who will, alone, give us everything that the infant within us wants, and that we are now responsible for answering our own needs appropriately from a number of sources. This perhaps is the most difficult part because it means facing the great sadness that now we are never going to get exactly what we want and because this is so profoundly painful it is sometimes easier to rage and protest than finally accept the truth of the inevitable. However, while we must rage and despair it is also necessary to develop all the abilities to strengthen self nourishment, to ask and to receive, with the ability to take refusal without a regression into the wound. There is a world outside, though not a cornucopia, that is generally willing to give in a fair and equal exchange.

Once we have come into the world, incarnated, literally entered the flesh, it is then necessary to separate from our mother and begin to establish an independent identity. This begins at once, leaving the womb being the most concrete of separations, and is furthered by our first faltering movements away and growing ability to speak and say 'no!'. For this to be possible we need to be encouraged in a full range of self-expressions that are appropriately mirrored and also sufficiently curtailed so that we also know that with power comes limitation. Failure to have this experience causes 'self disorders' that result in an alienation of our deeper feelings from how we have to appear to survive. Our parents in all cases have used us to fulfil their agendas and so great was the need that we entered a confusion where their needs overwhelmed our own. This is called a separation of the 'real self' from the survival or 'false self', and shows itself in the following three character styles.

The Symbiotic Character

Key Theme: Smothered, fused.
Age: Emerging 15 to 24 months and continuing.

In many ways the symbiotic wound is similar to the compensated oral wound, both share the problem of losing themselves in another. However to understand the basic difference it is necessary to remember that the oral wound concerns malnourishment and is a problem of finding a start in the world, while the symbiotic concerns a denial of self-assertion and is therefore developmentally later in sequence. A difference between before and after the first eighteen months, but with an obvious cross over period. Another possible confusion is that the word 'symbiotic' is also used to describe a state of (theoretically contentious) union between an infant and its mother that exists at birth. This is not the period we are speaking of here.

If we bear a symbiotic wound our parents are likely to be experienced as blocking and inhibiting our exploration of the world and our ability to affect it. Behaviours that seek separation, express aggression and want self-determination are met with either withdrawal or punishment, while behaviour that continues dependency and identification with the parents is rewarded. Both responses are equally discouraging and finally create in us the need to forgo our natural separation and remain merged within our parents. To enter this world we only have to remember the child who longs for the dangerous joy of walking along a wall while the fearful parent clings or even refuses permission from fear for the child's safety. Here the balance must be struck: enough care and safety balanced with enough letting go and toleration of anxiety.

For a person with a symbiotic wound the question is always 'Who am I?', for our sense of identity is weakened and we cannot easily separate what we feel and think from that of intimate others in our lives. This fear of loss of identity, giving rise to a compensating need for rigid distancing may then in turn create a fear of isolation and abandonment. This also leads to problems with being over-responsible for others' needs (as with the compensated oral wound), as we live to serve them.

The established defences of denying and projecting difficult feelings into others continue as does a third early defence called 'splitting'. When we do not have confidence in our mother's love or the benevolence of the world, we will not dare, for fear of rejection and abandonment, to protest when our desires for nourishment, and then later, separation, are not met. Since it is impossible for all desires to be met, in every child's life there comes a time when it must recognize that the giving and withholding mother are one. When the insecure infant reaches this point, unable to express both its gratitude *and* aggression, it splits them so that only the loving side is shown, with a quality of appeasement, and the frustrated angry feelings are repressed within the shadow. The same process is also used for the image of the parent. We imagine them as entirely good and that their withholding part, the 'bad', is a result of our own badness and so not part of them. In this way the insecure child ends up carrying not only its own repressed angry feelings but also feels responsible for the failures of the parent. By this means experience of the parent as the fulfiller of desires *and* also the source of frustration is avoided, as is the experience of ourselves as both loving *and* aggressive. However the cost of this splitting is having hidden feelings of being bad, worthless and guilty, deep down inside, while appearing loving and obliging on the surface. Furthermore, the repressed feelings of rage, engendered by our unmet nourishment needs, being unconscious, may then be projected back into our mother who will then be felt as attacking. This then reinforces the worthlessness (for we are also responsible for this), and the loop is closed. Likewise, later relations with the world retain this immature perception that serves the purpose of not having to recognize the more realistic but sobering reality that not only the one who loves me retains ambivalent feelings about me but also I share in them. That oneself, others, and experience generally, is not all good or bad but that it usually contains both in a middle ground. And so, halted before the fear of ambivalence (for if I am in any way unloving I may be even less loved), fearful of sacrificing the ideal for the 'good enough', we continue identified with the parental needs and our real needs 'slip out' around the edge of our lives in manipulation and stubborn resistance, the self expressions of the devoured.

Work on the wound will essentially revolve around the issues of closeness and distance. The aim is to start and support the stalled process of separation. We need to stop living our lives for others, put down the obligation, and begin to think and feel for ourselves without having to take reference from another. We also have to do this without being overcome by guilt that we are somehow hurting others by doing so or that we will be punished by others with abandonment. Self-expression is at the heart of this and everything that encourages self discovery and personal tastes is desirable. Also getting the personal and ancestral histories straight is important because it clarifies what belongs to whom and how patterns of wounding are handed down through the generations. All this strengthens and differentiates an individual sense of self in the greater collective self of the family. As work continues it will also become necessary to identify how we unconsciously maintain identification with others at a cost to ourselves by giving away our authority, choice and responsibility. Also we must recognize that either being merged with another or stubbornly asserting distance are both sides of the same coin, that the desirable balance is one where we can let someone touch and influence us without a loss of identity and also know the power of our influence on them. When this becomes possible the defensive strategies of manipulation, passive aggression and making oneself and others all good or all bad will become unnecessary. With the grief that one was eaten alive comes the joy that now I can be me.

The Narcissistic Character

Key Theme: Distorted self-esteem.
Age: Emerging 15 to 24 months and continuing.

There are two ways to view narcissism. The broad view recognizes that all wounds have their narcissistic element in that they create a false self that obscures the underlying real self. In this view immature narcissism grows into a mature form that leaves a confident individual who can also give to others. The narrow view recognizes that in addition to this there is a specific narcissistic wound that arises from precise parenting experiences. While the broad view could be called the collective wound of our time it is the narrow view that we are considering here.

In Ovid's myth Narcissis had problems with his inflated sense of vanity. Likewise when we are wounded narcissistically we suffer issues of self-esteem. Like the symbiotic wound we have to live life meeting parental needs. The natural central place that we expect as children, confirming our own individual nature, is usurped by one or both parents taking it for themselves (often because they themselves are narcissistically wounded). They require of us either that we shine for them, realizing their need to be unique, magnificent and special or that we be eclipsed and humiliated and so offer no competition. Sometimes one parent will want one thing and the other the opposite, sometimes both will fluctuate between both. Naturally this leads to a profound confusion about self-esteem and the system of checks and balances that give a realistic idea of our value remain immature and dominated by grandiose fantasies, initiated by parental demands, around self-worth. We also remain unbearably vulnerable to criticism because it confirms deep feelings of inferiority hidden in the shadow. We present ourselves as omnipotent, arrogant, perfectionistic, self-involved and obsessed with status and yet this false self is always in danger of breaking down into its opposite where we are vulnerable to feelings of shame, humiliation and worthlessness which in turn lead to a deep depression. With this come feelings of anxiety and a deeper fear of dissolution itself, for at bottom, without a sense of our place in the world and in relationship to others we have no self-identity or value. To avoid this painful experience we try to maintain the grandiose false self at all costs. All attacks on this from an intrusion of reality are dealt with by denial of criticism, blaming others, diminishing the value of others and unrealistically identifying with those idealized. When this collapses it is replaced by an equally distorted and exaggerated sense of valuelessness that is preoccupied with hypochondriacal anxieties and morbid cogitations around self-worth. Both these states together conspire to keep the real self at bay because experience of this may be felt as completely disorientating. However, with the searing vulnerability also comes a real connection to life and others.

Those around someone with a very visible narcissistic wound may feel that they are being used as a mirror, as if they were an object with no needs of their own. Alternatively, if the false-self has a high degree of simulated adaption, that is, can put on a good performance as a less self-obsessed individual, they may feel caught up in charisma. Kurtz calls this constellation of characteristics the 'psychopath' (because it only cares for itself), and names two strategies, the first is tough and generous and the second, charming and seductive. (Think male old Hollywood movie stars.) The idea is if we cannot remain on top one way then there is a fall back position, the vital thing is not to lose control because that feels vulnerable. When our narcissistic wound is not keeping us on top it is scouting for remarkable things to identify with and so share in their value. Beneath the surface of idealization the small child can be seen still trying to be inside the special parent or being that specialness and so meet the parental demand. All this activity really has little to do with relationship or true feeling, and because of this there is a phony quality to a narcissitically wounded person's feeling that neither rings true to oneself or others. However this is also a starting point because the desire for real relationship, that includes the willingness to expose oneself to criticism and learn how to balance it against real qualities, is essential for healing.

Working with this wound it is necessary to avoid the hierarchical relating that the wound engenders. Tempting though it is, taking the narcissist down a peg or two will only serve to re-entrench the defensive grandiose self more deeply. This unequal style of relating originally caused the wound and so its healing must be in an equal exchange between two people who accept the other's limitations and enjoy each other's qualities. Once this safe therapeutic vessel is created it will be possible not only to face the equally delusive positive and negative inflation but also the really dangerous experience at base of vulnerability and relinquishing of control. The vulnerability will include acknowledging feelings of deep sadness and rage at being let down by those idealized, and fear of letting oneself be vulnerable to disappointment again. Beneath this, the feelings of inferiority must be faced and accurately assessed, and beneath this again the emptiness and fear of fragmentation of the real self must be stayed with until this self begins to emerge from behind the wound structure. Like the new, naked real self of the orally wounded, this self will also need to discover just who it is but here the issues of trust and establishing a real concern for oneself and others is central. Realistic and ambivalent appraisal will be part of this, as will establishing mutually nourishing and equal relationships. Letting in others will be terrifying because they may use and abuse us for their own ends but the only end to the isolation and fragile self-identity will be through the nourishment of safe intimacy.

The Masochistic Character

Key Theme: Resentful submission.
Age: Emerging 18 to 24 months and continuing.

When suffering the third wound from this group our parents are likely to have been experienced as dominant and invasive. We may particularly feel overpowered in the areas of eating and excretion and eventually, when our resistance finally crumbles, assuming a compliant and appeasing persona, we join with the greater force and repress our own hostile and retaliatory feelings. However beneath this the rage and frustration from having been defeated continues and this may be expressed particularly by acts of passive aggression. If this has happened to us we can feel a chronic low grade depression that seems to colour everything with the flavour of defeat. All the life energy is not only hidden in the shadow but also seems to be felt as an alien force weighted against us. The expressions of long sufferance, complaining self-defeat and self-depreciation, along with helplessness, distrust and hidden anger, all add up to create a boggy place where this 'Eeyore' lives. Resistance, the last remains of the defiant self, now acts against our best interests as all change, even for the better, is seen as a challenge to the internalized controlling parents and must be subjugated to their rule. On the surface we say 'I give up' but beneath another voice says 'I will never submit!' and knows that it can endure its burden longer than anyone else and that this masterly performance of masochism will 'show them'. As with other structures this too is maintained by denial and projection, particularly of anything that may connect us with the underlying rage. We wish to see ourselves as one who serves others and meets duties and yet we also spoil any pleasure in this with endless complaints and feeling guilty for obligation failures. The cost of this is to feel caught and frustrated while both needing and fearing acts of spontaneity, fun and creativity. The only release this victim mentality may secretly feel is when we have defeated all attempts to help us with 'Yes, buts'. Evoking a frustrated attack from the would-be helper, we finally legitimize the expression of pent up spite. Or alternatively, their depressed defeat triumphantly reaffirms the immovability of our masochistic determination.

Any attempt to help us in this position is felt as an additional attack and so in effect the source of healing, a reconnection with the life force lost within the shadow, is furiously defended against. Naturally this will lead an inexperienced therapist into the trap of pushing harder which will only evoke the responses mentioned above. Somehow it is necessary to get round behind the defences and not play into the unconsciously desired theatre of rewounding in replica of the original hurt. In practice feelings of aggression and self assertion must be welcomed as must discovery of pleasure and creativity. This will mean recognizing and disidentifying with the internalized parental voices that demand service and induce guilt if they are challenged. It will also require the behaviours that maintain the structure to be understood and abandoned. These include flooding the therapist with material to assure nothing will move, disavowal of the violent, spiteful feelings, deep-seated pathogenic beliefs and the spoiling of any successes, particularly in the therapy. Indeed we will need to learn how to contain the anxiety evoked by expressing ourselves and exchange self-defeat for balanced self-assertion, self-respect and a trusting, equal relationship. This may all sound simple and straightforward but the determined self-defeat of this place means that it is not only difficult for the therapist to find an ally in the patient but that at every turn all healing will be systematically dismantled as it occurs. At worst therapy becomes a battle between a determined-to-heal-at-all-cost therapist against an equally determined patient who feels that his very existence rests on continuing endlessly in therapy while ensuring that it will never work. For this reason humour, a sense of the ridiculous and even very loving teasing may find an appropriate place in the work.

Once the symbiotic phase has been passed through, then between the second and third years we have started to separate, we next begin consciously to move into a wider orbit of relationships. Typically we discover not only that our mother, or mothering person, and ourselves are separate individuals but that there are also others in our world and this frequently will mean a clearer discovery of father. If we consider how by this point many of us will be wounded from earlier developmental periods, perhaps one compounding another, and then add to this the labyrinthine relationship dynamics that exist between three people, then we can understand how complex this gets. Johnson, following Freud, calls this the Oedipal phase and sees it dominated by the concerns of relationship, love, sex and competition, and suggests that like all other phases, it needs appropriate expression and limitation. When this does not happen we have the following two wounds.

Oedipal Character. The Histrionic Wound

Key Theme: Exploited/Unheard.
Age: Emerging around 3 to 5 years, then continuing.

This wound may occur when one parent uses us as a sexual object, or when one parent is cold, rejecting or punishing, particularly in the area of affectionate relationship, or when each parent takes each one of the above roles or even alternates between them. Here we are not necessarily referring to sexual abuse or extreme rejection but more likely a mother or father taking a level of inappropriate emotional and physical satisfaction from their child, perhaps because these needs are not met by the partner, or alternatively, that one parent withdraws because he cannot contend with the child's erotic explorations. Either way, these behaviours will result in a dislocation and distortion of our natural exploration of sexual desire, love and rivalrous feelings against competitors. Instead of developing a healthy pleasure in our ability to attract and be attractive we will feel ourselves used in relationships with future sexual partners or that, unless we perform, we will go unnoticed. The last twist is that it is also possible for the child to experience the parent as rejecting because the child is projecting its guilt for its own sexual and competitive feelings into the parent.

In this confusion of relationships it is not surprising that our emotional expression becomes distorted and no longer communicates what we actually feel. Playing up to the needs of the one parent or desperately trying to attract the attentions of the other we become larger than life, dramatic, exhibitionistic, theatrical and yet paradoxically, we are unfocused and emotionally and intellectually shallow. While seeming to be particularly attuned to the opposite sex and sexualizing ordinary communications, we in reality may be cut off from our sexuality and perhaps experience functional sexual problems. Indeed, behind the seduction may be hidden hostility not only to those of the same sex but also those of the opposite. These somatic symptoms symbolically express the separation between our own real sexual self and the sexualized false-self which we have become for the other or to attract the other. Beneath the surface we believe that sex and competition are bad, or, that we must be attractive to be loved. But beneath this again at the deepest level is the silent cry to be loved for oneself and to be allowed to express our love and sexuality in our own way. At base all the acting out, the overwhelming of any containment, the sheer noise, is a legitimate, if unconscious, cry to be heard. Of course the problem is that the original parents are no longer there to hear, and others tend to abuse or turn away and so, ultimately, it is only we who can hear ourselves. This wound is mostly found in women, though not exclusively, and it is important to remember that the word 'hysteric' etymologically links it to the womb. Ancient Greeks, believing that the womb unattended would roam lost around the body, held a posy of sweet smelling flowers at the womb's door to attract it back into its rightful position. Surely this tells us that when the womb, as symbolic vessel for the conjoining of male and female, is lost, it is the natural and the beautiful that creates healing and enables it to hold life again.

The therapeutic responses that particularly help when we suffer in this way meet the central need to be heard firstly by the therapist and ultimately by ourselves. All else follows from this. However this is not always easy because the loud, invasive, theatricality will either entrance the therapist and cause them to miss hearing the real voice within or more likely, cause them to become distancing and suppressing as they struggle to contain the hysterical expression. Thus the therapist becomes the absent parent (usually father). To hear properly and enable the patient to hear herself it is helpful to discourage all behaviours that maintain the false self; the use of large emotional dramas to mask the underlying feeling, the distracted acting out, the flitting from one subject to the next with no completions, the denial of personal responsibility, the use of sex for gaining affection and lastly, simplistic perceptions of men, women and relationships.

Conversely, all experience of the real self is encouraged by enhancing the ability to experience, stay with and express real feeling. Usually this includes distinguishing affection from sexual needs, that is actually listening to ourselves and what we really want. The inhibitions of love and competition, and the resulting shame and anger need to be worked through. Also the feelings of having been used or abandoned must be experienced and the sadness and depression this may evoke seen as a positive sinking down into real feeling. As always, healthy, realistic ambivalence is desirable. Finally, men bearing this wound will need to resolve their yearning for mother love against their rage for her holding and using them. This is frequently acted out by offering a seductive persona to women that hides a deep sadistic streak. The mythic image of the puer aeternus, the eternal boy. Women will have to resolve their dependency on father love (which costs them their own power), and the poisonous envy this may cause in them, by asserting their own authority. Again this is acted out later in fury at a society that has traditionally encouraged women to behave in a childlike way, the puella, while also persecuting them (i.e. witches) for holding hidden power. Indeed, the very name of this wound carries negative connotations whether we call it 'histrionic' or 'hysterical' and it would be better to find a description that was not tainted with denigration.

Oedipal Character. The Obsessive–Compulsive Wound

(Note: this is not the same as an obsessive–compulsive neurosis)
Key Theme: Control.
Age: Around 3 to 5 years, then continuing.

If the histrionic wound is characterized by a violation of natural boundaries then the obsessive–compulsive wound results from an over rigorous control of the same erotic and competitive energies and is found more frequently in men. (In other character systems this wound has been connected to an earlier phase where strict potty training is seen as partly its cause. Johnson argues, and I agree with him, that over-control of excretion, that is control of *self expression*, fits more accurately into the masochistic structure.) Strictly controlling, persistently rule bound parenting, dispensing punishment for any form of spontaneous, free expression, particularly if it is to do with sexuality and aggression, creates in us an ability likewise to tame and subdue our own vital animal nature. This is not the externally crushing control of the masochistic wound but rather the self-applied, introjected self-control of the parental discipline. The suppression of spontaneous feeling, personal choice and an ability to enjoy relaxation, an ability to be, leaves the familiar conscientious, correct, pedantic, rule bound, intellectually and emotionally rigid personality who is driven by a persecuting inner authority and who, demanding perfection, simultaneously creates a fear of failure. It is for this reason that procrastination and an inability to complete a task (from fear of getting it wrong) are also part of this pattern. Beneath this lurks a great anxiety, obsessive thoughts, sadistic and erotic fantasies and compulsive behaviours, checking, locking and washing, accompany the whispering secret voice, 'I have done something very wrong' and 'I must not lose control at all costs'. When we meet this person we are struck by their ability to deny feeling and apply reason while at the same time we may also sense the underlying hostility.

Healing this wound must include identifying the inner authority voice and challenging its supremacy. We need to let go of the tyrannies of perfectionism and control and realize that nature may never be absolutely ruled by the will. It is natural to fail, to be chaotic, to be imperfect, to be anxious and ambivalent. We do not need to block these out. We can accept these in ourselves and others. The Dionysian energies of sex and violence may be integrated in love and healthy competition. We can let go and the universe will not dissolve around us. Of course this is easy to say but in practice the fear of the anxiety that any small contact with the shadow unleashes, causes (similar to the masochistic wound), defensive moves that are designed to keep the structure in place. Because of this the tendencies to obfuscate by using all sorts of reasons why something cannot be changed, to flood with detail, to shift attention to the edge of the subject, to stay in abstraction, to describe endless complaints and to hide in indecision, must all be recognized and given up. What is to be encouraged is individual pleasure, delight, emotional immediacy, heartfelt warmth and, most frightening, good clean anger. From under the concrete emerges a vibrantly coloured flower.

THE MIDLIFE TRANSITIONAL CRISIS

It is not only the start of life that can create acute suffering. As well as traumatic experiences that may occur at any time, loss, disease, death, there is also the profound transition that does occur for some, but not all, at approximately the middle of life. The period on the Edinger/Somers map where ego and Self are most estranged. Jung (1931) recognized this as the onset of the second half of life where individual concerns are transcended and a connection to something larger than ourselves is made. Many writers have written on this theme picking up the old belief that once we have established a family we need something more that this has not satisfied. Others have challenged this, suggesting such a need can legitimately appear before midlife and cite examples of an earlier call. From a psychotherapist's perspective it is necessary to develop the 'nose' that can distinguish someone who has reached this point, a turning to spiritual concerns, from one who would hide in spirituality to avoid the pain of being simply human. And it is just as much a mistake to think all people need to experience this shift towards the transpersonal as it is to merely see all wounding as the failures of childhood. Michael Washburn (1994) charts this period well.

Washburn calls the development of an individual sense of being that functions in the world and can achieve satisfaction and meaning from doing so, the 'ego project'. At midlife and later, for some, this project begins to be less compelling because we either realize that we can never succeed in it or, having succeeded (unfinished patterns and cycles withstanding), find that its promise of wholeness was hollow. When this happens fundamental uncertainties in the shadow begin to emerge that up to now the ego project has kept obscured. We begin to feel a growing sense of being nothing beneath all our efforts and achievements and that whatever we do is not enough or right. Naturally in the face of this profound discomfort, not knowing exactly what is happening to us, we begin at first to try even harder to keep the dying system going. However this is doomed to failure and eventually we become defeated and are separated in feeling from ourselves and the world. This is the 'sickness unto death'. The wasteland. Washburn describes this as returning to a primitive narcissism in an attempt to shore up flagging self-worth followed by disillusionment with previous values, a frightening shifting of identity and depression as the world flattens and is withdrawn from. He also reminds us that these experiences are not solely the result of a midlife crisis and can also result from trauma, developmental arrests and biochemical imbalances.

In this description we can recognize the soul sickness that Jung described many of his middle-aged patients presenting and for which his particular way of working, facilitating a re-connection to the Self, was and is particularly effective. Unlike the character styles above, here we have no general guidelines that enable us to identify and respond to the wound. This is because there are no universal cures and each of us will quite literally have to find our own unique salvation. This being said the shape of the passage is the archetypal pattern of initiation; death, passing through darkness and rebirth. An example of this journey may be found in the Parzival story. Here the hero/ knight reaches a point of existential despair where he has achieved the 'ego project' but finds himself still as barren as the Waste Land he has failed to rejuvenate. At this pivotal point the unrecognized transformational feminine element in the form of Cundry, hideous precursor to the Grail, appears and galvanizes Parzival to complete his quest. He may not rest with King Arthur in the court of the familiar but must continue until he understands his deeper nature, represented by Gawain and Feirefiz, and his service as the redeemed Grail King. In this perspective the debilitating experience of ego dissolution begins to make sense, this is the death process that leads into the aridity of the liminal phase and finally renewal. Likewise, the inability to draw upon old sources of understanding is also important because it demonstrates that now a new source of guidance must be found. Now the therapeutic methods that Jung found so helpful; dreaming, active imagination, creative exploration and of course religious and spiritual pursuits, become important because in all cases they draw on areas that are beyond the 'ego project', that are transpersonal. Here also the difference between west and east becomes clear. While the notion of individuation continues to value a separate identity that now turns to face the greater Self in dialogue, the east practices methods of meditation and contemplation that seek to dissolve the very experience of separation as an individual self. This difference we will return to later. In practice this is a painful and slow wounding that ultimately is a healthy sickness if it can lead to a renewed understanding of who we are, replacing the old kingship of the ego and its values, with a new identification with a transpersonal centre. The night sea journey ends in a new dawn.

SPIRITUAL WOUNDING

Chogyam Trungpa Rimpoche in his highly perceptive book, *Cutting Through Spiritual Materialism* (1973), highlighted how even spirituality may be hijacked by the needs of an ego that seeks to consolidate itself. How we can fool ourselves into believing that we are 'spiritual', by holding beliefs, by following paths, by doing meditational practices etcetera and in reality all we are doing is maintaining the 'ego project' in extremely subtle disguise. The value of the book is in its ability to show how this unfolds from the most innocent looking desires, the desire to be *more* spiritual, and how once we step upon this road, on which the ego seeks to define itself by its fantasy of a 'spiritual' identity, it becomes downhill all the way. In addition to this almost universal inclination, specific and more serious wounds exist that arise from the conjunction of traumatic personal history and 'spiritual' beliefs, most particularly, the practice of meditation. In this next section therefore we will consider how the wounds described as character styles may become profound when they are mixed with so-called spiritual practice and belief in the 'transpersonal' in general.

  Mark D. Epstein and J. D. Lieff (1981) have outlined this for us. Firstly they remind us that a variety of psychopathological states have been recorded as having their genesis in meditation practice, these include deep destablizations of the ego in psychotic episodes, panic and anxiety attacks, and depression and suicidal fantasies. They also remind us of the conventional psychoanalytic understanding of meditative absorption as a re-entry into the earliest oceanic states of fusion with mother, and concentration upon the process of consciousness, a regression into primary narcissism, a place of self-absorption where only oneself is real. However they challenge this rather dire and bald interpretation and argue that we need a more differentiated understanding of the various levels of experience meditation can generate and also of the problems that each of these levels may create. Furthermore, picking up Wilber's (1995) 'pre/trans' fallacy, it is important not to confuse pre-personal states with trans-personal states. This fallacy occurs, on a personal level, when we delude ourselves into believing that our beliefs and our practices are about a dissolution of a separate identity when the unconscious intent is really about trying to *escape back* into a place of no anxiety or responsibility, and is therefore spirituality used as an ego defence. Not transpersonal but prepersonal. In my experience the reality is not so easy to divide. Certainly at the onset these two motivations may be mixed. Indeed part of the legitimate process is the identification of the regressive desires that causes one to make the mistake of wanting to be other than where one is.

Epstein and Lieff offer a model of three stages of meditation practice and the psychological problems that each can create. (For a fuller account of transpersonal psychology and meditation see Chapter 9 'Naked Presence'.)

Starting meditational practice

In many systems, it is usual to start meditation practice by developing one pointed concentration upon an object, thereby creating a mental state of slowed and reduced mental activity. When we start doing this we generally experience a great excitation and flooding from the contents of our minds, both conscious concerns and more disturbingly, the content of the shadow. Thoughts, feelings, desires, and daydreams are commonly experienced intensely as are audio, visual and somatic hallucinations. If this material has never been experienced before it may well be of fascinating interest to the novice and a common problem is that it becomes so captivating that the meditator is lost in the *content* of the mind rather than observing the *process* of its continuous manifestation, and so the practice does not proceed. More seriously, if our ego is fragile, the inundation of the ego by the shadow, can and will create intolerable levels of ego disturbance, drawing the practitioner into the mind's content and causing the ego to resort to the early defence mechanisms, denial, projection and splitting, to keep itself intact. Obviously then, if the object of practice is to be mindful of one's reality, then a fragile, heavily defended, ego will not find this possible. As a therapist confronted with this phenomena it is important to recognize the fragility of the ego and the undesirabilty of its destabilization and find ways to support it as has been suggested above. In serious cases meditational practice would be counter-indicated.

Engler (1984), has differentiated these wounds precisely. As a psychotherapist he recognizes a number of clinical features in students he has taught meditation to. These include the flooding by the contents of the shadow mentioned above, dwelling in fantasy, memories, conflicts, compulsive thinking and intense mood swings. Also the relationship with the teacher becomes distorted by the transference of the student's parental experiences. Typically, the student relates to the teacher as if they were a parent, both requiring elements of parenting needs that have not been satisfied and also displaying acts of aggression when the teacher is seen as a parent to separate from. This may be especially difficult for those suffering a self disorder who have yet to find a way to accept that the idealized parent (teacher) is also the one who is incapable of meeting unrealistic expectations. The struggle that the defence of splitting causes appears as wild swings where one moment the teacher is God and the next of no value whatsoever. These types of problem particularly occur for would be meditators in late adolescence and also for those passing through the midlife transitional crisis: groups who both show a marked interest in meditation. For all the issue is one of identity and self-esteem and involvement with meditation may become unhelpful when it is used as a (mistakenly) short cut to avoid the life issues that these painful phases throw up. This is particularly true when philosophical ideas about the non-existence of a self and non-attachment are used as a let out for feeling and personal responsibility, the ability to respond. For those who suffer having no real sense of a cohesive self, inner emptiness and fear of relationship, who may have borderline personality organization, and those who suffer a narcissistic personality wound as defined above, spiritual teaching is attractive. Notions of no self seem to mirror the borderline experience of lack of self feeling and non-attachment appears to legitimize avoidance of personal relationships. Likewise, the ideal of enlightenment, is immediately attractive to those of us with narcissistic wounds because it is the ultimate promise of a non-vulnerable state of total independence and exalted perfection that takes us beyond the common crowd. Or so it seems until the painful reality of sitting practice deflates the fantasy.

Stabilizing concentration

Once one has found a way through the possible problems that starting practice may throw up, one has an experience of the practice working. This is a relief because at times it can feel that it is all suffering and no reward. The practice now becomes the motivation itself rather than the more conceptual and emotional incentives that initially caused one to sit. This level of practice is experienced as growing moments, and then periods, where there is an ability to step back from identification with the contents of consciousness and find a place of rest where one can remain uninterruptedly concentrated on either the object of concentration (candle, image, letter, or breath), or more widely, the awareness of the movement of thoughts and feelings. Problems at this level of practice come from wanting to establish this experience so badly that one begins to strain oneself and create stress. Ironically the only way to actually establish the practice is to relax as this desire to be somewhere other than where one is, *is* the very root of the problem. A phallic driveness at this point will assure that no more development happens. To guard against this students may be advised to monitor their state of consciousness carefully and apply practices that compensate for imbalances as they occur. The response to serious problems at this level is not to stop but to relax.

The conjunction of calm and insight

For most of us it is unlikely that we will have the deepest levels of this category of experience. My personal belief is that it is unobtainable unless one is prepared to pour one's entire life into it and this would include a commitment to retreats. Others however (Tart 1994) seem to suggest that our everyday life is the place to practice and this is appropriate for our contemporary times. As with the category above, it does not seem correct to call the problems of this level psychopathology, rather, they seem to me to be natural fears from the perspective of the ego. Here, we are informed, the problems consist of becoming attached to the fruits of the practice, deep feelings of bliss for instance (Kornfield 1994). Later still the dissolution of the self threatens the practitioner with seemingly no solid ground to stand upon. Attachment to the fruits is recognized as an abuse of the practice and the dissolution of the self would become a psychotic break if the ego structure were not strong enough finally to contain its own transmutation. Once or twice I have been consulted on experiences that sounded similar to this and on each occasion have referred the person asking to an authority in the tradition they had most followed. Their symptoms could easily be understood as psychotic delusions, and indeed may have been, but I am wary to condemn something as insane when it may be recognized by someone more knowing as a valuable experience of opening. If indeed it is a fact that the practice has developed deeply then the only solution to ego's anxiety is more practice.

The essential thing is to recognize when a person's interest is a defence against a life they are afraid of living as opposed to a desire to live life more mindfully which will mean facing the pain and the fear. Those of us who use spirituality defensively usually do not practice a great deal and so the community or group who usually gather around the teacher act as a surrogate family which becomes the arena for acting out the repeat performance of family dramas. Teacher, Lama or Guru as parents and friends as siblings. Others who try to practice may distort the intention of the practice, really needing to grow a solid ego before they dissolve it, but here again I believe the practice itself is generally its own safeguard as it is difficult to muster the mental resources to continue unless one has a good, healthy, robust and intentioned ego. However there are a few who, though fundamentally unstable, manage to even enter long duration solitary retreats and it is in these that a real danger of unseating the ego can cause irreversible damage. If there is a greater understanding of 'spiritual' pathology, by both spiritual teachers and psychotherapists, then this never need happen.

CONCLUSION – FROM THE LEAD COMES GOLD

In each of these personality wounds we have primarily focused on the aspects that create suffering, however it is extremely important to remember that many of us go through our entire life with low to medium level wounds that are never articulated nor worked upon. While these may cause distress, particularly at times of crisis, for the rest of the time they are merely 'us' and are recognized simply as our personality. Indeed each of the wounds has its 'golden lining', even without any work on it, and these provide valued qualities and attitudes within our society. To greatly simplify; the inventive imagination and technical abilities given by a schizoid wound. Helping professions staffed by those with oral and symbiotic wounds and the arts with the narcissistic and histrionic. Masochistic and obsessive–compulsive behaviour is particularly favoured, providing perseverance and exactitude. Lastly, the midlife transition gives birth to what is ultimately the most valuable in human culture, something that may go beyond death. While psychotherapy can underestimate the value of continuing in unconscious defensive patterns, particularly since they break down at times of change, it is important to remember that symptoms are also symbols and as such each character is multifaceted and both represents a pattern of pain and also an individual expression of human life. As such, while it is genuinely useful to have a map of psyche's unfolding it is also necessary to recognize that the map can become a hindrance when the therapist, using it as a defence against the anxiety of not knowing, begins only to see the wound pattern and not the person. This is extremely easy to do. Imagine before you someone in great emotional distress. Their need is to have you understand their pain and remove it. At this point, identifying the constellation of their life pattern and the type of pain it may have generated appears to start the process of healing by making meaning out of the chaos. However, unless this is meaningful for the patient also, it has little value and at worst may actually harm the therapeutic relationship. Transpersonal Psychotherapy remembers this and while using the patterns of wounding to orientate the therapeutic response, primarily works from the place of health. While we all bear wounds these wounds are not all we are.

REFERENCES

Clements, F. E. (1932). 'Primitive Concepts of Disease' *University of California Publications in American Archeology and Ethnology*, Vol. XXXII, No. 2, 185–252.

Engler, J. (1984). 'Therapeutic Aims in Psychotherapy and Meditation: Developmental Stages in the Representation of the Self', *Journal of Transpersonal Psychotherapy*, 16(1), 25.

Epstein, M. D. and Lieff, J. D. (1981). 'Psychiatric Complications of Meditation Practice', *Journal of Transpersonal Psychology*, 13(2), 137.

Johnson, S. M. (1994). *Character Styles*. New York and London: W. W. Norton.

Jung, C. G. (1931). *The Stages of Life*. London: Routledge and Kegan Paul.

Jung, C. G. (1936/37). *The Concept of the Collective Unconscious*. London: Routledge and Kegan Paul.

Jung, C. G. (1954). *Achetypes of the Collective Unconscious*. London: Routledge and Kegan Paul.

Kornfield, J. (1994). *A Path with Heart*. London: Rider Books.

Kurtz, R. (1970). *The Hakomi Handbook*. Boulder: Hakomi Institute.

Samuels, A. (1989). *Psychopathology, Contemporary Jungian Perspectives*. London: Karnac Books.

Stevens, A. (1982). *Archetype, a Natural History of the Self*. London and Henley: Routledge and Kegan Paul.

Stevens, A. (1993). *The Two Million-Year-Old Self*. Texas: A & M University Press College Station.

Tart, C. T. (1994). *Living the Mindful Life*. Boston and London: Shambhala.

Trungpa, C. (1973). *Cutting Through Spiritual Materialism*. Boston and London: Shambhala.

Washburn, M. (1994). *Transpersonal Psychology in Psychoanalytic Perspective*. New York: State University of New York Press.

Wilber, K. (1995). *Sex, Ecology, Spirituality: The Spirit of Evolution*. Boston: Shambhala.

CHAPTER 5

Images of Liminality in the Masculine

Stephen Friedrich

Editor's note: In the latter half of the twentieth century, in the 'developed' world, men's position is both under radical assault and in transformation. For many men the impact of this has yet to be profoundly felt while for others this is a disorientation that frustrate the expression of the ancient archetypal masculine energies that continue to clamber in the depths, demanding recognition and expression. Here Stephen Friedrich charts these energies through the stages of adolescence, adulthood, midlife, old age and death, illustrating each with stories that reflect and reveal the tensions that each stage evokes. His thesis is simple: if we are to be whole then we need to grow into each part of our life fully and not tarry in fear in a stage it is time to leave. Today, societal changes threaten this evolution as fatherless boys fear to be men, men fear the feminine side of their nature and all finally fear death. It is as if men have come to a liminal point collectively where the voice of the masculine needs to change its tune but without losing its note. Perhaps our task today is to allow and encourage this change, for this is life itself, but also find a way to continue to draw upon our archetypal roots so they may both anchor, nourish and guide our growth into the future.

N.W.

INTRODUCTION

In a short essay called 'A Note on Story' (Hillman 1991) James Hillman writes that exposure of the child to myth, folk-tales and legends gives a perspective to life which is psychologically therapeutic. This process is unconscious and provides us with a psychic container for organizing events into meaningful existence for the stories are a way of showing us how the events in our lives can be understood psychologically. Furthermore, the exposure to these stories develops the imaginal life and thus, there is less need to repress the irrational, the threatening if our imaginal capability is more developed. We may pathologize the irrational and threatening if we take them literally.

These images of myths, folk-tales and legends which, for the sake of brevity, I shall call stories, appear also in dreams and fantasy and poetry and familiarity with them gives 'story awareness' as Hillman calls it. Story awareness provides a better basis for coming to terms with our own case histories than clinical awareness. The clinical awareness of case history pigeonholes us. We become the diagnosis, abandoned in a grey hinterland; with imagination we can walk the busy, populated roads of our own lives for imagination and fantasy is the dominant force in our lives. Hillman says that when we examine this we are brought back to the great impersonal themes of mankind as represented in story. Through the collective unconscious we share these in our own culture and find our connection to other cultures.

The stories that have shaped our Western consciousness are the stories of Greek, Roman, Celtic and Nordic myths, the Bible and legends and folk-tales. The Grimm Brothers bowdlerized the sexual content of the tales they collected. This process continues today when material of a threatening, baroque nature is expunged: the wolf in a modern version of the story of Red Riding Hood is invited to tea which only postpones the terror at the top of the stairs to another time. The child should experience the terror of these stories in the safe enclosure of a parent's arms where the fear of the terrible is held by the parent and the child becomes familiar with it.

Since these stories are the basis of our Western culture they are also the basis of our own psyches. However, they are not only containers but also give us the way forward. In meeting these stories as adults we also meet the stuff of our own psyches. The story development helps us to find unconsciously the path forward in our own pathologies. Every time we approach a story we meet something new, a new facet of ourselves is disclosed for we are not the same person that encountered the story the last time: time has passed, we have a different mood and different experiences have shaped our lives. Each time the story discloses more and makes us more aware, more conscious of ourselves.

When I first came across Hillman's essay I experience it as if a door had been opened for me. It seemed to me that he was writing about a great truth and like all great truths, for which no scientific demonstration may be available it is something that I accept. These stories are the matter of our souls and function in a timeless void. At the same time they are determined by their epoch and culture and are, therefore, also the way in which our ancestors reached towards self awareness. The stories reflect the struggles that is the task on hand and we are helped through transitions of our lives by recognizing it in the story even unconsciously.

I accept all of this to be an uninfringeable truth and this chapter is written from this standpoint. What I have tried to do too, starting with adolescence, is to show the developmental stages of the masculine and how the images of these stories, which have gone through many generations of development, reflect the anxieties, vicissitudes and triumphs of these stages. The stories are, therefore, a way in which we can come to terms with the problems which arise in our development. We meet images of the collective which may disclose, illuminate and make numinous the events of our lives. They will also enable us to accept that we are not alone.

The feminine aspect in story is a parallel but separate development and it is not the brief of this chapter to deal with this. Women tend to be more grounded in their bodies than men due to the reminder that is brought in the physical signs of menstruation, defloration, childbirth, lactation and the menopause and transitions tend to be marked by these events. There is, consequently less turbulence, less turmoil as if the body had already prepared the psyche for these stages. A girl's puberty begins with the menarche and initiations into life stages such as childbirth tend to be a claustral events, conducted quietly in confined spaces. Women may also be thought to assume a socially dominant role in old age since they remain rooted in the community and tend to live longer than men. In this sense too, they carry the traditions of the community onward.

The material available in story is predominantly heterosexual. The issues affecting gay men are not brought overtly in these stories. However, it is clear that we contain both masculine and feminine elements in our psychic make-up and that these can respond to stories, can open to them when they are touched. Aspects of our sexual identity will be influenced by developmental factors and this has certainly been the psychotherapeutic point of view in the past. But it is clear from today's perspective that this is not necessarily universally so. Hereditary factors may also come into play as well as cultural ones of choice as we respond to the feminine or masculine poles in our psyche.

Finally, one aspect of the title to this chapter may need explanation and that is the word 'liminal'. This word comes from the Latin 'limen' meaning threshold and means also the initial stages of a process. The liminal state, the crossing of this threshold brings disorientation, time wobbles and there is a general feeling of being disconnected from things around us. This liminal feeling also brings with it an unprotected openness to feeling, to being taken over by new impressions and insights resulting in a new way of being in the world. Experience of a liminal transition brings a shift of awareness. The stages of life described below are liminal in the sense that they represent thresholds which we must cross to attain a new way of being and if we wish to live fully integrated lives. The experience of the images is the threshold; they are the experience of the liminal.

ADOLESCENCE

The word 'adolescence' comes from the Latin 'adolescere' meaning to 'grow up'. It has, therefore, a sense of evolution, to arrive at a goal. Adolescence now is generally considered to define the period of life between the onset of puberty and the early twenties. It is a period which is marked by profound changes in the body. Body size increases so that at the end of the period the boy is the same size as the parents and has also achieved sexual genitality like his father. It is a process of transition and like all transitions is disorientating. It leads the adolescent to crisis in which existing defences are no longer adequate to deal with the internal and external demands and which may lead the young person into extreme forms of behaviour.

The relationship with parents has been based on dependency and indeed, the adolescent is still dependent but his task now is to become independent of his parents not only materially but also of the imago of his parents. The imago is the internal representation of his parents in the psyche which arises out of what the individual has made of the experience of his parents and how they have affected him. Issues of privacy arise in personal matters at this age. The adolescent becomes secretive about his activities, hides papers and will refuse to talk about his schoolwork or social life. This behaviour is also mirrored in a new focus on the body. The investment in the ego that is being made at this stage may be displayed by extreme narcissism. He will gaze into the mirror in a self-regarding way and suddenly find that a comb does have a use. The bathroom door may be locked and demands are made for locks to bedroom doors. Territory which hitherto had been open to the parents is now closed. Associated with this is also the development of a turbulent sexuality which initially may find expression in homosexual play, masturbation and which leads some developmentally to the search for a mate.

The adolescent will strike out into the world only to withdraw promptly to the safety of the parental home and values as it becomes too dangerous. There is an in-and-out as the adolescent tries to establish himself in the world and tests himself in it. In this, the values of the parents are seen as old-fashioned, twisted, without virtue and need to be subverted. Hence the fascination in the adolescent for 'counter-culture' activities, the pursuit of music, fashions and intellectual activities which go against those of his parents, the more violently the better. However, the attack on the parents and their values arouses feelings of guilt, mourning and loss and the need to make reparation. It is in the working through these feelings that the adolescent becomes independent of his parents and is thus able to achieve a new adult relationship with them. The individual may remain immature, stuck in the adolescent phase if these archetypal imperatives are not experienced.

This period of life is, therefore, a period in which remarkable growth takes place, both physically and mentally and yet somehow the adolescent has to be contained within that state. It is a regressive state in which the forces of the psyche are retrenched in order to integrate and find that ego strength that the individual requires in order to move forward psychologically to live as an adult. Edith Sullwold (Mahdi 1997) writes with insight of her experience with adolescent boys who used the element of fire to act out their inner turmoil. The control, tending and the extinguishing of the fire is the expression of the archetypal need to be contained. This active containment is provided by tribal societies in the contained ritual of initiation by the elders of the adolescent's tribe. Here, the boy is inducted into the mythology of the tribe and is put to severe physical tests to mark the differentiation between the boy and the man. However, the elders not only provide the containment but also the role model of what it is to be a man. Such a grounded initiation does not take place in our society and the effects are clear in the uncontained antisocial behaviour of many teenage boys.

Many folk tales exist which show the requirement for containment and the presence of the father. A Slav folk tale deals with this issue. This story is called 'The Son of the King's Daughter' (Weißenberger 1990) and concerns a King who so loved his daughter that he treated her as his wife and neglected his real wife, the Queen, thoroughly. A passing traveller saw the Queen's trouble and advised her to collect the scrapings of a grave bone, put it in her daughter's coffee and she would fall pregnant. This all happened and the King, mortified that his subjects would think the child was his, put his daughter on a boat with provisions and sent her out to sea. A son was born and grew up in isolation with his mother on the boat. The son was ill-shaped, precocious and powerful. Eventually, coming to land in another country he wrought havoc and repeatedly visited the local market where he collected food and refused to pay. He had no paternal model, no one to establish boundaries and his mother was unable to instruct him. She did not tell him that he had to pay for these goods. He thought they were his due. He behaved in a similarly obtuse manner to the King of that country. The King duly met his mother and married her. After the marriage, the young man took the King for a walk in the forest until they came to a tree against which were propped a number of rusty swords. The youth told the King he should behead him and, as the King hesitated, the youth said he would behead the King if it were not done to him. When the King performed the deed the youth changed from his coarse appearance to that of a fine young man. His mother would not believe that this was her son.

Here we have the need for containment – paternal authority and role model. Where is this today in our society where the archetype of the father has been driven underground? The son grows up without the authority of the father or of the father as a role model and behaves in a belligerent, exploitative way. He cannot obey the rules of the collective because he has been 'at sea' with his mother; his mother knew no better from a father besotted with her. It requires the father, the King, to reassert the paternal boundaries so that the son can fit into the world and become integrated with the collective. It is the son who takes the initiative with the King who has become his role model. It is the son who suggests that they walk in the forest for he 'knows' what he needs and what his task is. The task has not yet been achieved for the swords of discrimination are rusty through disuse. Thus the adolescent fights the parents against boundaries – what time to be home, how to behave, to do his schoolwork – yet he knows he needs these boundaries to be set and to see the role model of the paternal authority with which he can identify. He needs the swords to be used.

In late adolescence and early manhood, say between the ages of eighteen to twenty-five, the young man moves into the heroic stage of life in which his task is to establish himself as an individual in the world by separating finally from the enmeshment of his family and particularly from his mother. The developmental task of the early twenties is that the young man must now strengthen his ego identity to enable him to love and work as an adult. This archetypal need for ego development is similar in intent to the developmental phase of the two year old who is trying to separate from the mother/child dyad.

Physical separation is insufficient because the internalized representation of the mother, the mother imago, is carried within the psyche and it is from the imago that the adolescent must ultimately separate. We all have a mother complex which remains as part of us for our entire lives. This complex carries our accumulated experience of mothering and encompasses the objective mother as she was and the subjective mother as she appeared clothed in our own projections. It is called a positive mother complex when this experience is so powerful and fulfilling that it eclipses any subsequent relationship with women; it is called a negative mother complex when it is an experience of unfulfilled needs or abuse. Both positive and negative mother complexes frustrate separation because the former offers more than anyone else can give while the latter keeps us attendant in the hope that our needs will be met one day. Within both, within the shadow, lurks the unrealized need for independence which may be expressed in anger, yearning for the father and initiation into male maturity or hopeless depression.

Jung (1990) describes the typical effect of the mother complex on the son as 'Don Juanism, (which may represent a fear of intimacy with an underlying sadism), homosexuality (as a desire for male initiation) and impotence (which may represent a symbolic loss of the phallus). The mother complex, I also suggest, can sometimes be expressed as moodiness, resentfulness and a prickly touchiness as if nothing and no-one is good enough. Here, the adolescent may have become identified with the mother complex and so treats the world as the actual mother did when considering that it was not good enough for her son. Moreover, Jung also says, the boy's mother complex does not appear in a pure form in that it is only constellated around the mother archetype but is also mixed up with the anima, the feminine side of a man.

The anima is that part of the psychic structure which represents the soul-image, enhances the feeling function and creative possibilities of the man. The wholesome anima frequently appears as a guide. It is the essence of the legend which I wish to discuss which illustrates how the mother archetype and the anima are mixed up. How could it be otherwise? First love is love of the mother and we must move beyond that for every love of a woman is a reminder of that. The relationship with the woman is potentially influenced by the internalized image of the mother. A psychologically resolved relationship in which the anima is differentiated from the archetype of the mother and in which the son can see the feminine otherness without his mother and in which both the mother and the son are equals leads to more appropriate behaviour by the son.

Stories exist in most cultures which deal with the hero's journey to full ego identity. In Greek myth (Graves 1992) we have the story of Perseus' slaying of Medusa the Gorgon whose gaze petrified all living things. Anglo–Saxon myth gives us the story of Beowulf (Wright 1963) who slays the dragon, Grendel's mother, who lives in the depths of the mere (which is an image of the unconscious). In the Babylonian myth of Enuma Elish (Sproul 1991) the solar god, Marduk, conquers the powers of darkness and chaos represented by the mother goddess Tiamat in the form of a dragon. Many dragons in our Greco-Roman heritage are founded in the mythologies of the Near East: Sumeria, Babylon and Egypt and in these the overcoming of the dragon has a sense of overcoming evil and the powers of darkness. This idea is still contained in the devouring feminine now where the phrase 'She is an old dragon' is a way of describing an old woman who is seen to have a certain power which is experienced as threatening. So there is a fundamental congruence of the dragon symbol with the experience of the mother, particularly with the negative, devouring side of the mother, that part which does not want to let go of the treasure she guards so vigilantly which is the child.

The theme of the separation from the mother, the fusion of the mother/anima archetypes and the reward is the unconscious ground of the story of St George and the dragon. This theme has been painted by many artists but I shall discuss a painting by Paolo Ucello (1397–1475) which is in the National Gallery, London. It is a small painting and a similar one is found in the Louvre for which the National Gallery painting is thought to be a study. The Louvre painting is considered to be a panel for a *cassoni da nozze*, a bridal chest. This would have stood at the foot of the bed of the newly-weds and the theme, therefore, penetrates to the core of the relationship between the young man and his bride.

In the painting a young St George (a puer, a man who is halted in the psychology of adolescence) is driving the lance, the phallic divisive lance, into the dragon's eye. The dragon is held on a lead by the princess. What is their connection if it does not go to the root of Jung's statement about the confusion of the anima with the mother archetype in the unconscious? The colours of the princess's dress are also reproduced on the bull's-eyes of the dragon's wings; the princess's dress touches the dragon. Whose side is the princess on? She seems closely allied with the dragon. However, the princess is the reward and St George has to prove himself worthy of her by dealing with the dragon.

Does St George kill the dragon? A lance through the eye does not seem to be a mortal blow. But it is a theme which brings us back to the petrifying gaze of the Gorgon. What is it in the mother's gaze that immobilizes the young man and prevents him stepping out into the world? Perhaps it is the experience of the mother's retentive quality or his own regressive yearnings that must be psychologically destroyed. The young man fights to be released. In a painting of the same theme by Lucas Cranach (1472–1553) in the Kunsthalle, Hamburg, the fight between St George and the dragon takes place in the foreground and the thrust of the lance is delivered to the dragon's jaw. Again, this is not a mortal blow. In the background with their backs to us, going towards the city are St George, the dragon and the princess. The message is clear: the dragon mother has been tamed but is present and each day will be a struggle with her. The mother complex will not be eliminated but stays present in the psyche – it is held on the lead and it accompanies us to the city. This connection between anima and the archetype of the mother, in which the mother is in the foreground, resurfaces in adulthood when the anima stands to the fore.

Erikson (1995) holds that the psychological task to be undertaken at this stage of life is to learn intimacy. Adult intimacy in the presence of the mother is unthinkable for it touches on the incest taboo and the accompanying fear of loss of ego. Erikson suggests too, that failure to learn intimacy leads to self-absorbed isolation which prevents the man from reaching out and connecting with the world.

This dichotomy is shown in the dream of a man in his fifties, R, whose task was still to effect a psychological separation from the mother and establish a connection with his feelings. For him the dragon appeared in the form of a witch riding a pig (the pig, because of its fecundity, is also an archetypal symbol of the fertility of the mother). She chased him across a large square. He escaped by ascending a drainpipe at the side of the church. A young woman, representing the princess/anima, stood beside the drainpipe, smoking a cigarette. She had no interest in what was going on before her. R did not engage in the fight but elected to remove himself from the world and so continue his self-imposed isolation. None of the figures were connected in the psyche. The young girl was unconcerned about his fate and she did not fear the witch, implying a connection between them. The dream suggests that R was still in the devouring power of the archetypal mother and not yet ready to engage in a relationship with the girl/anima, that is, not yet ready to engage in feeling. The witch gives up but the struggle will continue. A good outcome is suggested with the drainpipe against the church indicating a spiritual dimension to the quest and a requirement for assertion of R's phallic power.

ADULTHOOD

The word 'adult' is also related to the Latin 'adolescere' which I discussed in the previous section. Here, the sense of 'adult', from the past participle 'adultus' has the sense of 'grown-up, of 'having reached the state of maturity'. Adulthood is the last phase of ego development and the individual is now established in the world and ready to engage in an intimate relationship with a partner and to take responsibility for the nurturing not only of his own family but also to provide a protective embrace to his society and culture. We may say that a position of ego integrity has been achieved.

This is the stage which Erikson (Erikson 1978, 1995) calls generativity. He means generativity in its widest sense, not only in procreation of children but also that the man works in a contributative and creative manner. The adult's generativity is based on trust, 'the assured reliance on another's integrity'. Erikson writes that generativity is essential for psychosocial and sexual development and without this the individual falls into the opposite pole of stagnation.

Stagnation leads through regression to a pseudo-intimacy and personal impoverishment in which the individual rather than the community and the outside world becomes the focus of concern. This is typified by early invalidism and an essential lack of faith in the future of the species. Children fail to be seen to carry the potential of the future because the adult is caught in stagnation and sees no future himself. This may also be a definition of narcissism. Some middle-aged men who live with their mothers are examples of this.

Against this, the integrated adult is independent, knows who he is and stands his ground. In Homer's tale of "The Odyssey' (Rieu 1988), Odysseus, the hero, learns how to do this on his return journey to Ithica after the ending of the Trojan War. The outer purpose of the journey is to learn prudence and develop craft, shrewdness and enlightened self-interest as Odysseus moves through adulthood; the inner purpose is the psychological task of making conscious, unconscious shadow components of the psyche. I have selected salient incidents from the journey to illustrate how Odysseus moves through this development.

The shadow part of our psyche are all those repressed feelings, impulses and desires which we, our parents and society have found unacceptable and which we have been forced to hide. It carries also a sense of our potential. We become who we truly are by bringing the shadow into consciousness. Repressing shadow is hard work and takes energy. Individuals frequently become more energetic when projections are withdrawn as part of the shadow is made conscious.

Odysseus leaves Troy with twelve ships and his first port of call is the town of Ismarus in Ciconia. He and his men kill and loot and plunder the town. 'I sacked the place and destroyed the men who held it', says Odysseus without feeling. The experience of ten years of war at Troy is all that he knows. He slays everything and has to move through battle lust to understanding who he is.

In one of the most important episodes of his journey, Odysseus meets Polyphemus, the giant, single-eyed Cyclops. There is no social cohesion in the land of the Cyclops for 'nobody cares for his neighbour'. Polyphemus imprisons Odysseus and his men in his cave and intends to eat them. Odysseus, biding his time, makes the giant drunk and pierces his single eye with a fire hardened olive branch while he is asleep. Polyphemus' neighbours ask who is tormenting him when the giant cries out and he replies 'Nobody', the name that Odysseus has given for himself and so Polyphemus receives no help. Odysseus and his men escape by strapping themselves to the underside of the rams which Polyphemus lets out to pasture in the morning.

Here, Odysseus is the hero. The hero may be understood as a symbol of the self-assertive struggle necessary for separation from the maternal matrix. The hero's journey has archetypal stages that take the hero through a process of leaving the familiar, death, rebirth and a return to the world, renewed (Campbell 1973). This episode may be seen as compensation for the uncompromising heroic mentality that must achieve its task at any and all costs. This is indeed the hero's life and death struggle to establish a connection with his own feminine qualities, the soul. The hero/adolescent must be full of unassailable intention and commitment to his own truth to do this, brooking no others. The subordination of the appropriately inflated self-worth is here symbolized by the defeat of the giant Cyclops. Moreover, giant mentality is traditionally stupid. Giants blunder through forests, uproot trees and are tricked by the little folk. Giant words are absolutes such as 'always', 'never', 'everywhere' – words which allow no compromise and live in the single-eyed vision of the giant. These words measure extremes which are the currency of the young who deal in absolutes and have not learned to make compromises. Hence, in the world of the giant there is no social cohesion because paradox is not admitted. It is Odysseus' task to leave behind the inflated, single-eyed vision of the hero so he becomes 'Nobody'. He will learn to accept the world in all its diversity and to understand that diversity from a new perspective in which he learns to make compromises and embrace ambivalence.

The episode with the Cyclops is not the only one in Odysseus' journey in which he must confront gigantic figures. In the land of the Lastrygones, Odysseus meets the monstrous King and Queen who may be said to represent the internalized image of the experience of the persecuting parents. Odysseus and his men scarcely escape with their lives as ships and men are killed when this pair hurl rocks from the cliff top. We see here, that an insecurely attached child's feelings of frustration and anger towards his parents, all part of normal development, will be experienced as dangerous since they may provoke retaliation. Left with unbearable emotions, the child must resort to defence mechanisms and deny, repress, split off and project his own rage into the very parents of which he is already uncertain. The parents are then experience twice as bad because they not only provide insecure attachment but also carry the child's projected feelings. This is the King and Queen hurling the persecutory rocks on the small figures below. However, that is not to deny that some children suffer real abuse at the hands of their parents nor that all apparent bad parenting results in fear of our own projected rage. I remember the surprise I felt, after listening to a patient's story about her abusive parents, when she brought family photographs to the session which showed the parents, children and pets in what appeared as a loving family. We will need to work through both real memories and projections of good or abusive parents if we wish to move into integrated adult life. This will include the authentic experience of anger and fear and the mourning of the loss or absence of loving parents. We can finally stop persecuting ourselves if we now work through this process as adults.

In order to deal with these shadow projections we do have to go into a deeper part of ourselves which Odysseus does in his journey when he is sent to the Underworld to consult the blind seer Tiresias. Tiresias has been both man and woman and can see into the depths of all things. An approach to the Underworld is to see into the depths and confront ego death so that we can leave parts of ourselves that no longer serve us just as Odysseus relinquishes parts of himself and, therefore, changes in the transitions of his journey. A change in ego consciousness is required for which the ego has to die in order to be resurrected. Each transition in our life's journey is a death as we leave behind what is known and, therefore, comfortable and move into a new land, the lie of which we do not yet understand. This experience is shown clearly in the following dream: *A patient, H, dreamed that it was the end of the war and that he was Himmler and that the only solution was to commit suicide. He does so in the dream by taking an arsenic pill. He lies on the bed, crunching the pill between his teeth and feeling his body relaxing into what he believes to be death. He describes the sensation as comfortable since he also knows that he will not die. A nearby clock shows the time which is approaching the time for his usual session. At one level this dream represented a descent into the unconscious which H does when he goes to his sessions. It also represented an escape from the considerable financial difficulties which beset him.*

We saw in retrospect, however, that this death was also the beginning of a new stage in H's psychological development in which rigid, militaristic attitudes were abandoned.

Also, it is by confronting death, by confronting our actual physical demise, that we are liberated from the fear of it. It changes our attitude to dying and transforms our way of being in the world; we no longer make elaborate preparations to stave off death but have enthusiasm to seize the day. It also prepares the way for the experience at the time of biological demise so that we can depart gracefully, reconciled to the living.

There are six encounters with the feminine in Odysseus' journey, the last of which is with his wife, Penelope in the hierosgamos, the sacred marriage. The journey has prepared him for this final blessed reunion with his wife, fully aware of who he and she is. The confrontation with the feminine, with his own anima, is an important part of that journey. Four of the figures which he encounters are all 'magic' figures which would seem to suggest that they are primarily undifferentiated anima figures, parts of himself which are deeply unknown and which still carry a large element of unconscious shadow and seductive, regressive feelings related to the mother. The anima is also the link between a man and the world and between man and his interior life and is thus also a guide to relationships. It is the embodiment of the 'aliveness' of an individual and brings relatedness into his life. The way we relate to the anima in our unconscious is also how we relate to the outside world.

We have discussed above that for the man the feminine function in himself is infused with the experience of the mother. Thus the man will be *unconsciously* reminded of the mother when he seeks the feminine outside himself in lovers and partners even though he may have effected the psychological separation from the mother at the heroic stage. What deep feelings are buried as we caress a lover's breast which was the source of nurture for our infant selves? And how threatening are the images of seductive ease and terrible fear of annihilation which was our infant world and which remain in the shadow?

There is something reiterative about Odysseus' experience of these anima figures which mirror the unhealthy patterns we repeat in our own lives until a shift occurs and we understand why we are caught in these patterns. A man will 'fall' into love with the same type of woman again and again and each affair will end in the same unhappy manner; or he may remain discontentedly in an unhappy relationship because he does not have the self-awareness to understand his plight. In the same way, in therapy, we return to the same issues repeatedly until we have brought a little more of the shadow into consciousness and become more insightful about our own behaviour. We can then move on. Odysseus can only move on when he knows enough to be free enough to see the world as it is.

In Circe, he meets the instinctual, maternal level of the anima. Circe turns Odysseus' men into swine (we have seen the pig above as a symbol of the archetype of the mother). The pig also represents the instinctual at a primitive infantile level in gluttony, lust and anger. Odysseus is able to withstand the enchantments of the anima infused with the mother complex and to escape the trammels of the primitive instincts with the help and advice of the god Hermes, the god of transition and changes, of liminal states.

A clinical example of the way instincts may dominate our feelings is found in the case of N' an anxious patient who had been weaned early and unsatisfactorily. He would consume large amounts of junk food on his way to sessions, devouring it greedily in the street: hamburgers, pizzas, gooey cakes, sweets. The anxiety about the forthcoming session, that he may not be given enough nourishment, had to be satisfied with this gluttonous behaviour in which he was feeding his despairing starving infant self. The behaviour stopped after the first year of therapy spontaneously as he recognized unconsciously that the process was giving him the nourishment he needed. He was rescued from his Circe needs by the hermetic experience of therapeutic intervention.

The Sirens are another image of the regressive power of the feminine and in their form also suggest the succubus which would have sexual intercourse with a man while he was asleep and wrest from him his strength. Odysseus' response is a phallic assertion of the ego as he stays conscious and ties himself to the mast of his ship. The mast may also represent the World Tree as a symbol of the universe, of wisdom and eternal life and that Odysseus, by withstanding the allure of the Sirens, is allied to these forces and earns his place in the world. *An example of this comes from a colleague who recounted her experience with a thrice-divorced patient who found irresistible women who emanated a certain kind of sexual promise. He married these women and as the enchantment fell away, as his projections were withdrawn from the current wife, he would fall in love with a similar woman with whom he would begin an affair which would lead to the dissolution of the current marriage. The marriages remained childless and the wives all had a striking physical resemblance to each other and to his mother.*

Unlike Odysseus, he had not found a mast to which he could tie himself.

Then, Odysseus meets the *vagina dentata*, the vagina with teeth, the devouring feminine in the encounter with Scylla and Charybdis. Here, he faces the elemental male fear of castration and annihilation in the sense that a man unconsciously imagines that he can be consumed by a woman he enters. This feeling is heightened by post-orgasmic detumescence with the attendant sense of loss of power. The *vagina dentata* is also a universal symbol of the castrating mother (the mother's iron gates of life) and suggests masculine ambivalence to the mother. To stay within that from which life emerges is to experience death. The fear of the devouring mother needs to be faced for without this a man may be impotent not only sexually but also in his relationships with others.

Calypso, the clinging feminine, is the last of the 'magic' figures with whom Odysseus is marooned for seven years. This is a full cycle for it is thought that seven years is the time required for every cell in our bodies to be renewed. He has lost all his men and ships and sits on the seashore weeping for his homeland. Through loss he has changed. Calypso has offered to make him immortal to keep him identified with the unconscious but he wishes to return to Ithica. Odysseus has found a grounding within himself by rejecting immortality and attendant grandiosity. He is able to relate to the world.

Odysseus' fifth encounter with the anima is with Nausicca, the royal daughter. He is shipwrecked and naked, exhausted and stripped of everything. He crawls from the sea as if he were being reborn and shelters under an olive tree in which the wild and cultivated stock are intertwined. Nausicca, the princess and as the helpful anima, guides Odysseus to her father's palace, the King, which can be said to represent Odysseus' encounter with the Self. Nausicca has the 'elfin' characteristic of the true anima (Jacobi 1968) which appears to the man after aspects of the unconscious have become differentiated and aspects of shadow have been brought into consciousness. We discriminate over our feelings and desires for they are no longer projected. Thus, we shall have achieved a certain independence once the contrasexual element in ourselves is known. From the arena of internal independence from projections we can make appropriate connection to the external world and the Self. Odysseus symbolically does this in the mystical hierosgamos, the sacred marriage with his wife, Penelope, with whom he celebrates a physical union, after he has dealt with the suitors, in the marital bed carved from a living olive tree. The hierosgamos is the final resolution, the meeting of the opposites in which each of the parts makes the whole and which was anticipated in the image of the wild and cultivated olive tree above.

Washburn (1994) calls this period of life the last stage of the ego project in which the individual has established a place in the world through work and love. The ego is now supreme and has no other challenges to meet. It has been a one sided but necessary development to deal with the tasks of this period of life. Now, new ways must be sought to restore equilibrium to the psyche to meet the obligations for the next stage of life.

MID LIFE

The period of mid life prepares us for new life tasks and the period can vary for each of us from the beginning of the forties to the early sixties. Up to this point, the ego project which has been moving us forward and which was important to enable us to deal with the world, hold down a job and nurture families comes up against a barrier. Suddenly, the things which were important no longer are. Perhaps the goals which were set earlier in life have been achieved. Now what? Everything else seems barren and a wasteland. Or the individual has failed to achieve his goals and reviews his life in terms of failure and the future looks equally bleak.

This is the time of life when a new psychological relationship is required with the world and with oneself. The ego has moved forward into an increasingly isolated position and this one-sided development is unhealthy. Other aspects of the psyche need to be acknowledged. The mid life period is, therefore, a period of adjustment in which new relationships will be established intra-psychically in preparation for a connection with spiritual values and a connection with the Self. Ideally, this stage of life in Indian culture is characterized by the man handing over the family affairs to the son and going off into the world to find his soul as sanyasii, as a mendicant.

It is a period of painful adjustment in which we have to give up the things we thought of as having value. However, not everyone goes through this turmoil, this crashing of gears to find a new meaning. Some, according to Jung, proceed on the smooth path of instinct. However, the disappointment in failing to achieve the goals or the disappointment in realizing that the goals are insufficient to provide lasting satisfaction lead us to reconsider the value of the goals. The fundamental questions that confront us may lead to disintegration of the world as we know it and into states of depression which are not associated with unhappy or tragic life circumstances or developmental failure. These are frequently concerned with fundamental questions about identity. Who am I? What am I doing here? What is my purpose? In many respects these are akin to adolescent questions about identity but are now based on what we had felt to be a secure adult identity. This makes them more difficult to acknowledge for there is no sense of future development. We are it! What now?

Here is a return of the repressed shadow and there is a strange shadowy behaviour at this stage of life. We feel, perhaps, that something has been stolen from us and we have to compensate for it. The theft is the goals which we have or have not achieved and for men, particularly, there are feelings about the loss of sexual potency. The compensation takes the form of thieving of spouses, the aberrant shoplifting of the middle aged; some men leave their families and take up with much younger women in an attempt to steal back the lost part of their lives. Geographical relocation is another way in which we try to find new meaning: 'If I now lived in the country/an island/ Scotland instead of where I do live everything would be better.' But would it? We take our internal states with us and nothing changes.

But we cannot see that there is another dimension to be achieved until we have gone through this phase of renunciation. In mythological terms we can turn to the Book of Jonah for revelation about this stage of life. Again, this story can be read at several levels but let us consider it from the aspect of the mid life experience.

What is Jonah's experience? The Lord calls him to go to Ninevah to do His work. This is the new relationship required between the ego and the Self, the spiritual dimension. Of course, it is difficult and Jonah does not want to do it. He tries geographical relocation in order to meet the intra-psychic requirements and runs away to sea: to the unconscious. But he is not free of his internal demand, for the Lord sends a great wind and the sailors wonder why this is happening and cast lots. But Jonah is missing. Where is he? He is in the bowels of the ship, fast asleep – a further denial, another defence against what is required of him and also pointing to his final stage of transformation in the belly of the fish. Finally, he does admit to the crew that it is through him that the Lord is causing this great storm and offers to have himself thrown overboard to save the ship. Jonah is now prepared to go into the unconscious to find the connection that the Self wants of him. He is swallowed up by a great fish in whose belly he spends three days and nights. This is the deepest part of the affliction visited upon Jonah, a liminal state, the alchemical nigredo where everything is chaos, darkness and despair. It is also frequently the state of mind that brings people to therapy which is the first step of transformation.

This stage of life has the quality of stripping down, of reducing so that we are faced with the awesome choice of becoming different, of moving into a different phase of our life. Behind that lie despair and nihilism. I came into therapy in my early fifties. My marriage had failed and I felt myself to be at a dead end in my work which I had never liked much. I was assailed by feelings of nihilism, by the flatness of experience where there are no highs and lows; the world was uniformly grey. I felt that my world was governed by others and I had no control. I was bored and had a feeling that any action was futile. I did not know who I was and the ego compensation was overwhelming grandiosity. I had to demonstrate that I was of value and had special insights. I made grandiose gestures in order to feel that I was effective.

This sense of boredom, nihilism and narcissism led to feelings of profound alienation. Ego not only loses interest in the world but also loses touch. This, Washburn writes (1994), is a double-sided process. The ego becomes cut off and the world becomes inaccessible. The individual feels depersonalized as I did. My view was 'All this does not matter. I am not connected to it.' Sounds came as if through a long tunnel and the world appeared flat, in a two-dimensional perspective. Of course, this also created anxiety because suddenly the known touchstones had vanished. Washburn calls this 'radical freedom'; since there were no constraints nothing mattered. The management of my company lost confidence in me and I was dismissed.

Thoughts of suicide became frequent and the possibility existed since this had already happened in my family. At this point, stripped like Jonah with the weeds about his head, I started therapy and began to connect with that part of my psyche which I had ignored for the last thirty years in the proper struggle to hold down a job and provide for my family. Without being stripped of the illusions which our ego has cherished we cannot move on to the next stage. Hence Jonah's sojourn in the belly of the great fish. Nothing more profound or worse could happen to him. Jonah, by being swallowed by a great fish, is granted a vision of the two worlds, the spiritual and the material. He surrenders his ego to gain a higher wisdom. This is also an initiation into the next phase of life, old age, with the preparation for death.

OLD AGE

We are faced with contradictions when we think of old age. On the one side we have the image of the wise old man speaking his words in a sonorous, measured tone and revered for his wisdom, the carrier of the culture of the community. On the other side rests the incontinent, physically frail, mentally confused individual bound to his armchair. There is, therefore, a paradoxical meaning to old age. Old age is certainly a time of depletion and loss of faculties as Shakespeare lets us know in *As You Like It* where he describes the last of the seven ages of man:

> Last scene of all,
> That ends this strange eventful history,
> Is second childishness and mere oblivion,
> Sans teeth, sans eyes, sans taste, sans everything.

There are profound changes not only in the physical capacity but also in the behaviour of individuals as they age. The sense of depletion of the body has concurrent patterns in ego consciousness. Ego functioning may be diminished and hence more primitive patterns of behaviour can emerge. The tendency to use projective mechanisms (Rayner 1997) increases. These had been either rationalized or repressed in adult life. The emergence of the repressed shadow in projections in old age may result in uncharacteristic quarrelsome behaviour, irrationality, inflexibility and rigidity; breaks with family, neighbours and friends may occur: think of the erratic behaviour of King Lear. Perhaps the old person feels smaller, less in charge, less autonomous. This may find expression in anxiety about road crossing, in dealing with the swirl and eddy of daily life or a crowded room as the diminished ego is overwhelmed. However, this change in ego functioning also brings a freedom in which conventional behaviour is overturned in favour of spontaneity as ego restraints are loosened.

While we have this sense of depletion and impoverishment, we do also have, as mentioned above, the cultural view of the wise old man, the senex. If we accept this idea we should also recognize the hierarchies of age in family, work, politics and the arts. We should accept the view that the old be given respect for their views and actions which is deserved for the weight of experience of life that these encompass. These hierarchies, though, no longer exist in Western culture. There is no sense that the younger generations must serve an apprenticeship or learn from a master. Each generation re-invents the wheel for itself and the inflexibility and rigidity of the old is seen to stop progress which makes them unsuitable for a market place where novelty and development are at a premium. Old age becomes a matter of perception when the cut-off date in company recruitment schemes is forty-five. A dynamic, profitable organization is one in which young managers have the hands on the levers of power.

There is, perhaps, from the perspective of the old person also a fear of coping with the new which results in the denial of the new. If the new is accepted then it will supplant what I know and how do I manage with my diminished ego capability? In the pre-Olympic divine dynasties Cronus castrated his father, Uranus, to supplant him and heeding Uranus' curse that Cronus would in turn be supplanted by his children, swallowed them as they were born. Finally he too, was tricked by his youngest child and overcome. It is part of the natural order that the old are overcome to give way to the young and for the old to resist the young lest they are annihilated.

There is, though, an inevitable sense of loss for the old which comes about through loss not only of physical and mental capacities but also of a loss of connection with the collective. The great Irish poet, W. B. Yeats (Yeats 1958), deals with this issue in the first stanza of 'Sailing to Byzantium'.

That is no country for old men. The young
In one another's arms, birds in the trees
– Those dying generations – at their song,
The salmon-falls, the mackerel-crowded seas,
Fish, flesh, or fowl, commend all summer long
Whatever is begotten, born, and dies.
Caught in that sensual music all neglect
Monuments of unageing intellect.

This poem was written in 1926 when Yeats was 61 (old age is not necessarily only chronological; some of us are old before our time) and included in the collection of poems published in 1928 in a volume entitled *The Tower*. He had returned from England to Ireland in triumph. In 1922 he had been awarded honorary degrees by Belfast University and Trinity College, Dublin. He had been appointed to the Senate by the President of Ireland and in 1924 was awarded the Nobel Prize for Literature. But somehow it was not enough for he was blind in one eye and deafness was coming on too. There was physical decay and the sense that the body no longer worked. So, the poems of *The Tower* are full of bitterness at a time of his greatest worldly triumphs but they did not compensate Yeats for the feelings of old age. The sense of depletion in which the being-all-right in the world had disappeared also brought with it for him, feelings of depression. There is also in the last two lines of this stanza the bitterness that the achievements of the old will be ignored as they are displaced by the young.

This ejection from the collective also deprives the old of a role. However, the lack of a role does bring a certain freedom. Conventional behaviour becomes unimportant. Old people may ignore someone they have never liked or they wear slippers to dinner parties (Guggenbühl-Craig 1991). Old people become emotionally more volatile and can laugh and cry with the spontaneity of the child. There is, paradoxically, a lack of rigidity behind the barriers of old age but it is one which is of benefit to society. The lack of restraint brings a certain grounding. Without being beholden to any authority the old can say things as they are and with the child cry, 'The Emperor has no clothes'. There is a madness in the freedom where certainties about life are laid down in the marrow-bones of experience, a devil-may-care attitude which Yeats captures so well in his poem 'The Wild Old Wicked Man' in which the wild old wicked man is also connected to the divine in his relationship to the 'old man in the skies'.

'Because I am mad about women
I am mad about the hills',
Said that wild old wicked man
Who travels where God wills.
'Not to die on the straw at home,
Those hands to close those eyes,
That is all I ask, my dear,
From the old man in the skies'

The old provide boundaries which are both containing and restraining. The containment is in the sense of family history and that things are set to go in a certain way. They carry the history of the family and of the community. The restraint comes from the external rigidity, the unwillingness to consider new ideas that stop progress; but the mental and physical depletions of old age bring the old to face the end of life. Feelings may arise about the uncompleted tasks, the regret for a life only half lived which may culminate in despair that everything is now too late.

However, the despair of the old may be transcended if the connection between the ego and the Self is achieved. This task was initiated in the mid life period. Then, there is a way forward to a spiritual dimension in which the past is recognized with a sense of achievement. In the second stanza of Yeats' 'Sailing to Byzantium' he considers the fate of the old man who has lost touch with the collective.

> An aged man is but a paltry thing,
> A tattered coat upon a stick, unless
> Soul clap its hands and sing, and louder sing
> For every tatter in its mortal dress.

It is the soul's clapping of the hands, the celebration of the body as it is and the sense of being alive despite the depletions of age which give old people, who have achieved a sense of integration and a sense of spiritual values, a feeling that life is worth living. If soul does not clap its hands for us then we are spiritually dead; we are reduced to despair and become paltry things if there is no transcendent connection between the Self and ego. We become that grumpy old relative who is shunted into a side room during family parties so as not to affect the rest of the family with his mood.

It is in the aliveness of the individual that old age is celebrated and paradoxically, this aliveness also comes from a readiness to face death. The connection between the ego and the Self which informs our lives with a sense of spiritual values enables us also to look back on our lives with a sense of achievement as being the life we have lived; it is the only life we have had and that it will do. There is a sense of letting go. We are able to face death with dignity because we are conscious of what we are about.

DEATH

If we consider that birth is an assertive, masculine act in which we move energetically into life then death can be thought of as a diffusion, a surrender and has more of a feminine quality and a return to the mother. This is an inscription on a seventeenth century memorial tablet in St Martin's Church in Cwmyoy, Wales which conveys this sense of easeful death so well:

> Thomas Price he takes his nap
> In our common Mother's lap
> Waiting to heare the Bridegroome say
> Awake my dear and come away

Though this slipping into the lap of the mother is a universal experience it is, nevertheless, an experience that some face unwillingly. It is the end and endings are difficult for they lead into the unknown. We are not that sure about resurrection though Thomas Price awaits the call. However, as Odysseus came to understand on his visit to the Underworld, it is only in facing and accepting death, in facing the unknown that we learn to live. Many documented examples exist of men and women who have had 'near death' experiences, who have been brought back to life and have then adopted another way of living intensively in the moment as if every moment were precious. It is as if they relished each moment of life because they have experienced the finality of death. However, we do not know how this experience is transcended for no-one can truly die and return to recount the experience. We have only unconscious fantasies, dreams and the writings of poets to give us an intimation of the kingdom of the dead.

Today, the subject death is also further removed from consciousness than it was for our forebears. We are no longer reminded of death in our conscious lives as were our medieval ancestors by woodcuts of the dance of death or depictions of the charnel house; nor do we see, except in picture galleries, paintings such as the pre-Enlightenment 'vanitas' pictures with the skull placed among objects which symbolize the pleasures of this world. We are not reminded that at the end there is the corruption of the body. We try to evade death: we undergo cosmetic surgery to preserve youth. We hope for immortality through cryogenic preservation. We undertake frantic diets, exercise regimes and consume vitamin pills by the cartload. We try to stop time.

The ancient Egyptians, however, evolved an after-life in which death was birth into a perfect life with the gods and all of life was a preparation for death. For the majority of Christians, death, too, is a joining with God which will be perfected on the Day of Judgement when the corporeal body is resurrected. In these faiths the individual must also live a good life in the here and now in order to gain the rewards of divine proximity in the next.

The Greek god of the Underworld, Hades, is seen as the enemy of all life and without pity. He is seldom worshipped since prayer and sacrifice have no effect and he is hated by gods and men. Only black animals are sacrificed to him. The ghosts of the dead are incorporeal images of their former selves without mind or consciousness in the realm of Hades. Are we strong enough to face these images which give us no hope?

What do dreams and fantasies tell us about what happens on death? Marie-Louise von Franz describes a man's dream in 'On Death and Dreams' (von Franz 1984) the night after he had been given a medical death warrant which he could not accept. He dreamed that he saw a green, half high, not yet ripe wheat field. A herd of cattle had broken into it and destroyed everything in it. A voice from above called out that everything seems to be destroyed but that the wheat will grow again from the roots under the earth. This dream suggests that while the corporeal body may decay with death, something does continue: the fundamental essence, the root of the thing continues.

Many examples exist in the early mythologies which show the connection between grain and resurrection. We find a picture of Osiris, the Egyptian Lord of the Dead, from the Book of the Dead of Hunefer painted on papyrus around 1285 BC (Hornung 1990) in which Osiris is laid out and new corn sprouts from his dead body which is being watered by an acolyte. Similarly, Frazer (1929) writes that the festivities of the ancient fertility gods Attis, Adonis and Tammuz were all associated with grain as a basis for sure resurrection. A Roman fresco shows a soul escorted by two funerary genii in which the soul carries an ear of wheat. In the Middle Ages wheat germ symbolized Christ who descended into the underworld and was resurrected. The resurrection through grain finds its most apposite expression in the sacrament of the Eucharist in which the transubstantiated body of Christ is offered in the form of grain as a communion wafer.

There is also something of the vegetable world at the source of the imagery of death and dying. It is almost as if the nitrogen cycle were invoked to take care of the corruptible body from which new growth emerges. Yet what remains of the psyche? Von Franz's interpretation of the dream above saw it as a hint that the life of the psyche continues somehow after death.

We rail against dying yet it is in accepting death that we seem to make an easy passage into death. Failure to accept death seems to bring dream images of violence, of shadowy behaviour, of burglars.

For a short time I had a patient, P, in her forties who was dying of cancer, a diagnosis which she refused to accept. This patient brought a dream to the first session in which her place of work was dilapidated and boarded up and a violent, dangerous man abducted her in a car and drove her erratically and dangerously to an unknown destination.

The abduction of the Kore by Hades was a strong association for me. Her refusal to face the possibilities of her death brought these violent images to her dreams almost as if the unconscious were trying to bring her to consciousness, to make her recognize that she was in the grip of life and that life was at an end.

Yet, it is part of the development of our life that we should come to accept death gracefully and with equanimity. An accepting attitude to death and the last stage of our life's journey enables us to deal with our affairs in the sure knowledge of what we are doing and to make appropriate leave-takings without bitterness. This quotation from 'The *New* Natural Death Book' (Albery 1997) is a source of reconciliation between the living and the dead in which the living partake of the finality of death: 'Often in the back country of Montana, a hole will be dug and the body, in a plain pine coffin or perhaps just wrapped in a tie-died cloth, will be lowered into the ground. Instead of a tombstone, a fruit tree is planted over the body. The roots are nourished by the return of that body into the earth from which it was sustained. And in the years to follow, eating the fruit from that tree will be like partaking in that loved one. It touches on the ritual of the Eucharist.'

CONCLUSION

The numinosity of these images live in the containers of the story, poem or legend and they only live in us if we approach them ourselves. We have to be alone with them in order to let them live in us and they do so the more frequently we attend to them. This chapter is an introduction to images which may not speak directly to you now. However, the important thing is to spend time with them: chant the same poem out daily until the images become alive, suddenly, what was mysterious in the language takes on meaning. If we read folk tales at bed-time we may find that our dream life suddenly becomes more vigorous for these images touch the unconscious profoundly. The stories are many faceted and we find what is meaningful for us in them and it is by exploring the meanings we receive from stories that we find connections. Our stories are based on images that have been sifted through the unconscious of our ancestors and are founded in the collective. This makes them relevant for all of us.

I feel that this was addressed in a dream which came to me while I was working on the conclusion of this chapter when I dreamed that an ancestor was giving me the wisdom of the age which he had written down. One of the messages of this dream seems to be the incorruptibility of ancestral memory. I have written of the personal mother and father but the dream seems to be saying that there are other family figures behind them which have also contributed to the way we are. We are not only the product of our parents but of our ancestral family. It also made me think of Philip Larkin's poem, 'This Be The Verse'. His theme is that our parents fuck us up because they were fucked up in their turn by their parents and so it recedes into history. Larkin recommends that we have no children ourselves to escape this misery. This seems somewhat radical. Perhaps a better answer is to become aware, to become conscious of the forces in the psyche so that we can understand what we are about and use our understanding to break the cycle.

One of the ways of doing this is by entering therapy. In therapy we try to explore the 'As if . . .' quality of stories. How do we use them in the therapeutic setting? First, by letting them suffuse our own imaginations and so, even unspoken, their patterns of wisdom will be present and mediated by and through the unconscious. Perhaps it is only when a therapist is in contact with his own archetypal experience that he will be able to constellate it in his patient. We may often find synchronous events occurring if there is this connection. I started recently with a new patient with whom I felt an immediate rapport. He was carrying a copy of Homer's 'The Oddyssey' when he arrived for the first session. He had not only picked up my own preoccupations while writing this chapter but had also found a way to start his own journey. Secondly, stories also provide supervision as they chart the patterns of psyche's unfolding. A patient may recount an event that reminds me of something in a story and the connection opens to an understanding that was not there previously. Finally, when appropriate, stories may provide amplification to personal associations, both in the understanding of dreams and the dream that is life. Jung has suggested (Jung 1991) that the second half of our lives open out into 'culture' where the small egotistical concerns of life broaden and expand, lifting and connecting us to the collective themes that have run through our lives since the beginning of time. Perhaps our existential 'aloneness' may be alleviated in this way as we connect to something greater.

REFERENCES

Albery, N. (1997). The *New* Natural Death Handbook, N. Alberry, G. Elliot and J. Elliot (eds). London: Rider.

Campbell, J. (1973). *The Hero with a Thousand Faces*, Bollingen Series. Princeton: Princeton University.

Erikson, Erik H. (ed.) (1978). *Adulthood*. New York: W. W. Norton.

Erikson, Erik H. (1995). *Childhood and Society*. London: Vintage.

Frazer, Sir James G. (1929). *The Golden Bough – A Study in Magic and Religion* (abridged edition). London: Macmillan.

Graves, Robert (1992). *The Greek Myths*. London: Penguin.

Guggenbühl-Craig, A. (1991). *The Old Fool and the Corruption of Myth*. Dallas, Texas: Spring Publications Inc..

Hillman, J. (1991). *Loose Ends*. Dallas, Texas: Spring Publications, Inc..

Hornung, E. (trans.) (1990). *Das Totenbuch der Ägypter*. Hamburg: Goldman Verlag.

Jacobi, J. (1968). *The Psychology of C. G. Jung*. London: Routledge and Kegan Paul.

Jung, C. G. (1990). *The Archetypes and the Collective Unconscious*, vol. 9, Part 1 of *Collected Works*. London: Routledge.

Jung, C. G. (1991). *The Structure and Dynamics of the Psyche*, vol. 8 of *Collected Works*. London: Routledge.

Mahdi, L. C. (ed.) (1997). *Betwixt and Between: Patterns of Masculine and Feminine Initiation*. La Salle, Illinois: Open Court/Steven Foster & Meredith Little.

Rayner, E. (1997). *Human Development*. London and New York: Routledge.

Rieu, E. V. (trans.) (1988). *Homer: The Odyssey*. London: Penguin.

Sproul, B. (1991). *Primal Myths*. San Francisco: HarperCollins.

von Franz, M.-L. (1984). *On Dreams and Death*. Boston and London: Shambhala.

Washburn, M. (1994). *Transpersonal Psychology in Psychoanalytic Perspective*. New York: State University of New York Press.

Weißenberger, M. (ed.) (1990). *Märchen von Vätern und Töchtern*. Frankfurt am Main: Fischer Taschenbuch Verlag GmbH.

Wright, D. (trans.) (1963). *Beowulf*. London: Penguin.

Yeats, W. B. (1958). *Collected Poems of W. B. Yeats*. London: Macmillan.

CHAPTER 6

Changes and Transitions

Valerie Coumont Graubart

Nothing in life is constant except change

Editor's note: In taking us on a journey into the myriad forms of change in adult life, Valerie Coumont Graubart illustrates the many different forms of change and rites of passage. She describes the process, with its shared sense of chaos, descent, not knowing and passages into the new, and the initiatory quality of transitions. She puts herself warmly, and sometimes fiercely, into the writing of this chapter, as a vulnerable human being and as a therapist with strong views about human life at the turn of the twentieth century. A deep concern for her is to name the reality of the anger carried collectively by women over hundreds of years which has had no voice, but often is suffused into symptoms such as depression, eating disorders and relationship difficulties. She challenges psychotherapists to embrace the power of this reality in terms of the historical, economic and social effects of the oppression of women, rather than using psychological theory as yet another burden for women to carry. Particularly evocative are the many vivid individual stories of change that she has shared with her patients, ending with the very moving images that remain of her grandmother's death.

E.W.M.

When I asked the *I Ching*, the Book of Changes, what it had to say about change, I got the character *Ku*, Work on what has been Spoiled. The Judgement began:

> Work on what has been spoiled
> Has supreme success.
> It furthers one to cross the great water.

The Commentary reads:

> The Chinese character *Ku* represents a bowl in whose contents worms are breeding. This means decay.

And in the *Tarot*, the card representing an image of change is a crumbling tower struck by lightning.

What makes change so difficult for us is that in order for the new to come, the old must decay, crumble or die, sometimes with violent suddenness. Change, even in its benign manifestations, always carries a component of loss, even when it is change for the better. We move from the known to the unknown.

In phases of change we stumble about, unable to take our familiar landmarks for granted, lost and alienated. We marvel that others can make jokes, go shopping, indulge in trivial conversation, blissfully unaware of that existential terror that grips *us*. We are in a new place where we have never been before; we feel exposed, raw; painful realities which our healthy defences could normally keep at a distance, such as frightening or horrifying news items, now seem to come right inside us. We wait, without hope, for we know not what.

Change naturally occurs at predictable points in our lives – birth, puberty, adulthood, marriage, childbirth, menopause, retirement, death – and also unpredictably, as in major illnesses or accidents, job losses, wars, natural disasters. It is easy to idealize change, but without security of the known, we feel lost, disoriented, even if we are leaving a negative situation; a woman who spent years coping with a feckless, alcoholic, gambler husband who burdened her with debts, bailiffs, reclamations and even the loss of her home, woke up one morning after her divorce feeling anxious and thinking to herself, 'I haven't got anything to worry about'. Far from feeling relieved, she was at a loss to know how to structure her life in the absence of crises, and she came into therapy feeling that she was falling apart. However, change can be welcomed, as when an individual is initiated into a religion or religious community, goes to live in another country, or assumes some special role in society. In ancient societies and some present-day ones, those events are marked by rites of passage.

A rite of passage or initiation ceremony both formally acknowledges change and transition in the life of the individual, and often serves as symbolic enactment of that process. Characteristically, the person being initiated is isolated from his normal environment or social group and undergoes an ordeal which takes him into the no man's land of chaos and terror where his known conscious self, or ego, loses all its familiar supports. The experience may be like, or actively simulate, the individual's own death. The old self having thus 'died', a 'new' self can be reborn and emerge back into the world from which he came with new insights, understandings, and an infant-like freshness and openness to life.

Death and rebirth, sacrifice and redemption, descent into the underworld and return, transformed, are recurring themes in myth and religion around the world (Mahdi, Foster and Little 1987, Perera 1981). Osiris is dismembered and resurrected after Isis devotes herself to gathering up and piecing together ('re-membering') his body. Jesus dies on the cross, descends to the underworld, and on the third day rises from the dead into everlasting life. Dionysus, the horned child, is torn to shreds and boiled in a cauldron by the Titans but comes to life again after being reconstituted by his grandmother Rhea.

Psychotherapy may constitute a containing ritual for change, and a high proportion of clients come into therapy at this point, be it a natural transition point in their life cycle or a change suddenly and unforeseeably brought on by an external event or crisis; crisis being, according to the Chinese character which represents it, both danger and opportunity. What can help a person to navigate the perilous straits of transition? The first thing is one beyond our control; that inner security that comes from secure attachment in early life. The second is a network of support and love. The third is the sense of a story which, however, sad, bad or frightening parts of it may be, in some way adds up, has meaning, is not, ultimately, 'a tale told by an idiot . . . signifying nothing'. The first patient I ever assessed for psychotherapy said to me, 'I don't ever seem to have been able to tell myself the right story about my life'. Stories make sense of our lives, bind them coherently together, and part of the business of psychotherapy is to help the client to find his or her story, to understand the inner logic that brought them to where they are, and to create the potential to move forward to the next chapter. At times they may recognize their own process of change in a poem, a story, an account of someone else's journey, and these may serve as a map to help them make sense of their own way.

The therapist's task is likely to change during the process. At first it is one of containing and supporting; the client, already overwhelmed by loss, pain, rage and disorientation is not helped by explorations of infant trauma, which can only further raise the stress level. Later on, as the dust settles and he or she begins to recover some stability, a time will come when it is useful to begin to put the current change in the context of a whole life-story; to help the client take an observer position and begin to understand what parts of him or herself had to be sacrificed in order to maintain the *status quo*, and how that locking away of aspects of the personality and of particular feelings may correspond to the losses sustained and sacrifices made in early life in order to find a place in the early environment.

Thus for example, Peter, a 33-year-old mathematician and keen amateur violinist, came into therapy when his wife unexpectedly left him. The first task was to help him find ways of surviving his terrifying loneliness, his feeling that life was now meaningless, and to begin, as he put it, to 'plug in' to the world on his own behalf, rather than through her. Later he came to see how the early loss of his father and his mother's ensuing depression and withdrawal had led him to 'unplug' himself and live an encapsulated life with her. This in turn had been re-enacted in his marriage, leading to a kind of smothering symbiosis that his lively, gregarious wife found intolerable. Interestingly, as he began to find his independence, she was able to come back and build a new kind of relationship with him, and they subsequently had their first child.

As therapists, we may have to tolerate the pain of watching disintegration happen; of simply being alongside our client, waiting for the unknown new to emerge. We may have to hold on to the sense of meaning for them when everything feels meaningless. We do them no service by trying to 'put things right', but our patient support is vital. This chapter aims to be a starting point for thinking about some of the more predictable changes and transitions of adult life.

ADOLESCENCE AND YOUNG ADULTHOOD

Adolescence is the gateway to adulthood; the time when we stop being children and become, very distinctly, boys and girls, young men and women. Body chemistry feels as if it is taking over. For most, it is a time of loss and disorientation as well as, or rather than, excitement. I have not met many women for whom their first period ('the Curse') was cause for celebration. Some were unprepared and thought they were suffering from a shameful illness; some had rather got the message from their mothers that menstruation *was* a shameful illness and not to be spoken about; a few simply found it a messy nuisance. Those who enjoyed easy camaraderie with the opposite sex found their playmates and siblings no longer so easy-going around them. For both sexes, fear of being left behind in the race to 'go with' someone, fear of not having 'done it' when everyone else has, creates pressure to 'perform' often before we are emotionally or even physically ready.

In adolescence our relationship with the opposite-sex parent may become complex and tricky. I have frequently listened to the story of the girl whose father had always adored her and then suddenly, unaccountably seemed to 'go off' her when she was twelve or thirteen. Daughters are certainly not ready to contemplate the possibility that their father is finding it difficult to manage his own sexual response to his increasingly attractive daughter, and awkwardly handles the situation either by backing off and seeming to ignore her, or by acting the authoritarian bully, forbidding her to have boyfriends, wear lipstick and short skirts, or stay out late partying with her friends.

Sons, on the other hand, more often feel they are betraying their mothers by becoming independent and forming sexual relationships, especially if the parental marriage is in difficulties. An extreme case was a boy who had slept in his mother's bed until his teens, who felt that the only way to leave home was to 'catapult' himself out into the world, which then seemed, for years to come, a dangerous, frightening and mystifying place. The boy who obscurely feels that he has won the battle with his father to be 'number one' with his mother is left burdened with guilt and over-responsibility, and may carry a lifelong fear of being 'possessed' by women, which is likely to stand in the way of his making committed and fulfilling adult relationships. Bob Dylan is the voice of such young men when he writes that having given her his heart she now wants his soul, and makes it clear later in the song that this is the reason he is 'travelling on' ('Don't Think Twice It's Alright', Bob Dylan, *Writings and Drawings*). However, travelling on will be difficult if alienation from father causes the world of men to be a frightening place.

Clients of all ages may enter therapy to make the transition from adolescence to adulthood which has never been satisfactorily completed. They may have remained tied to a parent, or stuck in a rebellious mode which leaves them ineffectually fighting what they see as authority, without finding an authentic sense of authority within themselves. If they are in the process of separating from a parent or parent substitute, it may be important for them to enact the rebellion that never happened – to become passionately engaged in whatever for them represents protest – music, alternative lifestyles, dress, sexual experimentation, ethical or political causes – as a way of expressing their uniqueness, their differentiation from the family of origin. The therapist, like the parent, will need to support the emerging ego while holding firm the boundaries which are likely to be pushed against in terms of missed sessions, lateness, failure to pay.

Jonathan was a young professional man who had crossed the globe to get away from an invasive and controlling mother. However, in spite of the geographical distance between them, he still found himself acting like a rebellious adolescent – not opening letters or answering phone calls, not paying bills, getting into debt, getting drunk and turning up late for work the next day. In therapy these patterns were also enacted, and the therapist cast in the role of controlling parent. In spite of her attempts to hold firm the boundaries, little seemed to be achieved, and Jonathan failed to turn up for his last session or pay the bill for it. However, unexpectedly, two years later the therapist received a cheque for the missed session and a letter thanking her, and saying that he had now understood what was going on, and was settling his debts and sorting out the backlog of chaos in his life. The therapist realized that it had been essential for him to do this in his own way and his own time, and not as yet another act of compliance with a resented 'parent', as part of the process of connecting with an authentic (rather than adaptive) sense of self.

The Hero's Journey

The journey of the twenties is the hero's journey, and its essence is that we are, for the first time, on our own, forging our own path, making our own mistakes, following our own direction. (Joseph Campbell (1972) has charted this journey well). This is an important journey for *both* sexes; we are emerging from a time when the majority of young women saw their objective as getting married to a man and then accompanying him on *his* journey. Like many women of my generation, I did this, and like many, later had to find a way to do the necessary journeying on my own. The hero's journey is often perilous – we struggle in a highly competitive employment market, we run the gauntlet of exploitative employers and landlords, sexually transmitted diseases, social isolation and plain old loneliness as we go on our Odyssey. Yet like Ulysses we must not succumb to the enchantments of our inner Circe-mother which would cause us to give up the quest and settle for a tame pig-like existence in her backyard.

Ian Gordon-Brown used to speak movingly of the young adults who enter a world that offers few opportunities for the heroic quest – the young who grow up, for instance, in areas of high unemployment, who see their parents in the dole queue and are lucky if they can have any other vision of their own future. How can we develop our own muscle if there is no arena in which to try our strength? Perhaps rising crime figures represent one of the answers. For young women, early pregnancy may seem to be another, yet both often land the young person in deeper entrapment.

The Puer and Puella

On the other hand, there is the 'young' man or woman (of up to at least 40) who gets caught at the transition to adulthood because the options of adult life seem stiflingly unattractive and deeply frightening. C. G. Jung called them the 'puer' or 'puella' (von Franz 1970, Hillman 1979, Schierse-Leonard 1983), the eternal boy or girl who lives in a fantasy-land of eternal youth, permanent in-loveness, intense and special. They have the capacity to soar, Icarus-like, on the wings of their fantasy and creativity, and they fear above all the clipping of these wings by the demands of everyday life, leaving them condemned to a life of soulless drudgery. Stereotypically, their vision of 'adult' life usually includes a mortgage and a family saloon, financed by a mind-numbingly boring job (often like the one their father did). Trapped in 'rebel' mode, they are frustrated by their impotence and relative poverty, but contemptuous of the 'ordinary' life which lesser mortals (as they see it) are doomed to. Often they seek out a partner to do their 'ordinary' living for them – the social worker/teacher/nurse who brings home the bacon while they prolong their adolescence indefinitely – like the long-suffering social worker wife of an artist who, at the birth of their first child, 'went his way in the name of art'. As these eternal youths grow older life becomes less and less fulfilling, and they may drift into therapy, rather expecting the therapist to play parental adult to their eternal child. The same-sex parent will often have been despised and devalued, and the challenge of therapy is to help them find their own creative way of entering the adult world without abandoning the sense of what is important to them, to begin to distinguish between 'ordinary good-enough' and 'mediocre', which have previously been confused in their minds. The therapeutic alliance is often strongly challenged when they suffer the necessary disappointment of discovering that their therapist, rather than enabling them to fly for ever, as they had hoped, is there to help them to forge a realistic connection with the world and relationships. At this point they will probably attempt to butterfly-flit to the next alluring flower, and the therapist will need to feed this observation back to them if they are not to perpetuate a lifetime of briefly exciting but ultimately unfulfilling evasions.

Adrian, a fashion designer, came into therapy in his late thirties because he found himself unable to make a commitment to his girlfriend of many years. He attributed this to the fact that, although the relationship was emotionally, sexually and intellectually satisfying, she was not the skinny, glamorous woman he had always expected to have on his arm in a world where looks are everything. As he explored, he met his own reluctance to face physical ageing as he approached 40 – his thinning hair, his need for glasses, the lines his face was beginning to acquire. His therapist too came under fire – perhaps she wasn't skilled enough/had the wrong approach. Perhaps, he felt, some *other* kind of therapy would fix the situation. Additionally, work abroad made him absent himself frequently, so that therapy mirrored the relationship with his girlfriend in its tenuousness. Sadly, despite confrontation, he finally left in the hope of finding a therapist who would somehow, magically, relieve him of the pain of giving up his dream of eternal youth.

However, the Puer/Puella archetype is not always experienced pathologically. To the emerging adult, fresh to the world, it enables the excitement of discovery and a vision of life's possibilities. This is an energy that is not afraid to go out and try things and through this exploration we come to know who we are to be. Only when it is identified with for too long and begins to obscure the equally necessary qualities of commitment, perseverance and completing, the arena of the senex, does it become a problem. Our work as therapists is to recognize this when it happens and help the client stand firmly on the earth but not at the cost of their creativity and inspiration.

ADULTHOOD

Our ego identity is not, and cannot be, separate from the cultural and political context into which we are born. Society provides the words in which we describe ourselves; our choice is what sentences we make with them. After centuries of being warriors, foragers, ploughers of furrows, builders of homes, providers and protectors, in relation to whom women were secondary beings, at best pampered and protected, at worst trapped and abused, men are facing a transitional time where some old roles are no longer appropriate or desirable, and new ones have yet to emerge (Bly 1991). Redundancy and unemployment strike devastating blows to men who see their identity in terms of earning power and the ability to provide. Physical challenge, and the experiences that traditionally 'made a man of you' are largely absent unless deliberately sought out, for example in risk-taking sports. No longer experiencing the comradeship-in-adversity of war and danger, men are looking for ways of bonding, being close, for which the office, factory or pub are not enough. As with all change, something has to fall apart before something new can emerge, and that something is male identity. As with all change, the experience is a difficult and uncomfortable one. As a male client, faced with early retirement after half a lifetime in the armed forces said: 'If I don't go in to work in my uniform, I'm not sure if I'll know who I am'.

The last hundred years have seen huge changes in woman's place in society; unlike our great-grandmothers, we have the vote, control over our capacity to reproduce and to earn, sometimes, five- or six-figure incomes. However, corresponding changes in the inner landscape will take longer, and the core wound of having learned to view and evaluate ourselves through men's eyes remains at the heart of many women's experience, and the pain and anger it engenders needs to be acknowledged by therapists working with women seeking a sense of themselves in their own right. Since the 1960s post-Jungian writers and feminist therapists (Woodman 1980, 1982, 1985, 1990, Perera 1981, Singer 1977) have begun to open up psychological theory from women's perspective.

However, I think it is still true, even today, that in general women dis-identify with power. If we spend a few minutes thinking about 'powerful women' what images come up? Is it the ruthless high-flyer, all padded shoulders and nail-hard determination? A generous and kindly professional woman, thinking after years of exhausting public service, of carving herself a modest niche in the private sector, dreamt of herself with the face of Imelda Marcos. Had she confused the outer symbols of power, having 'power *over*', which so often prevails in the political and financial arena, with the potency of authenticity, and an unwavering connection with her truth? Confronted with the misuse of power we find ourselves faced with three unsatisfactory options – to make a bid for our share of 'power over', to experience ourselves as impotent victims, or to rebel against overwhelming odds. Alternatively, the work of therapy may be a reconnection with authenticity, and then a search for ways of potentially bringing our truth into operation in the world in which we live. In this way we may become effective agents of change, the yeast in the social dough.

Nadine, a successful accountant, often spoke in her therapy sessions about the masculine ethos of the financial world and her own difficulty in staking a claim for feelings when she was with her colleagues. An emotionally deprived childhood, in which she had learnt to be self-sufficient, made her skilled at concealing her own feelings, but she was becoming aware of the cost. It was not, however, until a male colleague, whose sensitivity had marginalized him, committed suicide, that she realized the importance of her female perspective in humanizing the organization she worked in, and began to speak up for it, thus starting to redress the balance in her environment and in herself.

Susan on the other hand had, at 33, spent most of her adult life in the service of men who exploited her. Told that, as a girl, there was no point in pursuing her education, she took a factory job at fifteen, married, had two children, divorced her selfish and unfaithful husband and, when I met her, was on the brink of marrying Ricky, another charming but irresponsible man. The poor urban environment she lived in offered little to a single mother-of-two; she was lonely and her self-esteem was at zero. A therapy that helped her to understand present events in the context of her life history led her to the insight that the relationship she needed to build was with her *self*. She declined Ricky's offer of marriage, and when I last heard of her, she had completed her A-levels and was embarking on a degree course.

Jungian analysts have done much to reclaim the variety of manifestations of the feminine, which include the Mother, both as creator, bearer, nurturer, container, and as spider-mother, devourer, smotherer, possessor; the Lover, both as inspirer and as *femme fatale*; the Virgin, whose virginity is not physiological but spiritual, the single-minded follower of her own inner voice; the Amazon, the warrior woman with a cause; the Priestess-Healer, mediating and making sense of others' experience, and the Wise Old Woman, the Crone gathering in her lifetime's inner and outer experience for herself and those who come after her. There is too little space to explore them here, but they are a rich resource for women trying to make sense of their own journey and find their own myth (Whitmont 1983, Wolger and Wolger 1987).

For me the most satisfactory image for female experience is that of the web. Its strands link me to friends, family, colleagues, fellow travellers, chance meetings – but the web of the Feminine is a wider one, a connectedness to the whole of life. While the Masculine, bearing the sword of reason, analyses, dissects, illuminates and conquers, the Feminine joins and connects. In the one-sided Masculine development of the West, where the ancient male/female deities, Shiva and Shakti, Isis and Osiris, have been superseded by patriarchal father-gods, connection has been sadly lost by the conquering hero who subjugates Mother Earth to his will, forgetting that what he is destroying is his own ground, and that he has no other. Reconnection, and the resurgence of the Feminine may be humankind's one chance of a future.

Finding Partners and Maintaining Relationships

The search for a partner will probably preoccupy us somewhere between adolescence and middle age, and for many the threshold to commitment and having children is the next one to be crossed. The longing for the other is beautifully described in Plato's *Symposium*, in the myth of the creation of spherical beings split in two at birth, who spend their lives searching for their other halves. Linda Schierse-Leonard has written on this theme in *On the Way to the Wedding*.

What are we are looking for in a partner, and what is it that draws us to one rather than another? In the course of growing up, it is likely that some facets of ourselves will have been better received and nurtured by our family and education than others. An academic environment or family may nurture the capacity to think rather than feel; a practical one may value common sense, physical strength and the ability to make money more than the ability to write poetry; an artistic one may promote creativity and sensitivity but leave its children with little idea of how to handle the material world. Some personal qualities will be rewarded, others may be strictly off limits. We tend therefore to grow up rather out of balance, and what we often look for in a partner is what is least developed in ourselves. If we think for a few moments about what attracts us to a potential partner, and then reflect on what part these qualities play in our life, and the life of our parental family, we may find surprising connections.

A young man from a rather cold intellectual family went away to study in Spain, and immediately fell in love with the warmth and emotionality of the people there. Later he met and quickly married a Costa Rican wife, but within a short time the marriage was in trouble, there was a breakdown of sexual and emotional intimacy, and he found himself spending more and more time at the office, until her threat to leave him brought him into therapy. He both longed for and *could not handle* what she brought into his life. The business of therapy was to reacquaint him with the lost part of himself which had been projected onto her, so that he could be more comfortable with that in her.

Sometimes we meet someone and feel as if we've known them all our lives. More likely than not we have, because they dance exactly the same dance with us as our mother/father/sister/brother did. We know the reciprocating dance-steps perfectly – we've been dancing this dance since infancy. If the dance is a healthy, happy one, all well and good, but if it is a damaging and constricting one, we embark once again on the same old struggle from which we thought we had escaped. At worst the dance may involve abuse or violence, contempt, lying or possessiveness. The therapist's task is to help the client recognize his or her limited repertoire of patterns of relating, to challenge them in everyday life, and, where necessary, to learn some new, more helpful ones.

Once we have passed the honeymoon stage of falling in love, we are confronted with the tricky phase of recognizing who our partner really is when divested of our rose-coloured projections; in other words, we begin to meet them as separate from and other than ourselves. A woman who found herself chronically angry with her husband replied, very honestly, when I asked her what irritated her, 'Anything that reminds me he's different from me'. Otherness both attracts us and drives us mad; the sociable wife who first seemed to save her solitary husband from his emptiness by drawing him into her busy social circle may later be experienced as invasively robbing him of his privacy; the intellectual husband who at first seems stimulating and exciting may later be experienced as cold, detached and lecturing, not to mention the fact that he never takes out the rubbish or does the dishes.

If we can begin to reclaim the aspects of ourselves that have previously been projected onto our partners, and to live out the roundedness of our whole selves, we stand a chance of making an enduring adult-to-adult relationship, and not one that constricts and limits both our self and our partner.

One of the key struggles between couples is often about who is going to be 'parent'. Anger and resentment will grow if one member of a couple is always called upon to be 'parent' to the other; the sexual relationship is likely to suffer, and the birth of a real child will challenge the dependent partner to embrace parenthood or move on.

Another key area of negotiation between couples is that of distance and closeness. I have Dr Anthony Ryle to thank for the poignant image of the two hedgehogs on the freezing mountainside who huddle together for warmth, only to scurry apart when they get hurt by each other's prickles. When we are too close for too long we feel trapped, smothered, restricted and at worst begin to lose a sense of our individual identity. When we are too far apart we fear to die of cold and loneliness. Often we are unaware of what we crave, whether it is space or contact, and are in danger of concluding that our relationship is over. The issue of space may be graphically enacted in terms of our home; a woman who remarried late in life developed insomnia when she moved from a whole house of her own to a shared house with her husband where not a single room was hers alone. She had never dreamt that she would resent sharing her space with this kind affectionate man, nor he that she, single for so long, might experience relentless closeness as oppressive.

When a client brings relationship issues to therapy, the therapeutic exploration needs to clarify what, in the story, has to do with objective reality, and what has to do with the client's internal learned patterns of behaviour and the way in which these are reciprocated by their partner, with an understanding of how the patterns were learnt in the client's family of origin. If the objective reality is one of current abuse, the therapist's recognizing and naming it may be vital in allowing the client to step back and appraise the situation realistically, perhaps for the first time.

Homosexual Identity

As a heterosexual therapist, I write with diffidence about the homosexual experience. Psychology is in flux over the debate about whether homosexuality is a matter of nature, nurture or choice, an aspect of our 'seed' self, of who we are at birth, or a later adaptation to experience. I prefer a wider acceptance of the individual 'way' and story. I have worked with gay men and women who were perfectly comfortable with their sexuality (though not with society's attitude to it), gay men and women who were agonized by it and keenly felt the loss of a conventional family life and children, and men and women who were unsure, perhaps bisexual and who felt they had a choice to make. Most of us will have had the experience, during our school years, of that intense first love (for it often is just that) for an older pupil or teacher of the same sex, which is dismissed by anxious adults, and later by ourselves, as a 'crush'. Androgyny makes our society uncomfortable, and in the anxious rush to be identified with one sex or the other, we may lose precious contrasexual aspects (i.e. aspects normally attributed to the opposite sex) of ourselves. Thus boys quickly learn that sensitivity and sometimes even creativity are 'sissy' while girls can feel it is 'unfeminine' to be incisive, intelligent and dynamic; to be capable home-makers but not car mechanics. For some boys and girls the homosexual orientation remains, and I feel that adolescence is for them especially agonizing, particularly if they grow up in a homophobic environment. I have met young homosexuals who believed that they could never be accepted in the conservative environment they were born into, and therefore felt compelled to make a new life elsewhere, where a greater breadth of experience was accepted. I have met boys whose experience of others' homosexual acting-out at boarding school, often abusive, has left them confused about their sexuality. A boy with a strong feminine side does not necessarily grow into a homosexual man, but being labelled 'poof' at school because you play the piano and don't like sports can leave you confused, anxious and marginalized as you enter adolescence. Conversely, the experience of trying to be 'normal', dating the opposite sex while feeling no sexual attraction, or even some repulsion, is equally painful, but the relief of meeting the same sex partner carries agonizing choices about whether to 'come out' to friends and family, and how that will be received. No gay man or woman has ever told me that homosexuality was an easy option, though some have spoken of the relief of finally feeling able to be themselves. The AIDS epidemic has further complicated and stigmatized male homosexuality; at the same time it has enabled gays to discover depths of loyalty, care and compassion in their community which may be the envy of those outside it. As a heterosexual psychotherapist sometimes working with gay clients, I feel my position must be one of listening, holding the balance of their experience and doing my best to support their transition to being fully who they are, sexually and socially. We need to understand that while living our truth in a society which is often hostile to it can be difficult and painful, owning and enjoying a love denied or hidden for years and even decades can be the most fulfilling experience of a lifetime. Perhaps rather than puzzling over the aetiology of homosexuality we would do better to begin to understand the meaning of homophobia, to put it in its place beside racism, and to heal the wound in ourselves and our society from which it emanates.

Heterosexual therapists working with gay clients should beware their own unconscious homophobia, which may destroy empathy and lead to a subtly critical or attacking stance. Supervision is the space in which they can safely explore this, and an honest look at hostile counter-transference is worth a thousand liberal blandishments. A difference of sexual orientation also means that the therapist can take nothing for granted, must allow the client to invite them into *their* world and must never lose sight of the marginalization which is a part of their client's everyday experience.

MATURITY AND MID LIFE

Jung said that nothing prepares us for the second half of life. Somewhere between our mid-thirties and our mid-forties we cease to perceive ourselves as 'young' and take stock of where we are and where we had expected to be. A man entering this phase wrote a poem about lingering at a lakeside, always imagining he would move on, and at last realizing he had put down roots there. Sometimes we wonder how we got here, with a feeling of surprised pleasure or of dismay – how we came to be living in the city, or married to someone we thought we were having a casual relationship with, or a parent when we expected to become an opera singer.

Sometimes we are dimly aware that we have arrived where we are via the faulty patterns of relating and the coping strategies we learnt in early life, which served us well then, but seem to trap us now. The caring professional may be there not out of a passion for the work, but because of his or her early 'training' to be a carer for an inadequate parent. The performer who pushes himself on in spite of vomiting with stage fright before every performance may only have won attention through perform-ance as a child. The bright truant who never passed any exams, or the person who left school early to help support the family, or simply because the horizons were narrow, may find herself in a mechanical, dead-end job, or no job at all. The used and abused partner may have stayed in that deadly relationship, like the heroine of Roddy Doyle's *The Woman Who Walked Into Doors*, because they never knew anything else, and so hardly notice how bad it is. The man or woman who prematurely opted for a safe but unsatisfying relationship out of feelings of neediness, inadequacy and dependency may feel stifled by symbiosis, while the Don Juan may be tiring of the unending quest for permanent in-love-ness, or at least the excitement of the next 'perfect' sexual experi-ence.

Sometimes life has been satisfying, but one-sided; one or two aspects of our self have become highly developed while others remain dormant, undeveloped, unconscious; we are like a plant that gets the sunlight from only one side, producing abundant foliage and blooms there, but with a dusty, stunted other side in the semi-darkness.

Around the middle of our life, the seed self starts to stir, to grumble, to crack through the persona we have constructed to deal with the world we found ourselves in at birth, the world we have adapted to and coped with over half a lifetime. We feel vaguely dissatisfied, even though our circumstances appear satisfactory, even enviable. We may blame external circumstances – if only we could change our job, our partner, our home, our country – and sometimes these do indeed need to change, but often external changes will not be enough if no internal change takes place.

Matthew, a high-flying businessman with two young children whom he rarely saw, sat in my consulting room crying about the fact that they hardly recognized him any more. His wife had a similarly demanding career. He changed jobs in order to be at home more, but the old pattern of being valuable only through achievement got the better of him, and within weeks he was back in the old routine. His feeling self had so long been invalidated that he could not listen to its voice, though it was breaking his heart not to.

Sometimes it takes a huge jolt from life before we can start heeding that in us which longs to be given a life but has never been allowed one. We use words like 'breakdown' and 'mid-life crisis' to describe such experiences. We can see this, in terms of Edinger's map of the ego and the Self, as the point at which ego-control weakens as the pull of the Self is felt, at first unconsciously (Edinger 1972). Our body may suffer under the strain in the form of a heart attack or a life-threatening illness. Our relationship may break up. We may lose our job, have an accident, or simply find ourselves walking around in tears for no apparent reason, wondering what on earth is going on.

Such a crisis may bring us to see a therapist. We may speak of 'stress', 'menopausal depression'; we may wonder if we are going mad or whether something is organically wrong. We may feel alienated, disengaged from what we previously pursued with enthusiasm. We may be disturbed by our dreams which we will probably describe as nightmares. The death of a parent or someone close to us may remind us that our own life is time-limited. We feel lost, disorientated, like someone who has stopped pedalling and feels himself wobbling, about to fall off his bicycle. In order to come to a new place, we are forced to lose the certainties of the old one, and we feel exposed, skinless, and terrified. Such a death is the prerequisite of rebirth, a new beginning.

This had happened to Ray, an army officer in his late forties, with a distinguished career in the Forces. His mother had died, there had been some professional setbacks, and Ray, who had spent his life soldiering on, could go no further. Having at an early age had to cut off from his grief at the loss of his father in order to help his widowed mother support the younger children, he had left school early and gone into the army. Now he was overwhelmed and terrified of what was happening, of the loosening of the iron control he had always exerted over his unruly emotions, as over his unruly men. He dreamt of a faceless stalker trying to break into a house whose doors and windows he was endeavouring to bolt. As soon as he locked one, the bolt shot back on the previous one. It was the *facelessness* of the stalker that so frightened him – the *unknownness* of what might come in place of his soldierly self-control. He found himself exerting obsessional control over the household – making sure everything was correctly put away, yelling at the children if they stacked the saucers in the wrong pile or failed to hang their coats on the pegs – as his control over his inner world weakened. He believed he wanted nothing more than to be back in uniform, back on the job. But as the weeks in therapy passed, and the long-held-in feelings began to surface and be valued without turning him (as he feared) into a monster, going back into the old persona began to lose its appeal. He started to relax, to enjoy his children, to read, to pick up some of the threads that were lost when he left school. When I last heard of him he had retired from the army and was making a modest but happy living from writing and illustrating children's stories.

The changes we make or undergo in mid life have a powerful impact on those around us. Men say 'She's not the woman I married' as their wives detach themselves from domesticity and go back to university; women fear a loss of manliness when their husbands cease to be the main breadwinners, as do their husbands. The habitual dance is no longer danced, and we face the challenge of either adapting to change, or moving on. Some partnerships break up under the strain, and the *fear* of a break-up may cause us to accept an increasingly intolerable *status quo*, until breakdown forces us to accept that it has become insupportable.

At its most frightening, change involves a loss of ego–identity, a falling apart of the known self, as if all the jigsaw pieces were shaken up in a bag and we have to wait for the picture to be reassembled, a total loss of basic security, a descent into what feels like endless night. A bereaved woman said to me, 'I know time will heal, but what on earth am I to do in the meantime?'

However, the rebalancing of mid life is what enables us to move forward in what Jung called the process of individuation, the becoming more fully who we are, the flowering of the seed that continued underground for half our lives and now must find expression. Is this perhaps the meaning of maturing, of confidence – the feeling that we are who we are, take us or leave us? It frees us to offer what we have to the world, feeling neither bashful nor inflated, and to move fully into what we feel to be our place there. In the Hindu tradition, 50 is the age at which men whose role up to that point had been to earn a living, provide a home and support a family, may turn away from outer achievement and go on their pilgrimage, the beginning of a journey inwards, the journey back to the soul, the Self, the oneness of creation – whatever we want to call it – from which they came. This may help us to make sense of the crises of middle life.

Menopause

Menopause involves loss, and, coming as it does at the point when many of us may be experiencing the death of one or both parents, it reminds us that life is time-limited, that our bodies are not indestructible, and that we need to be making the most of what we have. As I pass through this phase myself, I am aware that being able to hike up mountains or swim in icy water is not something I will indefinitely be able to take for granted. As Germaine Greer says, it heightens our love of the world, but it also broadens it; begins, in my experience, to deepen our connection with the great web of life.

For some women who have not had children, there is grief of knowing that they never will. This may release them from the tyranny of hope, and free them to invest their energy elsewhere. If we *have* children, the end of fertility may well coincide with the end of mothering, in the sense that they may be grown up and leaving home. This quiet crisis leaves a huge gap – after two decades of a life focused on others, many women experience a collapse of structure akin to what many people experience at retirement. I feel that a period of depression is quite normal at this stage, and can be understood as that incubation, that going into the dark, which precedes the 'birth' of something new, the nature of which is as yet unknown.

During the menopause our bodies seem to take on a life of their own, unlike anything since pregnancy or, if we are childless, since adolescence. We wake in the night sweating, get aches and pains in our limbs, sore breasts, feelings of debility and exhaustion, and moments of extraordinary energy and clarity. Because our bodies seem to be running riot, we may fear serious illness. We may feel powerful mood swings, intense anger or sadness. It is hard to know what to attribute to hormones, and what to the pent-up rage of a lifetime of pleasing others, as so many women have learnt to do. Anger, especially anger in women, gets a bad press, but when we take hold of it and use it, it can move mountains. Anger can move us to confront social injustice, environmental destruction, nuclear weapons, or just the fact that our local supermarket makes no provision for the disabled. Anger is one of the greatest agents of change.

Germaine Greer (1991) makes the point that the menopause is our opportunity to move from being *women* to being *people*. Collectively in the West, we lack initiation rites and a sense of community for this transition, and indeed the anti-ageing industry, offering us plastic surgery, rejuvenating creams and pills, intensive exercise programmes, encourages us to deny our experience, and to chase the illusion of eternal youth. We must look further afield to re-find the images of the wise old woman (vestigially honoured, perhaps, in the role of the agony aunt), the crone, the soothsayer, the healer, the midwife, the layer-out of corpses whose experience is valued, and sometimes feared (the witch), in the community.

Psychotherapy, particularly if the therapist herself has passed through this transition, can both contain the grief of loss, the letting go of hopes that will never be fulfilled, and help a menopausal client to value her rich store of experience, her mature insight, and in many cases the completion of her child-raising years which sets her free to engage with the wider world in a quite different way.

Loss and Bereavement

The age at which we encounter loss or bereavement for the first time is unpredictable – for the abandoned baby or the orphan it may be the earliest experience. We may first meet it in the form of loss of health, loss of a limb, loss of a partner, loss of grandparents or even, and perhaps most terribly, loss of a child, but by the time we reach mid life we are unlikely not to have been brushed by the wing of the angel of death.

Loss is an experience like no other – it is almost impossible to describe and, perhaps fortunately, we cannot imagine it before we have experienced it. This means that those who have early bereavements, and particularly bereaved children, feel so terribly isolated – often there is literally no-one to talk to, no-one who knows how they feel. Unsure how to address their unfathomable experience or their grief, others tend to fight shy of the bereaved – a teacher, widowed in her early forties, told me how, when she returned to school, she would notice colleagues crossing the playground in order not to bump into her – it wasn't that they didn't care; they just didn't know what to say. Often all we can honestly say is that we feel inadequate to say anything, but it is our *presence* that counts, the food we cook, the cups of tea we make, the opportunity just to sit in our home which feels warm and full of life when their own is so unbearably empty and cold. C. S. Lewis (1961) in *A Grief Observed*, written after the death of his wife, recalled how he wanted people around him but was totally uninterested in anything they had to say. 'If only', he lamented, 'they would talk to each other, and not to me'.

Colin Murray Parkes in his essential volume *Bereavement* (1972) makes the point that it is not only the dead person who is lost, but oneself: the self whose world was in part constellated by the dead other. It is as if they were a weight-bearing wall without which the whole edifice collapses. Meaning and basic safety disappear. Lewis, a devout Christian, cried out 'Where is God?' A wise therapist said to me, 'It is as if you have no skin. Your skin will grow back, but it will take time.' In the meantime, the world feels a totally unsafe place. The chill wind of an empty universe seems to blow right through us. A late train when we are alone on an empty platform, or the snow falling outside the window fill us with an unspeakable terror, the terror of annihilation, of ceasing to be. A woman living alone after a recent and painful divorce recalled: 'The mornings were the worst. When I woke up I didn't know if I existed. I had to go down to the newsagents and buy a paper – as soon as I had spoken to someone, I knew I was still there.'

Loss reconstellates our earlier losses, and if these have happened at a point where the ego was insufficiently formed to deal with them – as for example in the death of a parent in infancy – the feelings elicited by a later bereavement may precipitate a stage of disintegration where we fear that we are 'going mad'. The terror is like what Winnicott calls the 'primitive agonies' of the infant – falling apart, falling forever, being the last person left on earth, the most fundamental fear that there is *no* 'me'. Our needs at these times are like those of a baby too – warmth, feeding, containment, the undemanding presence of another person. The wise Jewish custom of 'sitting shiva' provides this – the bereaved person stays at home and friends and relatives bring food and take care of material concerns.

It is generally agreed that a bereaved person will need at least two years to begin to feel anything like 'normal', and of these, the first six months will be the most terrible. Murray Parkes names the stages of bereavement as numbness, anger, pining, depression and letting go, but makes the important point that grief is a process, not a set of symptoms. One thing we can be sure of is that, quite literally, we shall never be *the same* again. As therapists, our task is to sit in the darkness with our client, for as long as they need us there, to allow them to rehearse over and over again the harrowing unspeakable details, to hold the tender memories, perhaps with the help of photographs or treasured objects, to rage at injustice and abandonment, as they gradually accept the reality of loss, withdraw the energy invested in the lost person, and finally become ready to invest it in a new situation.

RETIREMENT AND AGEING

Retirement and ageing can no longer be spoken of in the same breath. High-flyers in the City plan to make their first million and retire by their mid-forties; 'voluntary redundancy' and 'early retirement' mean many of us will stop work in our fifties – for some people, with increasing expectations of longevity, this may mean they retire when they are not much more than half way through their lives. While, classically, retirement was a drawing back from the world into a more inward-looking life, today it may be seen either as a devastating blow to personal identity, if we have derived this principally from work, or a god-given opportunity to live out the parts of ourselves that had to be put on hold in order to do a demanding job or raise a family.

If we are psychologically and materially fortunate we shall be able, in our fifties, to start getting out of the fast lane. We may be in a position to reach and nurture the talents of those who are coming up the ladder after us, rather than feeling them as a threat, just as in the family a mother graciously steps out of the limelight to allow her grown-up daughters to take centre stage, rather than jealously competing with their liveliness and beauty. It goes without saying that both are easier to do from a place of security and satisfaction. If these are missing, it will be harder to let go.

Stepping aside allows us to develop other parts of our lives. For many of us, our creativity will find space to surface for the first time. We will have time to think, to reflect; increasingly people are going to university in retirement, some for the first time. If thinking has been our primary occupation, we may discover another side of ourselves in cooking, gardening, sculpting, dancing.

I watched with interest and respect as a loved colleague, in her late sixties, took the brave step of withdrawing from what had been her life's work. The beginnings were not easy – living on her own she faced unstructured time and an absence of demands which sometimes left her disoriented and depressed. Little by little her creativity began to build new structures: she went travelling rather as students do – for months at a time, on a low budget, making personal contacts wherever she could in all parts of the world, trekking in the Himalayas and involving herself in a women's project in Southern Africa. She took up writing, started a reading club and an art therapy group, involved herself with social and political projects. Ian Gordon Brown used to say that as we age we either shut down, getting narrower and narrower, or we broaden out, embracing more and more of the world; she has done the latter.

I feel fortunate to have known people who have modelled a rich and generous ageing process: Marion Milner attending Winnicott seminars in her nineties, Jean Gibson walking her five dogs at 6 a.m. in her eighties: they are a far cry from the stereotypical 'old lady' of my childhood (possibly not very much older than I am now) who seemed consigned to a homebound life of waiting for the all-too-infrequent visits from her far-away children. Doris Lessing (1996), writing about falling in love in one's sixties (*Love, again*) talks movingly about how 'old age' is largely an external perception; from inside we do not feel 'old' – our passions, beliefs, thoughts, feelings are as fierce as ever. We look in the mirror and are surprised by wrinkled skin and white hair. An older woman in therapy, accustomed to painting demure water-colours, drew 'a small grey person with her belly full of fire'.

One of the ugliest features of Western civilization at the present time is the ghettoization of those who make us feel uncomfortable. Whether they are the profoundly physically or mentally disabled, dying or old, we tuck them discreetly away where we can't see them. Looking at old age is painful; we are looking at what will almost certainly be our own future, and if we have decided that the old are of no interest, to be consigned to the scrap heap, then our own future is bleak. Unlike some less 'developed' society, we have lost contact with the archetype of the elder, the wise old man or woman who is a rich resource of experience for the rest of the community. When such people *are* there, they may be a lifeline to the young: it is interesting how often, in therapy, someone whose childhood seemed devoid of parental love names a grandparent as the one person who was able to be unconditionally loving and present, the person who will always be recalled with gratitude.

Recently, I heard of a therapist working with old people suffering from Alzheimer's disease. She brought into the residential home objects, clothes, pictures from the period of their youth. Little by little, communication began to open up as memories surfaced and they started to reminisce. They had stopped talking because no-one had seemed to be interested; they had become objectified, infantalized, condescended to, and so they had learnt to behave like objects.

Few people come into therapy after age 60. If they do, they are likely to do so because of loss in one form or another: bereavement, illness, retirement, debility, a sense of mortality, of time running out. As (usually) younger therapists, we need to ask ourselves whether we can tolerate this material; we need to be aware of the pitfalls of either trying to 'make it better', or being pulled into despair alongside our client. After all, it is our own mortality we are looking at, and we will need the containment of supervision for our own terrors about ageing and death. While I believe it is true that the inner journey has the potential to expand and intensify as the outer one contracts, nothing could be more infuriating than an able-bodied young therapist shifting the focus to spirituality when the client needs someone to hear that his knees have given out and he can no longer walk. Real losses must be acknowledged and grieved before an exploration of the dreams and visions of the inner life can be accessed.

DEATH AND DYING

The people who have lived the most fully seem to fear death the least (von Franz 1984). A woman in her nineties openly expressed a longing to die, not because she was ill or in despair, but just because she was so deeply tired. If we are called on to work with a terminally ill client, we face the challenge both of recognizing the reality of our own death, and of being unable to 'save' them, which may be hard to accept. A colleague who worked with terminal AIDS patients felt guilty about her own health, and ineffectual in the face of their inexorable disease, until she recognized how precious was her steady unflinching commitment to see them through to the end, to stay with their rage and pain in such a way that sometimes they came to feel that they lived more fully in those last weeks than at any other time in their lives. Those who have had near-death experiences or been pronounced clinically dead, but resuscitated, speak of the experience as one of deep acceptance, letting go into something which, in Ram Dass's words, is 'totally safe'. They often describe passing through a long tunnel with a source of radiant light at the end of it, feeling a loving and receiving presence waiting for them there. When in the seventies Grof and Halifax used L.S.D. to enable terminal cancer patients to go through a similar experience, almost all were transformed by it, and lived out their remaining days free from the fear of death, in an open-hearted and trusting way. No hospice-worker I have ever met has told me the work was depressing; on the contrary, the knowledge of an imminent death often seems to free their patients to be more totally alive, honest and present than ever before, to speak to their loved ones openly, from the heart, because there is no point in doing anything else.

My grandmother, in her nineties, died after several strokes. She could no longer speak, sit up or feed herself. She had become like the tiny baby I once was in her arms, and as I nuzzled her and stroked her hair I felt the simplest, most straightforward communication of love between us, unhindered by thoughts or words. We didn't need to *say* – we just *knew*.

REFERENCES

The writing of this chapter was informed by teachers, writers and clients too numerous to list. Instead I would like to name the following whose work has helped frame the thinking behind this chapter: C. G. Jung, Frances Wickes, Ann Shearer, A. C. Robin Skynner, Ian Gordon-Brown and Barbara Somers, Elizabeth Wilde McCormick, Dr Anthony Ryle, D. W. Winnicott, Ram Dass.

Bly, R. (1991). *Iron John*. Shaftesbury, Dorset and Rockport, Mass: Element.

Campbell, J. (1972). *The Hero with a Thousand Faces*. Princeton: Princeton University Press.

De Castellejo, C. (1973). *Knowing Woman*. New York: Harper & Row.

Doyle, R. (1996). *The Woman Who Walked into Doors*. London: Jonathan Cape.

Edinger, E. (1972). *Ego and Archtype*. New York: Penguin.

Greer, G. (1991). *The Change*. London: Hamish Hamilton.

Grof, S. and Halifax, J. (1978). *The Human Encounter with Death*. London: Souvenir Press.

Hillman, J. (1979). 'Senex and Puer'. In C. Giles (ed.) *Puer Papers*. Dallas Texas: Spring Publications Inc.

Lessing, D. (1996). *Love, Again*. London: Flamingo.

Lewis, C. S. (1961). *A Grief Observed*. London: Faber & Faber.

Mahdi, L., Foster, S. and Little, M. (1987). *Betwixt and Between: Patterns of Masculine and Feminine Initiation*. La Salle, Illinois: Open Court.

Murry-Parkes, C. (1972). *Bereavement*. London: Tavistock Publications.

Perera, S. B. (1972). *Descent of the Goddess*. Toronto: Inner City Books.

Schierse-Leonard, L. (1983). *The Wounded Woman*. Boston and London: Shambhala.

Schierse-Leonard, L. (1986). *On the Way to the Wedding*. Boston and London: Shambhala.

Singer, J. (1977). *Androgyny: Towards a New Theory of Sexuality*. London: Routledge and Kegan Paul.

von Franz, M.-L. (1970). *Puer Aeternus*. Santa Monica, Calif: Sigo Press.

von Franz, M.-L. (1984). *On Dreams and Death*. Boston and London: Shambhala.

Whitmont, E. C. (1983). *Return of the Goddess*. London: Routledge and Kegan Paul.

Wilhelm, R. (1951). *I Ching*. London: Routledge and Kegan Paul.

Wolger, R. J. and Wolger, J. B. (1987). *Goddess Within*. New York: Fawcett Columbine.

Woodman, M. (1990). *The Ravaged Bridegroom: Masculine in Women*. Toronto: Inner City.

Woodman, M. (1985). *The Pregnant Virgin*. Toronto: Inner City.

Woodman, M. (1982). *Addiction to Perfection*. Toronto: Inner City.

Woodman, M. (1980). *The Owl Was A Baker's Daughter: Obesity, Anorexia Nervosa and the Repressed Feminine*. Toronto: Inner City.

CHAPTER 7

Masculinities and Femininities, Women and Men

Ann Shearer

Editor's note: There is no concept, however much it may speak of expansion and otherness, that can not be unconsciously perverted so that it actually functions for the ego as a defensive structure. Now that ideas about the inner man and woman have become common currency within the collective culture, these too may be used in the service of bolstering our identity against uncertainty. In this way, though we may speak of the feminine soul and the masculine spirit as relationships that open to transpersonal experience, by limiting their definition, they may also be used to close down and control the Mercurial nature of the collective unconscious. Here, Ann Shearer, from the perspective of a Classical Jungian Analyst, leads us deeper into the labyrinthine world of gender identity, the archetypes of the anima and animus and their often contradictory imagery. Revisiting Jung she finds that he shared many of the questions that today are endemic. Her suggestion is that we look again at our certainties and question whether the comforting and familiar organization of qualities that we have assigned to women and men, to animus and anima and to the archetypal feminine and masculine are quite as certain as we would wish them to be.

N.W.

Of all the great collective waves of the past century or so of Western consciousness, the one which has swept over time-honoured understandings of what it means to be woman or man, masculine or feminine, is surely one of the most powerful. The intensity of rage and bewilderment, battering and bruising among and between both men and women that has come with it amounts to more than the painful sum of individual distress. The wave has swelled, it seems, from the depth of the collective unconscious, and we have been swept off our collective psychic balance by the force and speed with which it has broken in our generation.

It has been a long time swelling, as the historians' recent reclaiming of individual women's voices can tell us. But it is only just over a century, after all, since married women in Britain were legally permitted to own property, since higher education for women was first institutionalized, or – most amazingly – since it was conclusively demonstrated that the creation of new human life came from a fusion of egg and sperm. So we have been buffeted at every level of our old understandings about our nature and relationships, from the most basically biological and the socio-economic to the life of mind and spirit.

And beyond those too. The mythic structure within which we have lived for more or less the past 4000 years, the era of the sky-gods, can no longer contain us. We can draw on many stories of how that structure was made and its glories as well as its profound psychic costs in the dishonouring of 'the feminine principle', as Anne Baring and Jules Cashford have so invaluably done in their *Myth of the Goddess* (1991). But the story of how we are living with the structure's crumbling is only now being told through our individual and collective lives. How can we be attentive to it?

The question touches us all, whether we work as butchers or bakers, makers of candles or cabinets, psychotherapists or those who consult them. There is nothing so privileged about psychological understandings; psychology's approaches to the interplay between the individual and the collective can not but be informed by the material realities of the economists, the spiritual ones of the theologians, by the sociologists, insights into the way we live now and the historians' stories of the way we lived then. Most particularly, perhaps, in trying to understand more of this story between and within contemporary men and women, psychology can draw on contemporary efforts to understand the difference between sex – as biologically determined – and gender – as culturally and socially constructed (Connell, 1987).

But psychology has also its own lenses to train on the age-old wonderings about how far are we self-created, how far determined (of which the gender debates are among today's expressions). For me, the particular value of Jung's psychology is that in its attention to the *logos*, the laws, of *psyche*, it insists that we attend to both the subtle movements of the individual soul and the collective in which it is set. In the theory of archetypes, it gives us the means to do this. So we can ask, for instance, what it means that in a century when Western women have howled a mounting crescendo of rage at 'the patriarchy', depth psychology from Jung to Klein to Winnicott, Bowlby and beyond has rested on a myth of maternal influence far beyond that of the father. We can notice, at a time when our human natures seem increasingly to be genetically fixed, that the very notions of 'masculine' and 'feminine' are in flux as never before. For me, such questions are far from simply intellectual; they have to do with the very stuff of our psychic lives. So we could wonder, for instance and in terms of Jung's psychology, about collective compensations, and ask ourselves how the energies are striving to find a parallel balance in the unique lives and relationships of individuals.

In his own explorations of the movements of masculine and feminine energies within and between women and men, Jung knew that he was only at the start of something. 'We are concerned here', he says in his essay on 'Anima and Animus' 'with a new questioning, a new – and yet age-old – field of psychological experience.' And he warns against premature certainty about what is going on. 'We shall be able to establish relatively valid theories about it only when the corresponding psychological facts are known to a sufficient number of people. The first things to be discovered are always facts, not theories' (Jung 1938, para. 340). These days, we hardly heed his caution: his writings on the nature of man and woman, masculine and feminine, have become both so much part of the way we conceptualize these things and so much debated that we forget, perhaps, just how ground-breaking they were in their day.

Yet Jung was born into a social and scientific community which still took as axiomatic the inferiority of woman to man, in her physical and intellectual structure as much as her moral one. The inherited myths of the Judeo-Christian tradition and Aristotelian biology had interwoven over hundreds of years to ensure that this was so. And as Hillman (1978) has fascinatingly argued, those mythologies have had a profound effect on our 'modern' depth psychologies as well. To alert ourselves to this essential fact of our own psychological inheritance, we need only, perhaps, remember Freud's perception of the psychology of woman: his notion that it is based on the envy born of an essential lack is in some sense at least a faithful echo of Galen's teaching, first formulated some 1800 years earlier, that the female genitalia is an imperfect version of the male.

Against this background, Jung's theory of anima and animus can seem positively startling. After so many centuries of agreement that what was *inferior* in man had been removed in that first, divine surgical operation in the Garden of Eden, to leave him forever made of physically as well as morally superior stuff, here is a proposal that he not only contains a 'feminine' element, but that his very wholeness as a human being depends on his relating to her with the utmost respect! In the wake of an outbreak of grave concern among leading European and American physicians that the higher education of women would lead to a breed of denatured monsters and deterioration of the race (Showalter 1987), here is an assertion that not only does 'women's nature' inevitably contain a 'masculine' element but that, again, we ignore it at our psychic peril!

These days – and that is thanks largely to Jung's explorations – the idea that there is a 'feminine' element in everyman and a 'masculine' one in everywoman is hardly psychologically surprising. But what do we do with the perception – and what does it do with us? The questions multiply. What do we mean by 'masculine' and 'feminine'? Can we define a 'true nature' of everywoman and everyman to which psyche is leading each individul woman and man? What relationship does the first bear to the second? Again, such questions are not at all simply for intellectual debate. They are brought into countless consulting rooms, doctors' surgeries and lawyers' offices, from the intimacy of countless shared bedrooms and the loneliness of countless single ones, by women and men who are angered, hurt and bewildered by the lack of clear answers about their own identity and that of the Other.

Jung, of course, had his own response to the questions, and much debated it has been in recent years. The very fact of the criticism tells us that consciousness has moved on; personal reactions to both the theory and the critics can maybe help individuals situate themselves in the whole vexed business.

About the 'nature of woman', it seems, Jung remained sure. 'No one can get round the fact', he wrote in 1927, 'that by taking up a masculine profession, studying and working like a man, woman is doing something not wholly in accord with, if not directly injurious to, her feminine nature' (Jung 1927, para. 243). And 'Man's foremost interest should be his work', he said towards the end of his long life. 'But a woman – man is her work and her business' (McGuire and Hull 1980, p. 236).

These certainties can not but be intertwined with Jung's theory of animus, as I have examined in more detail elsewhere (Shearer 1998). He confessed himself scared of it (Jung 1930, p. 487). And it is sure that while Lady Soul, for all her dangers, remains bathed for him in life-giving numinosity, there seems little positive for him in animus at all. Back in 1922 he was teaching, according to one of his students, that 'a man must take up a feminine attitude, while a woman must fight her animus, a masculine attitude' (McGuire and Hull, p. 45). If she can overcome the perils of animus-possession, then it will become a 'creative and procreative being'. And then? Will she find new intellectual strength, a purpose in what used to be known as 'the man's world'? No, for Jung these creative seeds will fertilize the feminine side of man! (Jung 1938, para. 336).

The view is time-honoured, as John Milton knew centuries earlier when he was dividing the psychic labour between Adam and Eve: 'He for God only, she for God in him'. Given that Jung was a child of the European nineteenth century, born into the modest bourgeoisie of a small, mountain-enclosed nation which has only recently, a generation or so after his death, accorded all its adult women the right to vote, such views are perhaps not so surprising. But now for the Rorschach Test: how do we react to them? For some, and particularly women, they are a patriarchal howler, enough to discredit Jung's whole discussion. For others, and not necessarily men, they are not to be too swiftly dismissed, now that a generation of (privileged, middle-class, Western) women has been able not just to 'take up' but often to excel in 'masculine professions', and the popular prints as well as consulting rooms are full of tales of the personal costs (Singer 1989). For yet others, it is still worth working to reconcile Jung's theories with contemporary feminist understandings (Wehr 1988).

The distance we have travelled between the first and the second is nowhere more apparent, perhaps, than in Jung's persistent identification of 'the feminine' with women and 'the masculine' with men. In his day, I suspect, any other view would have seemed seriously eccentric; in ours, it can seem little short of abusive. Yet is there still something to be rescued?

Is there still value, for a start, in Jung's formulation of the great governing principles, masculine and feminine, as Logos and Eros? Important, perhaps, to underline his vision of their essential interrelatedness: 'It is the function of Eros to unite what Logo has sundered' (Jung 1927, para. 275). So Logos, the masculine principle of Word and spirit, of rationality, objectivity, judgement and discrimination, is in constant interplay with Eros 'the greater binder and looser', the principle of relatedness. Neither one is superior or inferior, each needs the other for its completion in action, separating what has been united, uniting what has been separated, over and over in the great rhythm of life. This is the action of psyche itself, imaged in the progressive refinements of the alchemical work that was so important to Jung as metaphor for psychic process. As the alchemists knew, the volatile must be fixed and the fixed made volatile, over and over in a continual *circulatio*.

Alchemical transformations are made from the interplay of energies we take as masculine and feminine – imaged as Sol and Luna, Apollo and Diana, King and Queen – as the alchemist and his 'mystical sister' work and pray among the sealed vessels in their enclosed laboratory (Klossow de Rola 1973). That the images are often bizarre and frightening, always extraordinary, tells us that this is a story not simply about men and women dressed up in funny clothes, but rather about our deeper and other selves. It is when Jung brings these psychological energies of masculine and feminine that he calls Logos and Eros out into the world, to identify them with actual men and women that something seems lost. From the mysterious containment of the laboratory we find ourselves in a convolution of conceptual pathways which lead us to a not unfamiliar place. 'In men, Eros, the function of relationship, is usually less developed than Logos. In women, on the other hand, Eros is an expression of their true nature [Ah!] while their Logos is often only a regrettable accident' (Jung 1950, para. 29). In simple words, and stripped of the qualifications ('usually', 'often'), aren't we back to 'men think, women feel'?

But before some of us throw the book across the room, let us just unhook the men from the thinking, the women from the feeling, and stay with the notion of two great currents, one of which discriminates and separates and one of which associates and brings together. We could even call them, for shorthand and knowing that ego can never do more than touch the archetypal depths, Logos and Eros. Whether we are woman or man, they flow through us all uniquely, according to our constitution, typology and life experience. As the feminist writer Marilyn French puts it, in her own version of the same story: 'The feminine principle is the pole of life, the masculine, of civilisation. And life is the highest value for "feminine" people, whereas control is the highest value for "masculine" people' (French 1985, p. 94).

Once the notions of masculine and feminine are released from identification with men and women, we can let some imaginal air into the age-old debates. Take, for instance, the issue we came in on: the supposedly superior thinking capacity of men. Marilyn French again: ' "Feminine" thinking is reflective, associative and circular – found in some masculine poets. "Masculine" thought is rational, logical, linear' (ibid.) This is not at all far from Jung's characterization of masculine consciousness as solar and feminine consciousness as lunar – the second not inferior to but simply different from the first. The difficulty begins when he identifies the first with man and the second with woman:

> Personal relations are as a rule more important and interesting to her than objective facts and their interconnections. The wide fields of commerce, politics, technology and science, the whole realm of the applied masculine mind, she relegates to the penumbra of consciousness; while, on the other hand, she develops a minute consciousness of personal relationships, the infinite nuances of which usually escape the man entirely. (Jung 1938, para. 330)

Another Rorschach test? But just to underline the point, it is Jung's equation of sex and gender – as in his description of the 'lunatic logic' of woman which 'can drive the rational [i.e. male] mind to the white heat of frenzy' – which these days can drive female astrophysicists and male psychotherapists to frenzies of their own (Jung 1954, para. 228). The idea that some people are more gifted in human relationships and others in abstract thought is hardly exceptional.

These personal equations have their archetypal resonances, as Jules Cashford, for instance, emphasizes in her own critique of Jung's views, in which she reaches for the essence beyond gender of the deities themselves. Her beautiful description of Aphrodite, 'the golden one', 'lover of laughter', evokes, as does the goddess herself, 'a world of relationship between all the forms of creation'. Aphrodite's imaging as a woman has nothing to do with either women relating better or men relating badly, for what she symbolizes is an invitation to 'a celebration of the beauty of daily life' which is open to all. 'She would have us entranced with the minute particulars of lived reality for their own sake, beautiful in themselves . . . ephemeral even, but nonetheless vital to bind us to each other and to life.' For me, this Aphrodite images the *function* or *value* that Jung characterizes as Eros, and Cashford's brilliantly youthful Apollo, 'god of the silver bow, who kills from a distance', that of Logos. And Apollo as 'image of the still point of orientation that gives birth to a point of view . . . the beauty of distinct form . . . a consciousness that is not implicated in what it sees and knows' is no less available to us all than is Aphrodite (Cashford 1998).

Now that the gods are evoked, other images, other altars, present themselves. Apollo's is the brilliance of pure thought, unrelated to consequence. But there are other modes of thinking on Olympus too. *Nous kai dianoia*, Mind and Thought, was one of the later epithets of Athene. But she is also Workwoman, Many-Skilled, Mistress of Crafts; her patronage covers the whole field of applied technology. She is the one who understands the essential relationship between mind, eye, hand and material to be worked. It is her *sophia*, an essentially practical wisdom, and her understanding of the fitness of things, which could yet save our planet from ecological ruin (Shearer 1998).

Like Apollo's, this way of being in the world is surely open to all, whether women or men. Isn't consciousness beyond gender? And yet, and yet, Athene's consciousness is so very different from that of Apollo . . . I find myself recalling Freud's conviction that women had little sense of justice, because of the huge role that envy inevitably played in their penisless lives. This want of moral sense, of the capacity to discriminate right from wrong, he could also have characterized – if he had spoken the same psychological language as Jung, or even been speaking to Jung at all – as a want of Logos. Yet what Carol Gilligan found in her important studies of women's moral decision-making, was that their approach had far less to do with abstract notions of 'right' and 'wrong' than with weighing conflicting responsibilities to actual relation-ships (Gilligan 1982). For at least these women, then, morality is an 'applied' matter rather than a 'pure' concept; they are under Athene's protection rather than Apollo's. Is this acculturated? Intrinsic to their nature? Can we begin to discriminate a distinctive 'feminine consciousness'?

So Logos works its distinctions for Eros to unite, over and over again. And so Eros craves expression in our Western collectivities, as we become more keenly aware of the limits of rationality, of the one-sidedness of post-Enlightenment thought, of the alienations of over-discrimination. Yet so repressed have its values been, it seems, that many of our reconnections can come only through its shadow. We long for a sense of relatedness to each other and our planet – and we find it through wars and exploita-tions. We seek 'community' – and find its shadow simulacrum through the Internet. We seek connection to our earth in fantasies of the 'one life' – and we shop its resources to exhaustion. In the desperation of our search we mistake sex for *eros* and sexualize all manner of encounters – only to fall into the shadow of relatedness when a gesture of tenderness, concern or even courtesy from adult to child, man to woman, can appear the prelude not to relationship but to abuse.

Yet the longing remains – and not so long ago, we saw it burst out in the intensity of reaction to the death of Diana, Princess of Wales. The distaste and even fear with which the rational mind dismissed the events of that unique week as 'mass hysteria' is further demonstration of the alienation of Logos and Eros in our times. For whatever else was projected onto those slim shoulders, it seems to me, Eros was part of it. For those days at least the image of Diana carried the yearning for relatedness and its expression, in those tears for the never-known but so vividly-imagined. The very sentimentality of those altars of poems, hearts and flowers attests to our clumsiness in articulating Eros; these days, its language comes from the unconscious. And in those repeated images of the glamorous, privileged and lively Princess literally touching (no Royal gloves!) people who were diseased, or marginalized, or dying, or simply ordinary, we could be touched by the possibility of connection among opposites, of relatedness in an alienated world. (Haynes and Shearer 1998 discusses these and many other psychological aspects of the events.)

If conscious reconnection of Logos and Eros is what we collectively long for, therapeutic reflections of this longing are not far to seek. We are by now well used to hearing that men 'should be' relating to their feminine/serving their anima, while women 'should be' honouring their masculine/setting their positive animus to work. The media plays its own part in such prescriptions, offering us collective templates against which to measure our own New Woman, New Man, Lad and Ladette.

Yet alchemy's images can remind us that the unions of insufficiently differentiated masculine and feminine may produce hermaphrodites rather than the Divine Andro-gyne who is the goal of the work. Hermaphroditus himself prayed that his own curse of barrenness would be visited on anyone who bathed in the lake where he had been forced into hated symbiosis with the besotted nymph Salmacis, and the gods granted his prayer. In this great rhythm of coming together and separation that is the work of Eros and Logos, we know that it can be the very longing for relationship that may bring us to that barren lake, as we seek to dissolve differences and subsume the Other to ourselves, ourselves to the Other.

And who is the Other, who ourself? When we urge, for instance, that men 'should relate to their inner feminine', are we thinking of such qualities as frugality, vehe-mence, hardness, saltiness, dryness? Or such images as fire, lightning, coats of mail and helmets, lances and weapons? Or such actions as smashing and breaking apart? I suspect not. When we urge women to 'honour the masculine within', are we relating to such images as pod-bearing plants, water, ditches, defective chariots, the moon, doors and openings? Is it keeping still, melancholy, the earache we have in mind? Again, I would be surprised. Yet these are all images and attributes drawn from commentaries of the same *I Ching* as the one from which so much of our contemporary 'knowledge' of the feminine (earth, receptive) and masculine (heaven, creative) is drawn (Wilhelm 1975, pp. 274–9).

Such surprises remind us of our relationship to the archetypal realm. We know we cannot comprehend the archetypes as such; our small ego-consciousness cannot encompass the whole psychic structure within which it is embedded. We also know that we risk madness if we do not keep ego's respectful distance from the archetypal energies, just as the ancients knew that if they approached divinities too closely they would be destroyed. Jung recognizes the frustrations, but he knows the reality too. 'The discriminating intellect' he writes,

> naturally keeps on trying to establish (the archetypes') singleness of meaning, and thus misses the essential point: for what we can above all establish as the one thing consistent with their

nature is their manifold meaning, their almost limitless wealth of reference, which makes any unilateral formulation impossible. (Jung 1954, para. 80)

So one task of psychotherapists – those who *attend*, who *wait upon* the soul – is to try to keep open the manifold meaning of the archetypes, to allow their energies to connect to consciousness in as much amplitude as is ego-possible. So in our imaging of the 'feminine', for instance, we may honour the ancient goddesses, remembering that Inanna and Ishtar of Sumeria, Egyptian Neith, Greek Athene and the Celtic goddesses Morrigan and Brigit were all lovers of war as much as of the peaceful arts – a psychologically essential paradox whose implications I have explored elsewhere (Shearer 1998). So in our evocations of 'the masculine', we may honour Dionysus, that deity of nature's own erotic relatedness to which the antagonism of Logos, as Euripedes so horrifically reminds us, can only bring tragedy (Euripedes 1986). We can remember Hermes, as close to us in the hurly-burly of life's market-place as his brother Apollo is distant, his ways as devious as Apollo's arrows are straight. In green and fertile, lush and plashy places, we can remember his children Pan and Priapus (Lopez-Pedraza 1977), and in this little island's fast-disappearing natural crannies we may still catch a glimpse of our own guardian of vegetation and holy places, the Green Man.

In such amplifications, imaginings and connections, through archetypal images as they appear to us in dream and reverie or the fascination which draws us to a particular place or work of art, we can collectively perhaps begin to release both women and men from the old prescriptive equations that tell them what their nature 'ought' to be and stop chastising the 'masculine' businesswoman and 'effeminate' man. And then, will we have fewer of the relational disasters which begin something like this?

> He: (before marriage): 'She is the most womanly woman I can imagine. Most men become more of what they are around her: a phoney becomes more phoney, a confused man becomes more confused, a retiring man more retiring. She's kind of a lodestone that draws out of the male animal his essential qualities.'
>
> She: (commenting on some notes he's written on their honeymoon): 'It was something about how disappointed he was in me, how he thought I was some kind of angel, but now he guessed he was wrong, that his first wife had let him down, but I had done something worse.' (Steinem 1987).

Oh Lady Anima, spinner of illusion! This time, the couple entangled in her web were Arthur Miller and one of the most potent and tragic anima figures of our century, Marilyn Monroe. But their tale of bitter disillusionment is surely told over and over, as couples of all sorts and conditions find themselves in the dark when the glow fades on the projection that has held them. Theory would suggest that if men and women were more able to explore and relate to their own 'feminine' and 'masculine' sides (allowing for the moment that such exist), the projections of both would seem less painfully potent, because containing fewer of their own unlived, yet yearned-for aspects. Can we imagine a future when that might be true?

What we already know is just how hard it is, here and now and despite the conceptual puzzlings, to free ourselves from traditional understandings of gender and sex. And we know too quite how much bitter and violent raging, both individual and collective, can accompany our efforts to get beyond them. We have historical, socio-economic and psychological explanations in plenty. How can we work with them now?

For me, the starting point is still the time-honoured identification of woman with nature and so the principle of life, and man with civilization and so nature's dominance. For centuries, it was at the root of the perception of woman as inferior, in physical substance as much as intellect and morality; we have seen some of its echoes already in this chapter. In our own times, and in one of those great psychic upheavals that feels like a search for a new collective balance, the tables have turned: women have used the perception against men, in the insistence that it is men who bear responsibility for all that is violent and destructive – from the fighting of wars and the destructions of technology to the despoilation of the planet and the abuse of individual women.

The myth behind such perceptions, it seems to me, is that of 'the matriarchy' – that Golden Age benignly ruled by the Great Goddess when all was harmony in nature and we humans with it. Whatever the historical facts, the psychological force of the myth can not be doubted. It becomes the more precious, perhaps, when such a dominant account of our individual beginnings is the very much less peaceful one imagined by Melanie Klein. How can the myth be protected against the reality of our world's violence? We know the psychological mechanism and we can feel its effects, in the huge collective projection of aggression onto not just 'the masculine' but men.

More than a century ago those policemen knew what it meant to bear it when the indomitable Mabel, the Major General's daughter, sent them off to fight the Pirates of Penzance:

> Go ye heroes, go to glory,
> Though ye die in combat gory,
> Ye shall live in song and story.
> Go to immortality!
> Go to death and go to slaughter;
> Die, and every Cornish daughter
> With her tears your grave shall water.
> Go, ye heroes, go and die!

And the policemen can only reply:

> Though to us it's evident,
> These attentions are well-meant,
> Such expressions don't appear,
> Calculated men to cheer,
> Who are going to meet their fate
> In a highly nervous state.
> Still to us it's evident,
> These attentions are well-meant.
> (Gilbert 1994, pp. 129–30)

Fewer than forty years on, there was no joke left when women were singing 'We don't want to lose you, but we think you should go' to a generation of young men being sent to bloody and senseless slaughter. Not all women, of course. Many showed extraordinary bravery in their resistance to the war, in a collective movement overtly based on the identification of woman–nature–life that has been echoed in women's peace movements ever since. Yet others again were sending white feathers to those they suspected of cowardice. And any soldier who was either overwhelmed by or challenged the madness would of course be shot as a traitor. In those days, after all, men were men and women were women and everyone knew what that should mean.

These days, we are a lot less sure. At the same time, we know that there is no projection without a hook to catch it, and we are very much better informed about the realities of men's violence to women, both individual and collective, historical and contemporary. But if the hook is one part of the story, the projection is the other. Theory tells us that psychic energy unlived builds up in the shadow and turns negative, and that shadow disowned is projected. Does that help us to see how it is that while many contemporary women have identified themselves as 'victims of the patriarchy', the experience of many contemporary men is that it is Eris, 'insatiably raging' who has been released? She is no less terrifying in her compulsions than her brother Ares, god of war. 'Once she begins, she cannot stop', as Homer tells us. 'At first she seems a little thing, but before long, though her feet are still on the ground, she has struck high heaven with her head . . . It was the groans of dying men she wished to hear' (Homer 1975, pp. 88–9).

Theory also tells us that the projection of shadow is the first step towards it becoming conscious. Are we beginning to see a time when women can consciously reclaim their aggression and so use it more positively, thus freeing both themselves and the men who have been burdened with it? To many (privileged, middle-class, Western) women the question may already seem redundant: they're doing it, aren't they? But in terms of the underlying collective, we may yet have a way to go before 'the feminine' is understood to include also its own aggression and the great goddesses who preside over war as well as the healing arts are once more fully honoured. (And isn't there still something, for many people, well, rather *unnatural* about those women who fight their way to the top in what can still, amazingly, be termed as a 'man's world'?)

Old perceptions die hard. And just in case we reach any prematurely conclusive new ones, here come the gender-benders, the transvestites and the transsexuals, to tease and challenge our assumptions. That is their symbolic job, it seems, their images appearing at transitional times to turn the old order upside down and clear the way for the new. They appeared in their numbers to fascinate the last *fin de siecle* through life, art and literature (Showalter 1991). And now, at the end of our own century, their images are the more available to us in the streets, in performance, and in projection on screens both large and small – images of our other selves and of new unions.

'Theory-building', as Jung reminds us, 'is the outcome of discussion among many' (Jung 1938, para. 340), and not a few people have been working to restore and adapt his psychological structures for our times. James Hillman, for instance, has gone straight to the foundations to dig out Jung's perception of anima as the feminine soul of man and animus as the masculine spirit of woman. Rather, he insists, both animus and anima are at work in each of us, whether women or men.

For Hillman, 'The *per definitionem* absence of anima in women is a deprivation of a cosmic principle with no less consequence in the practice of analytical psychology than has been the theory of penis deprivation in the practice of psychoanalysis'. The logical outcome of Jung's formulation, that women somehow *are* soul, because of their feminine gender, is for him untenable: 'psyche, the sense of soul, is not given to woman just because she is born female. She is no more blessed with a congenitally saved soul than man who must pass his life in worry over its fate. For her to neglect soul for the sake of spirit is no less psychologically reprehensible than it is in man who is ever being told by analytical psychology that he must sacrifice intellect, persona and extroversion for the sake of soul, inwardness – i.e. anima.' And again: 'Women are as salty in their weepings and resentments, as bitchy in their gossip, as abysmal in their dour broodings, as men . . . Why do we call the same behaviour in one sex "anima" and in the other "naturally feminine" or shadow?' (Hillman 1986, pp. 61, 63, 59). (And, we could add, men may be every bit as opinionated as women. Why is the same behaviour in one sex 'animus-possession' and in the other natural masculinity or shadow?)

So for Hillman – and for others too (Kast 1986) – the work of soul and of spirit, the relating with anima and animus, is the work of us all. (And were not Marilyn Monroe and Princess Diana every bit as much 'anima figures' for women as they were for men?) Others again – and the lead, significantly, has come from the experience of gay people for whom the old structures simply do not work – have been refurbishing the fabric of masculine and feminine. Robert Hopcke, for instance, writes of the insuperable problem for men, and particularly gay men, when 'even the anima's most positive qualities, summed up perhaps most succinctly in her role as Eros carrier for men . . . are not seen as available to men *as men*, but rather as available to men only through women, only through the integration of anima femininity, not as inherent in their masculinity' (Hopcke 1990, p. 90). He reclaims Eros as the phallic god, who far from being identified with 'the feminine principle', has been there in his generativity since the beginning of time. For Hopcke, then, it is an aspect of their own essential masculinity with which men need to connect. And the soul-guide in this work, the anima, may well appear, as it did for one gay man, as an insistently fascinating, beguiling, beckoning, 'Young Dark Man'.

Others have also been reworking the fabric of 'masculine' and 'feminine' to extend their boundaries. For John Beebe, for instance, masculinity is both solar and lunar, as is femininity, and the task for men is not so much to rush Jung's goal of union with the anima as first to bring together their own solar and lunar aspects – something which, he says, women have long been willing to do within themselves (Beebe 1993). That last perception finds a fundamental embodiment in Genia Pauli Haddon's image of the womb's function as both receptive and nurturing and 'exerting, pushing forth'. 'If we were to define femininity solely in accordance with the womb's birthing power, we would speak of it as the great opener of what has been sealed, the initiator of all going forth, the out-thrusting *yang* power at the heart of being.' It is time, she says, for women to reclaim their pushiness, to recognize that sometimes being assertive is being feminine (Pauli Haddon 1987, 1991). Here, the psychic pole of the archetype, imaged in those great goddesses of warfare and the peaceful arts, finds its completion in the biological.

Sol and Luna, Eros and Logos, Aphrodite and Apollo, Athene and Dionysus, the transvestite at the threshold and Marilyn Munroe, the Young Dark Man and the golden Princess ... Who are they all, and the myriad others who also crowd in dream and fantasy into our inner landscape, but images of that Other which is also ourselves? So should we be surprised at their multiplicity, or that they should appear to us, whether we are men or women, now as ragged girl, now as diva, now as bookish boy, now as gigolo? They are images of all that we are not yet, and their function is to lead us towards it. As Warren Colman reminds us in his delicate and thoughtful revisiting of Jung's theory of the contrasexual archetypes, it is this *function* of these images of what he calls 'the unknown soul' that matters, and to remember that takes us beyond the debates on the image and its gendering (Colman 1998). That is what Jung himself was after. As he said, 'it is because we are not using them purposefully as functions that they remain personified complexes'; once their imaged message had been integrated, it would be simply as *function* that they would be felt (Jung 1938, para. 339).

For most of us, that time is not yet; what we mostly know is the yearning for our own inner unions and completions that give to those fleeting images their numinosity. For many people, the Other will still most often be imaged above all as of the opposite sex. As Jung explains it (for men): 'What is not-I, not masculine, is most probably feminine, and because the not-I is felt as not belonging to me and therefore as outside me, the anima–image is usually projected upon women' (Jung 1954, para. 58).

But many women and men, whatever their conscious sexual orientation, know that the 'unknown soul', and our union with it, will image itself also in a variety of guises.

–   A man dreams he is being pursued by an androgynous creature, covered with hair. He's terrified!
–   A woman dreams she is being raped by another she admires not at all. It's horrible.
–   A woman dreams of The Lady with the Doves, a figure of powerful numinosity, who most sweetly welcomes her.
–   A man dreams of an invitation to join the Navy and set sail with all these fellow-men for the other side of the world.
–   A man dreams he is making love with a woman with male genitalia. How pleasurable!
–   A woman dreams she has a huge phallus, erect and thrusting to reach the sky itself. The power of it!
–   A man dreams that he, as himself, is making love to a woman – and realizes that he has female genitalia!
–   A woman dreams: 'I was myself and also a man with a penis, making love to a woman who was also myself!'

'Not for a moment', says Jung, 'dare we succumb to the illusion that an archetype can be finally explained and disposed of. Even the best attempts at explanation are only more or less successful translations into another metaphorical language . . . The most we can do is to *dream the myth onwards* and give it a modern dress' (Jung 1951, para. 271, his italics). The style and shape of the dress is collective, perhaps. But in its colour and texture, and the intricacies of the weaving, we all have our part to play.

REFERENCES

Baring, A. and Cashford, J. (1991). *Myth of the Goddess: evolution of an image*. London: Viking Arkana.

Beebe, J. (1993). *Integrity in Depth*. New York: Fromm International Publishing Corporation.

Cashford, J. (1998). 'Reflecting Mirrors: ideas of personal and archetypal gender', *Harvest: Journal for Jungian Studies*, **44**(2).

Colman, W. (1998). 'Contrasexuality and the Unknown Soul'. In I. Alister and C. Hauke (eds), *Contemporary Jungian Analysis*. London: Routledge.

Connell, R. (1987). *Gender and Power: society, the person and sexual politics*. Cambridge: Polity Press.

Euripedes (1986). 'The Bacchae'. In *The Bacchae and Other Plays*, trs. Philip Vellacott. Harmondsworth: Penguin.

French, M. (1985). *Beyond Power: on women, men and morals*. London: Jonathan Cape.

Gilbert, W. S. (1994). *The Savoy Operas*. Ware, Hertfordshire: Wordsworth Editions.

Gilligan, C. (1982). *In a Different Voice: psychological theory and women's development*. Cambridge, Mass.: Harvard University Press.

Haynes, J. and Shearer, A. (1998). *When a Princess Dies: reflections from Jungian analysts*. London: Harvest.

Hillman, J. (1978). *The Myth of Analysis*. New York: Harper and Row.

Hillman, J. (1986). *Anima: an anatomy of a personified notion*. Dallas, Texas: Spring Publications.

Homer (1975). *The Iliad*, trs. E. V. Rieu. Harmondsworth: Penguin.

Hopcke, R. (1990). *Men's Dreams, Men's Healing*. Boston: Shambhala.

Jung, C. G. (1927). *Women in Europe*, vol. 10 of *Collected Works*. London: Routledge and Kegan Paul (1970).

Jung, C. G. (1930). *Dream Analysis: notes of a seminar given in 1928–30*. London: Routledge and Kegan Paul (1984).

Jung, C. G. (1938). *Anima and Animus*, vol. 7 of *Collected Works*. London: Routledge and Kegan Paul (1966).

Jung, C. G. (1950). *The Syzygy: anima and animus*, vol. 9, ii, of *Collected Works*. London: Routledge and Kegan Paul (1959).

Jung, C. G. (1951). *The Psychology of the Child Archetype*, vol. 9, I, of *Collected Works*. London: Routledge and Kegan Paul (1968).

Jung, C. G. (1954). *Archetypes of the Collective Unconscious*, vol. 9, I, of *Collective Works*. London: Routledge and Kegan Paul (1968).

Kast, V. (1986). *The Nature of Loving: patterns of human relationship*, trs. B. Matthews. Wilmette, Ill.: Chiron Publications.

Klossow de Rola, S. (1973). *Alchemy: the secret art*. London: Thames and Hudson.

Lopez-Pedraza, R. (1977). *Hermes and His Children*. Zurich: Spring Publications.

McGuire, W. and Hull, R. F. C. (eds) (1980). *C.G. Jung Speaking: interviews and encounters*. London: Picador.

Pauli Haddon, G. (1987). 'Delivering Yang Femininity'. In *Spring*. Dallas, Texas: Spring Publications.

Pauli Haddon, G. (1991). 'The Personal and Cultural Emergence of Yang Femininity'. In C. Zweig (ed.), *To be A Woman: the birth of conscious femininity*. London: Mandala.

Shearer, A. (1998). *Athene: Image and Energy*. London: Penguin Arkana.

Showalter, E. (1987). *The Female Malady: women, madness and English culture, 1830–1980*. London: Virago.

Showalter, E. (1991). *Sexual Anarchy: gender and culture at the fin de siecle*. London: Bloomsbury.

Singer, J. (1989). 'The Sadness of the Successful Woman'. In *The Goddess Reawakening: the feminine principle today*, comp. S. Nicholson. Wheaton, Ill.: Quest Books.

Steinem, G. (1987). *Marilyn*. London: Gollancz.

Wehr, D. (1988). *Jung and Feminism: liberating archetypes*. London: Routledge.

Wilhelm, R. (trs.) (1975). *I Ching or Book of Changes*, rendered into English by C. Baynes. London: Routledge and Kegan Paul.

CHAPTER 8

Dreaming in Depth

Barbara Somers with Elizabeth Wilde McCormick

Editor's note: Readers of this chapter will enjoy the experience of being in conversation with Barbara Somers. As a founder of the Centre for Transpersonal Psychology, London, she brings alive both her rich and varied experience of working with dreams over the last 45 years and her deep love of the work. The chapter affirms the prime place of dreams in the work of therapy and their powerful systems of information. It looks at how therapists may begin to work with dreams in a session, particularly the first dream of a therapy, series of dreams and 'big' dreams. Through association and amplification, through understanding the order of the dream, therapists learn the drama of the inner life and have a link with the inside story of unconscious life. The dreams' gossamer threads, treated as delicte life in preparation, and linking image, feeling, symbol and archetypal force, all serve to awaken a wonder in the therapist as the unfolding landscape of the patient is revealed.

N.W.

THE INNER WORLD, THE OUTER WORLD, AND THE INTERFACE

EM: So why do we dream?

BS: My guess is that that's how we're geared; we are created as creatures who dream. From ordinary scientific testing (for example of Rapid Eye Movement sleep) we know that the majority of human beings do seem to dream. Babies dream; animals dream; possibly even the foetus is dreaming. It seems to be our nature to be dreamers. But – is it we who are dreaming?

EM: Like the butterfly?

BS: Yes, just like the butterfly. Chuang Tsu [1974, p. 48] said: 'Last night I dreamt I was a butterfly; am I a man who dreamt I was a butterfly, or a butterfly dreaming that I'm a man?' I have pondered this ever since I was a child, becoming altogether fascinated by dreaming and imagination, by the extension of the senses into the arts, story-telling, myth, fairy tale – image-creating. Are we, indeed, beings in a multi-dimensional universe – and does that universe dream us? If it's the Self that is the Dreamer, then are we being dreamed?

So why do dreams come? Maybe, living out of mere segments of ourselves, we all have the potential to be in the round. Dreams come to fill in some of the other segments, perhaps showing us how we expect ourselves to be in the outside world: 'Could it be that there is more to you than you've ever begun to express? Are you trapped in the old patterns, the old ways, simply because you were told you were?'

Dreams prepare us to reach out towards the fullness of our natures, develop a greater awareness, live more fully, more purposefully, more consciously. And what is the underlying, or overlying, reason for consciousness? The whole of life is a great stream of consciousness, coming from the One, returning to the One – the Creator.

I live by the sea – I have this sea-house; I can sit in my office at the computer, or be completely encompassed by the walls of the kitchen, doing what I have to do and loving every minute of it. But occasionally I glance up. Then – I notice the view outside. I step out through the doors to the sea-wall, to a completely different universe: sky, ever-changing cloud-patterns, stars at night and play of moon on water. It was there all the time; I just didn't see it. I can't believe I bring that into being, or that it's been created just for me to find it outside. It's an initial waking up.

EM: And the night-dreams are there all the time?

BS: I think so. I believe that we are dreaming all the time. At night, when the body and the senses are still, we can begin to move towards levels of consciousness blocked off from our everyday senses. We reach out to dimensions where past, present and future all merge into the timeless; where the usual parameters of up and down, in and out, North, South, East and West, merge into a spacelessness that is the quality of the dream.

EM: That's how dreams get through? They bring a charge with them, breaking through into consciousness so that we can't not notice them?

BS: And if they really have something to say (and dreams often do), they tell our external, narrow, confined life about this wider universe, this wider dimension. Our lives are probably about our growing towards the wider context.

EM: By 'wider context' you mean – bringing in our own unconscious?

BS: Well, it may be a universal consciousness. We call the Inner side 'unconsciousness' because we're basically unconscious of it in our everyday mode. But who is to say it's unconscious? It could be that it's an ever-widening context of consciousness, and when we are quiescent it can come to us. If relatively awake, we can move towards it and make contact with it through meditation, contemplation and the use of our imagination – it's a two-way dance.

Take the map of the Inner, the Outer and the Interface [Figure 2]. The idea is to help the dreamer make a bridge across between Inner and Outer. The dream is offering them information; their outer self is being invited to turn towards the Interface, re-entering the inner world, seeing the cross-connections.

EM: You can become so familiar with dreams that you can ask for a dream?

BS: Yes; you become aware of the language, the possibility of it. It's like learning to become a dressmaker or a carpenter: once you concentrate your attention along a particular line, you begin to notice a great deal more than you otherwise would.

The dream often follows the shape of a play, of theatre. The typical dream-shape is four-fold and the dream is in four acts. Act One sets the scene, introduces the characters, place, time and mood, and the play begins. Act Two states the plot, amplifying the problem or question to be explored. In Act Three, the plot is woven; this is the backbone, the pith of the dream, the action. Then Act Four is the outcome, the dénouement, where the dreamer may be shocked awake. It brings a conclusion, a suggested resolution. Something has broken through into consciousness, so the dream can stop.

And the beauty of it! The glory – the wonder – tautness – spareness – economy of language – of the dream. It must be seen to be believed! This is the greatest dramatist of all at work; and the more you work with it, the more you learn to trust that emergence, and to recognize the sheer artistry of it all.

EM: Recording dreams helps you make that bridge. Would you encourage your clients to dream, and keep a dream book?

BS: Yes, but only if it's their language. It can't be forced; some people are very frightened by the idea that there may be something over and beyond the parameters of their known world. But others are trying to reach further, to a deeper understanding of what life is about. I encourage those people to relax, open up, hear the language of the inner world coming to them. It's not unfamiliar to most clients; they knew it as

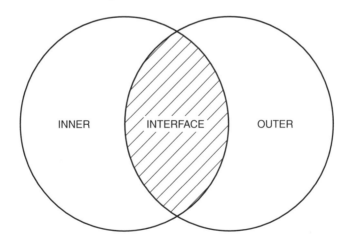

Figure 2 The Inner, the Outer and the Interface

children, dreaming their dreams or playing their play – being the engine driver, then becoming the engine, going on fantastic journeys through the reaches of imagination. It was difficult then to know which was the reality, the inner or the outer.

But educationally we were got at, taught what was outer and what was inner, and the separation began to be made.

THERAPY

EM: Let's move into therapy. Why do we work with dreams? What, and how, does it add to the therapy?

BS: Many who come towards therapy are living out of a fraction of the totality of their nature. Caught and trapped into the narrow confines of the outer world, they come to feel that's the only reality. Involved in other people's expectations and attitudes – their own expectations and attitudes – they begin to live very partial, lopsided lives, losing half their identity. More and more cut off from it as the years go by, they wake up one day and realize they are in a prison, a very cramped, small, airless space. Much of what is true to the fullness of their being is pushed down out of the way and suppressed. They're told: 'It's all imagination. It's not something you ought to feel. You feel like *this*!'

Nevertheless, there's a sense of something greater. Very many people expect a dimension of reality beyond what the world itself presents. Over and over again I hear, 'There should be something further!'

EM: And the dream is a way in?

BS: Yes, because it comes to them, unexpectedly. They don't create it, it comes to them. Look at 'Assagioli's Egg' [Figure 3]. We can – roughly – map on to it the question 'Where do dreams come from?'

First, at (a), the dot in the centre, is the everyday 'I', the self with a small 's'. Then round the centre at (b) is the Field of Everyday Awareness, containing the semi-conscious material to which, like the data bank of a computer, one has fairly ready access. 'What is that person's name?' – and five minutes later it pops into your mind.

At (c) is the Middle Unconscious. Probably clearing dreams are from this region, the 'hypnagogic' dreams that come as we go into sleep, processing the material of the day. They're a mix, a merging of what's been happening in the day-time with the movement towards deeper night-time sleep. Say you've been to the Chinese Take-Away; that's where the dream starts, but then it takes off, far from the Chinese Take-Away, into something behind the scenes.

The bottom part of the Egg, at (d), is the Lower Unconscious. As meditation helps clear, relax, let go of day-time attitudes, so the night-time dreaming state allows things repressed, suppressed, uncomfortable to admit and acknowledge in consciousness, to come out and present themselves. This is where they've been deposited, put down in a kind of 'dustbin of the unconscious', as it has often been called. As the 'on-

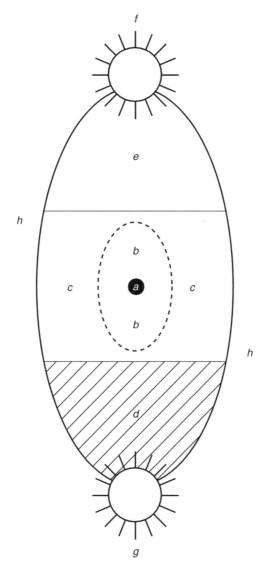

A permeable egg

a **The Ego**.
b **The Field of Immediate Everyday Awareness**.
c **The Middle Unconscious**, surface memory, accessible with a time-lag.
d **The Lower Unconscious**. Often thought to be the dustbin of the psyche, full of things too painful, too irrelevant, expendable. But it can also be the compost for the seeds of future potential and creativity.
e **The Higher Unconscious, or Supra-conscious**. Deeper, inner area. Intuition. Future potential, just beyond reach, the evolution of consciousness.
f **The Higher Self**, overlying, underlying and through all, not just on the top.
g **The Self in the Depths**. Transpersonal Psychology adds the Self also in the deep; the Self which chooses the life, knows, intervenes.
h **The Collective Unconscious**. The domain of the Archetypes.

Figure 3 Assagioli's Egg: the psychosynthesis map

guardedness' of everyday consciousness is rested back into sleep and day-time consciousness is less alert, what has been held down and disregarded has a chance.

This material can be very painful – it was put there for safeguarding just because it was so painful. It often comes up as what we call 'nightmare', and can feel – and be – frightening. The dream says to us things that in consciousness we have tried all our lives to keep under. It holds a back-mirror up to us and we see, not the conscious presentation that we've chosen to put out to the world, but its other side! That can be frightening, the more so the more we have been holding at bay.

EM: This is some part of themselves that has had to be repressed or rejected? The Shadow?

BS: The Shadow-self, yes; the part not acceptable in consciousness is tucked down there, but it takes the opportunity of night-sleeping to present itself again.

EM: Barbara, can you say something about the timing of those more unconscious, repressed, Shadow aspects when they emerge in therapy?

BS: I always look at it as a good sign for the well-being of the dreamer. Their own psyches are presenting them with aspects of themselves that they don't choose to recognize; yet, if recognized, they're very valuable energies to have alongside. I believe all these dream-images are containers of energies that have been repressed – and of one's creativity.

EM: Have you any examples?

BS: Yes. A man came to me with a series of dreams. He was being slowly and inexorably pursued by a *Frankenstein* monster-like figure, dragging and shuffling towards him, totally paralysed down the left side. Wherever he went – into his office, his home, his bedroom, his garden – this shuffling figure implacably followed. Looking back over his shoulder, he'd catch flashes, glimpses of it and its face was as if all made up of spare parts! It was horrifying.

Through talking about the figure, he finally had the courage to draw it. This allowed him to address and set up a dialogue with it. He realized it was the other side of himself, and it was all made up of spare parts – other people's viewpoints, attitudes, ideas as to how he should be – all bits of himself! The figure wore an artist's smock, very torn and paint-stained. Whatever had happened to the artistic side of him? Was it in the paralysis of this deeply, profoundly sad face?

In ordinary life he'd kept up a wonderful, intact front; on the ball, briefcase under arm, very smart. But occasionally, on dark days, he'd see himself in the shaving mirror half paralysed down one side.

EM: Was this a balance, a compensation?

BS: It was – and more. Dreams can sometimes talk about things that haven't happened yet. It isn't always repressed material that takes the opportunity of the dream. Those that come in these nightmarish ways are intending to be seen; sometimes they're bringing the seeds of unknown, untouched potentiality up from the unconscious. And the timing of it! These are energies that need no longer be held down in the unconscious – they can't be!

EM: You are looking at the compensatory but also at the transformative nature of dreams. Would you always look at both; or would there be times when you would hold back on what is in potentia?

BS: Oh yes. He came to it in his own time. The back–mirror was held up for him to look into, whether he wanted to or not. As he began to explore it, the figure revealed its potential.

EM: So the dream brought him into it, and he came to his own subjective understanding; rather than its being your – the therapist's – objective understanding? There's a lot of talk about dream interpretation, isn't there – wading in there with one's own ideas?

BS: Which is to take the dream away from the dreamer. Since that dream came to that dreamer in that form, better encourage the dreamer to dialogue with that aspect of his nature and discover what it has to say to him – and why at this particular time in his life.

EM: And you'd keep any ideas about it to yourself?

BS: I would, yes, unless specifically asked. And then I would say, 'Could it be that . . .?' or 'Might you consider that this is part of yourself?' But only if asked.

EM: Might you ever be tempted to say 'Could this have anything to do with X?' – if, say, you felt someone's ego was trying to take over the understanding of the dream?

BS: I wouldn't come in with anything while they were still working on the dream. When they had brought out everything they possibly could, then I might help with a few bridging words or speculations. Interpretation I would avoid.

ASSOCIATION AND AMPLIFICATION

EM: Imagine a therapist is training with us and her client says 'I've got a dream'. How would she approach and work with that dream?

BS: Well, sometimes the dreamer likes to tell the dream. As therapist, I'd ask them to enter the dream mood from the beginning, to say it in a dreamy way . . .

EM: Even closing their eyes?

BS: If closing their eyes is appropriate – and for the majority of people it is. Ask them just to enter, re-enter, the mood of the dream as they recall it, and tell it at a slowish, dreamy pace. That allows me time to write it down, not interrupting, letting them go right through to the end. Then I ask for their feeling on waking? Did any title come to them? Quite frequently one does, and it can be full of impact. Then together we work on the text of the dream. I stay as close as possible to the way in which it was presented, which is the freshest and most immediate.

Sometimes they bring in a written text, but I still ask them to read it in a dreamy way, not just gobbledegook: 'Enter the dream mood – contact the feeling of the dream'. Then we begin to follow along, as one would in a play, starting from the entry point of the dream, not interpreting at all, just going through. And I read it back to the dreamer, stanza by stanza, using exactly the words they've used: 'It starts at night, in this darkened street, and you've said it's not a place that you know. What's the feeling of that? Does it suggest anything to you? Does it remind you of anything?'

EM: That would be 'association'?

BS: It's their own very personal associations. I gather the associations they give without querying them, writing down for them just exactly the words they use for later usage. We go through, stanza by stanza, following the shape as closely as possible. I pause; I say in dreamy tones: 'So then – as you turn the corner – there's a lit-up door – you enter the doorway – and you see a flight of steps going down . . .' I'd stop there and say 'just follow that through – what is the feeling of that? What is the mood – what is your sense as you go through – what does it remind you of?'

EM: Almost inviting them into it . . .

BS: Yes, into it, so that they're re-enacting it. 'What does that mean to you?' 'Ah-ha's' often come up as they are making their associations: 'Oh, I hadn't thought of that!' or 'That reminds me of another dream!' By the end we have a whole network of associations going out from the stanzas of the dream. I try never to use a word that they haven't used; I stay exactly with their words, which will often evoke something. 'That was really, really scary!' they say. 'Stay with the feeling. What kind of scary? Does that 'scary' remind you of anything?' They're being invited to re-enter the dream – but now from their waking self, beginning to interact with their dreaming self.

So that's one way of working at that level with a dream, through associations. There are many other modes of working on the dream. The person can become different parts of their dream (the Gestalt way of working). If it's a dream with movement in it I may invite them to walk the dream, re-enacting it silently, going through its stanzas first as the dreamer, then as the 'dreaming self'. It's done from the point of view of the body: perhaps the dreamer was walking along a road, or going down a flight of stairs . . .

EM: You get them to walk it in their imagination, sitting in a chair?

BS: No. If that particular client can do it without embarrassment, I invite them actually to walk it. A huge amount of extra information comes in through the body's feeling. Though not apparently present, its senses have taken in a great deal.

EM: Barbara, when would you use 'amplification'?

BS: Amplification is the texture, the wider context of the dream, over and beyond the personal dreamer. For instance, a snake in a dream is the dreamer's snake; they make their associations to the snake. But the snake has always been related to human beings; from the beginning human beings have had views about and ways of seeing snakes. Cross-connecting into the wider context from 'What is the meaning of "snake" for you?' may help them to discover the wider meaning of 'snake' for the whole of humankind.

EM: Like the *Frankenstein* man?

BS: Yes. He'd read the story and seen the film, and that's what the figure in his dream looked like. But it was very specifically his Frankenstein figure. Presumably this dream was dreamed by many dreamers long before Mary Shelley wrote *Frankenstein*!

EM: The idea of the monster . . .

BS: . . . the monster, the scapegoat, the unacceptable being, the terrifying Other that once tyrannized small human beings in large places. It's part of the context of their imagination, their story, their folklore from the beginning of time. It's making that cross-connection. Here's an example of amplification.

A man recalled how, between the ages of three and fifteen, he'd spent most of the time in hospital, pinned down on a board on traction, endlessly tyrannized by an appalling harpy of a Matron. The only thing he discovered on that ward was that he had the most beautiful voice; he developed it in secret, singing quietly for the other children at night when Matron had gone.

When he came to see me he said he was an Aquarian. I chose to say something amplifying: 'How extraordinary! Did you know that the myth of Aquarius is – Prometheus?' I told him a little about how Prometheus was tied down on the rocks, suggesting he might read the rest of the story for himself. And so he read: Prometheus stealing fire – in the Underworld – pegged out on the rock – his liver pecked out each day by a carrion bird – (he associated this to the Matron, whom he called an 'old harpy'). And at night the liver re-grew – he associated that with singing his songs at night.

As he researched, he realized his story had a much wider context, a profounder meaning; it ceased to be just a terrible incident that had happened to 'poor him': it had happened to other human beings before him. He took courage and began to sing in public, speaking of it as his 'fire voice', his stolen fire.

EM: So he moved from the personal . . .

BS: From the very personal, the very narrow, the almost unredeemable situation, to realizing that the story belonged to the whole of humanity. It wasn't just his; it was much wider, opening up the fountain of his imagination and the reach and range of what that could mean.

EM: And so the imagination begins to do its own healing. There are some people for whom that doesn't work, aren't there; some people who can't go over that bridge and make it their own, or enter into that space?

BS: Yes; and that's never to be fought against. One uses amplification only after one has all the associations.

EM: And how important is that amplification! I have known trainee and other therapists bursting with information and stories; but if they tell them, it's the therapist's story rather than the dreamer's.

BS: That's right! Here's another story of amplification. A man had a dream of a small, circular mediaeval city with a square in the middle. In the centre of the square was what he called a 'plague tree'. I said 'A plague tree?' 'Yes,' he said. 'It's all withered. An old woman by the tree tells me it's the plague tree. In the time of the plague lots of cities had them. When the plague was coming near, the tree would begin to die. And she said,

"This is the tree of your life". I woke sweating in horror about this; what on earth could it mean?'

He'd never heard of a plague tree – I'd never heard of a plague tree either. I suggested he drew the tree. And he kept putting little green leaves on it, saying 'I realize it isn't totally dead'. What were his associations – 'What might a plague tree mean for you?' And then he remembered how he'd always longed for rapport with his father, but was always pushed away with 'Go away, you plaguey little nuisance!' 'I cut back my growth,' he said, sobbing as he started another picture, remembering how he'd felt.

He looked down. His hand had been drawing another tree for him. A sapling putting out green shoots. 'Where did that come from? Did I really draw that?' Then, cross-connecting: 'Am I still a plaguey little nuisance?' Consciously, he'd been talking; unconsciously, his hand had been drawing something different. The tree he didn't know he'd drawn had, like the dream, come through at the unconscious level, setting it all in a wider context, showing him why he was so narrow, so tentative, always thinking other people would find him a nuisance or a bore. His contexts were widened because he allowed other possibilities to penetrate and enlarge him.

THE DEVELOPMENT OF DREAMS

Childhood

BS: Let's go back to the Inner and the Outer [Figure 2]. As very small infants we come into incarnation from the unconscious Inner, over the Interface, in order to live an external life. And, having happened into the Outer world, our bodies begin to develop in adaptation. But the child, to begin with, carries an enormous number of connections with where it came from. Perhaps not quite 'trailing clouds of glory', it does have access to the unconscious side of its infant life, sharing both conscious and unconscious with its mother. It picks up what is unstated by the external world, knowing, for instance, whether or not it is truly loved. (However much it's told it's loved, if it doesn't feel itself to be, then it knows it's not.) It has a profound ability to know the world, sensing beyond the senses. Many children find it very difficult to adapt when something in them knows better than what they are being told. Sometimes, knowing a truth greater than the one presented to them, they may sense that they are older than their parents.

Dreams are the bridge for children. My own little grandson, at four or five, would talk about 'his mountain' that he came from. He had many dreams of being on that mountain. He 'helped the Mummies look after the children'. His parents asked him if he was a Daddy with lots of children? He said, No, he wasn't a Daddy – he 'tied up the legs and helped them look after the children'. He was trying to say that he was a healer of some kind. He referred back again and again to his mountain. It has a great reality for him.

Frances Wickes (1977, p. 192) tells of the little boy who had a dream of having a spark within him, a bonfire spark, there for him in his dreams:

'I have a friend, he is little as a twinkle and as big as pitch-black dark.' He described Twinkle as 'littler than a star, but he really is a star, but Twinkle doesn't go out, he stays there.' So at night he would always be there to help him, this little spark in the darkness. In the daytime, when Pitch Black Dark frightened him – when he was scared at school – he would have to concentrate to remember him: 'Pitch Black Dark can walk right into the daytime, and then I have to think very hard to see Twinkle.'

EM: Are dreams always good, containing a potential of the Self? After all, the Self is beyond judgement and can bring both positive and negative. Can they sometimes be malevolent?

BS: I think dreams are potential carriers of raw human experience, of energy. Energy is neither positive nor negative, malevolent or benevolent, it just is. It's what you do with it that counts.

EM: How the ego takes it in consciousness?

BS: Yes. The energy contained within the dream is from the beginning. The dream is carrier for the potential of the fullness of our nature. Whether it turns to evil or to good is neither here nor there. It's just a great energy unfolding itself.

The small child is very closely connected with inner reality, with 'the Unconscious' as we would now call it. As they come out over the threshold into the world, it's essential that the Interface between Inner and Outer begin to be more opaque, less transparent. If the child retained its contact with all of the Inner World it could scarcely function outside. Typically around age five or six the senses develop in relation to the outer world, but they close down in relation to their extrasensory ability in order that the child can function.

This is the period of so-called 'nightmares', when children are usually experiencing a collision between Outer and Inner experience. A lot of big impacts are hitting them. The adults (the gods) are disagreeing with each other. School is a Big School for them. They question the big issues: What is life? What is death? Where do babies come from? The huge figures in their dreams are there to be transitional objects, to help take them into the outer world.

Children take in a very great deal. One child had parents who were considering divorcing but never let it be known to her, showing a front of unity and friendliness to each other 'for the sake of the child'. The child had dreams of great giants rolling dice, knowing the way the dice fell could mean the difference between her being allowed to live and being asked to die.

These big dreams, full of impact, are very close to fairy tales and stories. It's important that the child has some access to stories, with their Big Baddies and Big Goodies, their Chocolate Factories, their naughtiness, outrageousness, joyfulness, playfulness, their disorderly conduct – handling all that! The child is trying to bring itself – or sometimes it's being painfully brought – into line with the external world. And it's all being acted out, there in the stories! And it's very often being acted out there in their dreams, too, helping the child align itself to the external world and giving it the aid and the widened recognition of something greater than itself. Fairy stories are wonderful, bringing in all the good and naughty characters – hobgoblins, leprechauns, fairy godmothers; the stories help carry the child's over-exuberance of energy and life, and show ways in which it can be ordered. After all, the witch can always be pushed into the oven and the door slammed on her.

EM: And the stories give it straight from the Inner; it's not explanation . . .

BS: Fairy stories were once somebody's dreams. They were told as stories, from village to village and place to place, till the fairies and the witches took on the qualities of the divine and the secular – the good and the bad. It's all human experience. But at some earlier point, it was somebody's dream that had been turned into a tale and picked up, together with other people's dreams and visualizations and imagination, and given the form and shape of story, so helpful for the growing child.

I often wonder how children make any sense of the adult world. They have to align with it when, from their point of view, it's often crazy. But the dreams do help to make sense of it. All right, you've dreamt of your pirate under the bed. But if, waking up, you can be cuddled and warmed, you discover that the pirate may after all come out from under the bed! And he won't always be there – occasionally he will, but it's all right, you can survive; you hold on to your teddy bear (your 'transitional object'!) and you can survive in the world, however trying.

Adolescence and young adulthood

BS: Next, the child crosses the threshold into Adolescence. At the Interface the veil is opaque. The thrust of life is outwards, into a wider life. In my experience, a lot of young people hovering on the threshold have dreams that would once have been part of tribal rites. Dreams act as the puberty rites of initiation and separation once did, leading away from the roots, the matrix, leading out of the boys' hut and away from the menstrual hut of the girls, into apprenticeship to life and to the Sun and the Moon, the ancestral gods.

Nowadays, this often means the tension of separation-anxiety. It means leaving home – parents – the known and familiar and cosy – to seek new paths and new leaders. It doesn't mean staying in wish-fulfilling daydreams, but taking the courage to experience 'life out there'. It means moving from dependence to responsibility as the 'learning' boy or girl, towards our potential as an ego-Self. The Lunar world of the Shadow falls behind – to be met again later.

EM: Would the initiation rites have been shared in a group; or would they let someone on to the next stage, helping with a rite of passage?

BS: It's rather that dreams now come in to replace the lost initiation rites that would once have been experienced. I can remember a boy of twelve, good neither at sports nor educationally. At school he felt himself to be in no place. He dreamt he was in a match: he fell down in the scrum and – covered with mud, he was being kicked all over the place. It turned out he was the ball! He sat up and started to cry, but a big man in a padded greatcoat said, 'Come on son, don't cry. Feel into your mouth.' He felt into his mouth – and he'd lost his two front teeth. 'It was terrifying – terrifying!' I asked him, 'What sort of terrifying – what was the feeling of "terrifying"?' And he said, 'I felt I'd gone through something – I'd had my two baby teeth knocked out, and I was a real man.'

Some of the initiation rites in Africa included the knocking out of the two front teeth; getting rid of the baby teeth meant moving over into manhood.

EM: Sometimes dreams of losing teeth are to do with ageing?

BS: Yes. But they can also be about people's grip on life, how much they're taking life in and ingesting it, biting into life, masticating the nourishment they're given. Are they losing their grip?

EM: Hanging on by the skin of their teeth!

BS: Exactly so! Beautifully put. But that theme would have a different meaning at different ages. This boy was on the threshold of adolescence, and his dream is just one of the many initiation modes that were used collectively in the past. I have another example, this time from a girl of about sixteen:

I have inherited my mother's jewellery; I also have her liver in a plastic bag, all flabby and dead-looking. I try to pass through customs, but the official says 'These are not yours. You are trying to smuggle them through. You must give them up, or go back to where you came from.' He is both fierce and friendly. He's right – but what will Mother say? Mother is indeed the Dragon to be slain.

Now, the young person must make even more adaptation to the external world. Now may come the first dream sightings of the 'beautiful beloved' or 'the handsome prince', as in the fairy stories. This is the first sighting of the 'otherness', the contrasexual side of our own nature. Now we meet the possibility of relatedness in the world, and of our relationship to ourselves – or the lack of it.

As people come up to their late teens and early twenties, into youth and young womanhood or manhood, they often dream of thresholds. A young man of twenty-four dreamed:

I'm leaving school. I'm seventeen, but wearing short trousers and my cap. I'm scared of a gang of older boys who want to beat me up, and I decide to escape by the back way. Suddenly, a huge bear stands in front of me, with an axe in its paws. I am terrified out of my wits. 'Kill me', says the bear and hands me the axe. It seems I have to behead it and climb inside its skin. I'm torn between sadness for the bear, and knowing I could frighten off the bullies if I were in a bear's skin. The bear says, 'You have to choose.' I raise the axe – and wake up in shock.

The middle years

BS: In adulthood, around thirty-five to forty-two, dreams very often bring the realization of how far we have come from our inner reality. On the map of the Inner and the Outer and the Interface [Figure 3], we've moved over to the right, the Outer, the extremity of the external world. This is when dreams come in to show us how lopsided is our development, how much of our true Selves, our true nature, has been left behind.

EM: Like the sounding of a gong?

BS: It is the sounding of a gong – it's a resonance, as if of the main chord of our life. It begins the wake-up alert, for us to realize . . .

EM: . . . the beginning of the descent of the Ego?

BS: . . . yes, but rather than 'descent' it's a return to the surface in a spiral progression. Now we're at the peak point, at noon, furthest from the unconscious. And when that resonance sounds through, the dreams draw attention to how much we've lived by other people's scripts. The *Frankenstein* dream was a perfect example – the dreamer was in his middle years. The thrust of the development of the dreams seems to be to take us through those years, gathering up parts of ourselves as we begin the rites of incorporation and return.

Gender issues arise, both outside and within, as we come to know our own contrasexual side, the Anima and Animus. The dreams are often uncomfortable, coming at us from our blind spots to challenge and to strengthen. Emerson said they give us 'an answer in hieroglyphics to the question we should pose'.

Dreams bring Shadow issues from below the threshold of consciousness, showing us our hidden, denied, perhaps unknown face. We meet the tension of opposites within ourselves as we struggle with polarities: head versus heart; inner versus outer; intended goal versus actual ability. And dreams raise Shadow stuff, that which is not in the light of consciousness. Can the ego withstand the meeting with its Shadow? Or, remaining blinkered, will it deny it?

The Shadow in dreams is usually a figure of the same gender as the dreamer, negative or positive. In its negative aspect it's threatening, scary, 'nightmarish'. Sometimes it's ludicrous – the dream may be sending it up, and that needs to be listened to. It sends urgent messages from the unheard, denied parts of our nature; it gives focus to attitudinal problems and their solutions, both inside us and in the outside world; it exposes our ego-limitations, helping us to enlarge and amplify; and it invites us to risk change, risk the unknown. Will we regressively repeat the old patterns? Or learn from the dream's comments, and be less lopsided, more in the round?

Here's a dream of a man of forty-three, an intellectual, a real know-all. The dream was saying that parts of the ego were due to die:

I am walking towards a fine sunset, and am terrified to find I cast no shadow. Am I real – do I exist? It's a nightmarish feeling.

And a woman of thirty-six:

I am hosting a dinner party. I lead the guests into the dining room and to my horror, see the washing line with all my underwear hanging across the room. And among the clothes are some shrunken heads!

She realized the dream was saying, 'I don't want my friends to see my hang-ups!'

Scary, nightmarish dreams often pre-empt a death, not usually of the dreamer but of some ego-attitude. Since this death is required, or in process, or to come, the dreams often include dying – death – dismemberment – murder – mayhem – warning of change needed. 'I am at my own funeral – I am to be beheaded – my feet are being chopped off . . .' (which may be about standpoint) – 'I'm being torn apart, I'll be put in the cooking pot!'

Positive Shadow figures, like Mercury or Hermes, are often threshold keepers. They're porters, frontier-guards, customs officers, ticket collectors, ferrymen, asking if we're ready to cross to new territory. Often friendly and helpful, they are boundary people – wanderers, old bag-ladies, odd-job people, tramps, Sherpas, cleaning ladies, plumbers. A man in his fifties, who says he is up in his head, out of touch with his feelings and a workaholic, dreamt:

I am at the dining table, writing on an important business matter. Suddenly water first drips then gushes through the ceiling, falling on my documents. What to do? The plumber, a big man, warm and friendly, arrives, looks upstairs and asks if I have 'a first aid kit' to mend the pipe. I say, 'I only have a hammer.' 'That's your problem, Guv!' he says. I wake, very upset.

Another man, forty-two and near to burn-out, had this dream:

I'm lost at night on a country road. It's frightening, and I'm wet and famished. I see a fire, and an old tramp by it. I say: 'I've lost my bearings.' He says, 'And I've lost my wits. Come and share my bread with me.' He hands me a bowl of steaming stew and a hunk of rough bread . . . And here the dreamer cried uncontrollably, and could hardly finish telling his dream.

At this noon point, furthest from the unconscious, we are 'alone out there'. The dreams tend to state polarities so that we can experience the tensions before reconciling them. With sexual dreams we need to recognize that 'the other' is also ourselves. What we do to the other, we do to ourselves. Therefore, a woman's dreams of the masculine are also comments on her relationship to her inner Animus; and a man's dreams of the feminine are also comments on his relationship to his Anima.

These dreams, of a woman of twenty-nine, a teacher in training, cast light on the synthesis of the ego and the persona. The problem was the parental script:

As teacher to young children, I'm writing on the blackboard, in white chalk. There is a big, hairy, frightening man standing alongside me, writing too:

I write 'good'; he writes 'bad'.
I write 'polite', he writes 'randy'.
I try to write 'nice', but I write 'B-randy, Brandy' instead.
He writes 'spirit' with a great flourish.

He then leaps at me and wrestles me to the floor. I smell his sweat, his bad breath. He has big teeth. He kisses me. I am sexually aroused – but 'not in front of the children!' I wake up in alarm and horror.

Then I go back to sleep:

Now, I'm wandering along a dark street of high-rise buildings, through graffiti and filth. I must find 'my baby'. I'm frightened I'll be attacked – but determined. I turn into an alleyway, a 'blind alley', to shelter and 'cover my back'. I hear whimpering – and in a dustbin is my baby, a girl, most beautiful with a soft petal face. She's three months old, and wrapped in a torn blanket. I pull back the blanket, and see she has a hairy body and a small, erect penis. It is his child.

So, our dreams carry us towards the marriage of opposites, into a wholeness. They move us from ignorance, grasping, lust, wanting to have others carry our inadequacies, towards courtship in the courts of love.

Maturity

BS: Now we are coming towards – maturity! Here the ego's Heroic Quest begins to lose its power. The journey to maturity and self-integration is less about worldly success, power, possession, prestige, and more about allowing the maturing person to come towards psychic wholeness, including both inner and outer values. For this, the claims of the ego need to be subordinated to those of the wider Self. There's no ego-triumph in this. We learn that heroic strength of the muscle-flexing type doesn't help much.

Dreams now often teach us about the acceptance of a wider context. We can't succeed by guile; there's no bribing this initiatory door-keeper. All that counts is who we really are, our own intrinsic worth, our true journey and meaning. We need the patience to stay with it, being prepared to let go and not try to possess or keep control. Jung said, 'When an Ego-position fades, the Self is born a little more.'

In the child, and also in the life of the ego, the Self is largely unconscious. Maturity is about becoming more awake, more porous, re-opening the threshold and allowing it to be less opaque again. In childhood, the Self gives birth to the ego: in maturity, the ego gives birth to the Self.

Even though the climacteric can, and often does, feel like loss, it can be a move to 'wizening' – or 'wisening' – for both men and women. The loss of youth, energy and sexual identity make us feel we're no longer masters in own house. Dreams of burglars, intruders, death motifs may bring a subtle change of viewpoint, of values, which seems antagonistic from the ego's viewpoint. But the dreams often reveal that what seems loss is also a gain. A woman of sixty dreamt:

My home has been ransacked; most of my valuables are gone. I have to move on: but at least I have my many books and all my clothes and furniture. I try to ram these into boxes and suitcases, but it's impossible. I'm crying with frustration. Then, someone quietly hands me a box of matches! Of course that's the solution!

There's also a need, at maturity, to bring the opposites together, away from 'either-or' to 'both–and'. The polarities of body and spirit, Soma and Psyche, need to unify, to marry. This raises profound issues. What about reincarnation? Can Matter be transsubstantiated to Spirit, as in the Mass? Does Spirit descend to matter? Can the Body become a gateway to the Spirit; as it was, at birth, a gateway of the Spirit into the flesh? The Body, with its dreams as well as its symptoms, enters in here.

And now our 'home', the ground of our being, begins to form under our feet. We realize that to be in the Now, linked to the Past and to the Future, is Eternity. 'We still feel pain, but it doesn't hurt so much.' Humour gives us a sense of proportion and perspective. Traditionally, the 'elder' was the guardian and repository of the connective thread, holding it and 'spinning the yarn' to help make the transition from one world to the next. Those who seriously address death can take life more gratefully and joyously. This is where dreams of wholeness increasingly come in. A woman of forty-five dreamt:

I am baking a cake. All the ingredients are prepared. I only have to mix them and stir them in a circular bowl. The oven heat is just right for baking.

Some of the best aids to keeping open the dialogue between the Inner and the Outer are arts, crafts, storytelling, song, poetry, therapy, meditation. Also, aware living; dreamwork; active imagination. A man of fifty six:

A huge jigsaw puzzle is nearly completed. It shows a square castle with four entrances over a moat. Many of us, both men and women, are working on it. One piece is missing. They turn to me: it seems I have it in my pocket. How can this be? I fumble about, feeling embarrassed by their expectation. But there it is, in my pocket. I click it into place, so locking the whole puzzle. How extraordinary!

Here's the dream of a woman of forty-six. The actual context: 'I have three brothers, and we all had trees planted for us at birth. They always teased me, calling my tree "the crab apple".' In the dream:

I go to the orchard at night. My brothers' trees loom dark and tall. I feel sad for my tree, and turn towards it. It is aglow with light, and I see that the full moon is hanging in its branches like an apple. I wake, crying with joy.

Such are dreams of Wholeness.

Ageing, dying, death, rebirth

BS: By now we have come full circle. The Inner and the Outer are turned, and we are coming home. Our dying, or our dream deaths, mean that we must readdress the threshold, and the 'guardians'. We have to prepare, packing for the journey. Could it be that we are magnetically drawn by the Self? Does the Self come seeking?

Initiatory dreams come at any stage in life; what follows applies to thresholds of death and rebirth in earlier ego-life, as well as to old age. Let's look at some of the motifs of ageing.

People have spoken of increased anxiety dreams, 'nightmares', as they are separated from the hold of the ego. Dreams of loss and invasion can come, especially if one is afraid of death and life. The values of this world are being eroded and dissolved, and this often raises fear and disorientation, which can be added to from outside as physical ageing advances. Jung (1995, p. 337) said:

Death is an important interest, especially to an ageing person. A categorical question is being put to him, and he is under an obligation to answer it. To this end he ought to have a myth about death, for reason shows him nothing but the dark pit into which he is descending. Myth, however, can conjure up other images for him, helpful and enriching pictures of life in the land of the dead. If he believes in them, or greets them with some measure of credence, he is being just as right or just as wrong as someone who does not believe in them. But while the man who despairs marches towards nothingness, the one who has placed his faith in the archetype follows the tracks of life and lives right into his death. Both, to be sure, remain in uncertainty, but the one lives against his instincts, the other with them.

An old Zulu woman held her palm turned upward and said, 'That's how we live.' She then turned her hand palm downward: 'That's how the ancestors live.' In general, the dreams tend to be less personal and more transpersonal, more collective and archetypal, as we approach the threshold of the invisible world. At this stage, motifs for life and death appear as processes, stages, passages. Actual death rarely comes as death itself, but as a Game or a Dance. Life is presented as a play, as theatre, as a journey, a road, the Way. Images come of crossing water – perhaps the river, perhaps the Great Ocean – by a bridge, a ford, a boat, a barge, a raft. There may be alchemical transformations. Ladders and staircases often spiral up and down. We dream of changing trains, vehicle, direction. There are ritual enactments, initiation rites, dreams of 'embarking'.

This next dream was reported by Dr Jay Dunn of a patient, and cited by Marie-Louise von Franz:

She sees a candle lit on the window sill of the hospital room. It suddenly goes out. Fear and anxiety ensue as the darkness envelops her. Then, the candle re-lights on the other side of the window and she awakens.

She died the same day.

My stepfather dreamed this after four and a half years of cancer, aged eighty-four. He did tapestry as an amateur:

I am in a large hall, like a jumble sale place. Nothing attracts me, except an easel with an old tapestry – stained, worn and faded. As I'm squinting to see the picture, a 'person of light', probably female, says to me, 'We'd like you to repair this'. She takes me round to the back of the easel. I see broken threads. She gives me a needle with some black thread and I weave in the ragged ends, all the time telling her I'm not an expert and don't really know what I'm doing. She puts a finger on my lips, smiles, leads me to the front of the easel, and points. The tapestry is stunning, radiant and – I just can't tell you [tears] – so – stunning . . .

Twenty-four hours later he went into a coma, and died peacefully three days later.

All in all, we need to realize that the deaths we die, the sleeps we sleep, the dreams we dream, are rehearsals for the threshold. We go by individual ways to the One. In dying, we may only step outside the 'event horizon' of the living, but still exist in an observable state. Jung (1995, p. 18) again:

Life has always seemed to me like a plant that lives on its rhizome. Its true life is invisible, hidden in the rhizome. The part that appears above ground lasts only a single summer. Then it withers away – an ephemeral apparition. When we think of the unending growth and decay of life and civilizations, we cannot escape the impression of absolute nullity. Yet I have never lost a sense of something that lives and endures beneath the eternal flux.

BIG DREAMS

EM: Let's look, finally, at Big Dreams.

BS: Well, I suppose the Big Dream is bigger than the person dreaming it! This map is about the dream that comes from the Collective and Supra-conscious level [Figure 3] and partakes of the multidimensional universe. It isn't simply an individual human experience – or if it is, it's for all humanity. There are times in many people's lives when a dream of that nature comes to, and through, them with a particular resonance. They know it has impact; if they could analyse it, or immediately access it fully, then it wouldn't be a Big Dream. It carries a resonance over and beyond. It would have been a tribal dream in the past, dreamed by Shamans, Seers, Dreamers, people trained to have dreams; a dream for the tribe, for the nation, for something much bigger.

As therapist, I'd be profoundly concerned for somebody who came with an influx of dreams of that nature. It could be an inundation from the unconscious which their personality is not able to contain; too much of it could lead to a cracking open.

EM: To psychotic episodes?

BS: Yes. The boundaries of their personality are far too porous, and they're beginning to perceive that. I would not work with such dreams immediately, but would begin to ground and anchor the person, bringing them down to the here-and-now, the practical reality of the everyday.

But the fact remains that quite a few people will have a dream which leaves them with a profound sense of something other. Something has happened to them; it has a sense of 'otherness', of the numinous. It often brings them to a state of some humility; they don't rush into it. As therapist I too would treat it with respect and humility, not assuming we had to start pulling it apart and exploring every part of it.

EM: Would it be a transpersonal dream?

BS: It is what I would call a transpersonal dream, yes. For me, the 'transpersonal' means all that is personal, emerging from the multidimensional realm of which we're all part, and yet also going beyond it. To an extent, that Plague dream was a Big Dream; it certainly had a big impact. Black Elk, in the book *Black Elk Speaks*, spoke of the dreams he had of the tribal rings, which were about his nation's future as well as about himself as a young man. He was speaking for something much bigger.

A woman of fifty-four dreamt this:

I'm on a raft in a dark, heavy sea, with six or eight others. I appear to be in charge. I seem not to have anything aboard, but realize we'll sink if we don't jettison all their belongings. How am I to tell them? I'm in deep distress, knowing how much they've already been through.

At last I manage to say: 'We must let everything go if we are to survive.' To my surprise, they give a cheer, and delightedly toss everything they possess off the raft. One of them says, 'There's one more thing that needs to go', and throws over into the water a birdcage – and inside is a canary, joyously singing its little heart out as it bounces on towards what I can now see is approaching land.

I sob with gratitude and love for these friends who turn pain into celebration. One of them says, 'It was only painful to you when you thought you were the captain of this raft!'

There in the raft the dreamer had felt so moved, so touched by their laughter, by their willingness to let go, that she realized even then that it was a big statement to herself of her own need to let go and not be in charge. With that feeling she began to cry; and they said, 'We're part of you, and we will take you through; just leave yourself in our hands.'

She took the dream forward from that in Active imagination. The raft became a Death Raft on which, knowing she was dead, she was being transported over the dark waters towards new land. In the dream, she went through the hands of the embalmer, was placed in a sarcophagus, carried across to the Underworld for the measuring of souls, and moved towards resurrection.

Her life was transformed through the depth of meaning of that single dream. She was engaged and enchanted by the readiness of parts of her nature – other than her controlling mind – to let go. She felt the canary was her soul, singing away there in hope that one day, out of this dark sea, there would be landfall. It helped to feed her. She's now creating pots, breathing spirit into new containers of life and energy. In her external life she has come through the passage out of profound mourning and grief. And she has become a therapist herself: feeling now that each human being is a living container, she wants to help them to breathe too, and their spirit to emerge.

I would call that a Big Dream. It has all the motifs of deeper things: the dark sea; the crossing of the water; the movement through the death-process; the embalming; the sarcophagus, the time of waiting for the renewal of life, and the breathing again. It has all of the fertility rites of Egypt. But the important thing is it didn't stay at dream level; she had the courage to re-translate it, to understand it, to draw it, to paint it, to remember it into her everyday life, until it transformed the living substance of her life. It has enlarged her usefulness in the world, given her hope, and taken her from death to resurrection.

REFERENCES

Tsu, Chuang (1974). *Inner Chapters*. A new translation by Gia-Fu Feng and Jane English. London: Wildwood House.

Jung, C. G. (1995, first published 1963) *Memories, Dreams, Reflections*. London: Fontana.

Neihardt, J. G. (1932) *Black Elk Speaks*. New York: Morrow.

Wickes, F. (1977, first published 1927). *The Inner World of Childhood*. London: Coventure.

CHAPTER 9

Naked Presence

Nigel Wellings

*One does not become enlightened by imagining figures of light but by making the
darkness conscious. (C. G. Jung)*

---

*Editor's note: This chapter beautifully illustrates the influences of Buddhism and European and
American approaches to transpersonal psychology upon the practice of transpersonal psychotherapy. It challenges every reader, whatever their background in psychological or philosophical
thinking, to extend their understanding of authentic spiritual experience by knowing it from the
inside. Nigel Wellings writes with devastating clarity about the many confusions that arise when
trying to formulate transpersonal experience into words, and he explores them thoroughly here. His
chapter demands that we are mindful of, and in constant relationship with, the seductions offered
by a collapsing back into prereflective consciousness, rather than the moment-to-moment raw
experience of the now, as a preparation for stepping back beyond duality.*

*He describes the technical methods that transpersonal psychotherapy uses to diminish the gap
between experience and reflective observation, such as spot imaging and focusing, and tells us why
they are important. Then he moves on to spiritual practice itself, describing and analysing the
stages of witnessing, bare attention and mindfulness as the bridge which, because of its nature of
unconditional presence, is truly transpersonal.*

E.M.W.

An Indian wisdom story goes like this: A group of blind men came upon an Elephant
and as each clasped the beast they shouted out their findings. One said 'It is like a
great twisting snake', the next said, 'It is like the trees of the forest', and the third, 'It
is round like a huge drum'. As a blind man who also knows this story I am aware this
is a contentious chapter that could be written by any number of people and each time
would come out differently. The problem is that Transpersonal Psychology is not a
religion with an agreed canon of beliefs but rather many ideas in a melting pot moving
together and creating and recreating different understandings. Certainly there are
shared views, many of these will have emerged in the proceeding chapters, but there
are also areas that engender hot debate and certainly when we talk of the relationship
between Transpersonal Psychology and spirituality we enter such an area.

In this chapter I am simply going to stick with my part of the Elephant and share
what has interested and influenced me as a psychotherapist who also feels that
meditation and contemplation have a central place in the deepest experience of healing.
In practice this will mean spending time with C. G. Jung and Buddhism (though not
so visible, a primary source), as well as others who have had a very large influence on

the form of transpersonal psychology taught in England at the Centre for Transpersonal Psychology. We will also extensively visit Transpersonal Psychology in America.

THE ANCESTORS, FREUD AND JUNG

Traditionally psychoanalysis has been dismissive of experiences in people's lives that they themselves would call 'spiritual'. Freud suggested (1930) that the yearning we feel for spiritual experience is a regressive yearning in disguise for the earliest oceanic bliss of symbiosis with mother. The existence of religion (1927) was also seen as a need for a father who would provide lifelong protection against existential vulnerability. Jung however, took religious and spiritual experience at face value from the very start of his professional life. During his student days, at the turn of the nineteenth century, hypnotism and spiritualism were enjoying a vogue, and Jung, sensitive to the times, shared in this. Later, after his break with Freud and psychoanalysis, following his dreams, he became interested in mythology, Gnosticism and Alchemy, writing extensively on these subjects as well as on Christianity, Hinduism, Buddhism and Toaism (*CW* vols 5, 11, 12, 13, 14). Indeed it is largely due to Jung that these subjects remained the legitimate concern of (analytical) psychology and have found their renaissance at the end of the twentieth century.

However, despite Jung's and Jungian acceptance of numinous or spiritual experience as a legitimate expression of the archetype of the Self, there still remains, with some Jungians, a prejudice against 'Westerners' actually practising religious and spiritual systems of meditation and contemplation that come from Asian traditions. This is because Jung felt that although these systems were rich in archetypal study they were not psychologically appropriate for European minds, deeply saturated, as they are, in Greco/Judaic myth. Exactly why is unclear unless we consider that they never really gripped Jung in the way his beloved Alchemy did. Now, nearly fifty years since *Psychology and Religion*, a period in which we have seen a migration into the west of teachers from many of the schools of Buddhism and Hinduism, it is not enough to make sweeping generalizations, we now understand much more, both the exact experiences of Westerners successfully practising these traditions and the psychopathologies that can and do occur when they are practised badly. We also know that while inter-cultural comparisons are valuable, it is not possible to understand something truly alien by attempting to find its equivalent within one's own traditions. Thus, even though Jung has provided the major and most viable of the transpersonal psychologies, he and many other early twentieth century investigators and propagator's of 'Eastern teachings', are now seen to be principally valuable for their introduction of entirely new material rather than for their accurate understanding of it. A greater understanding is only achieved by fully entering the other and knowing it from the inside.

However, the propensity for muddle and misunderstanding continues. Before we explore further it may be useful to consider some of the confusions that can arise in and around our understanding of 'transpersonal' and how these may affect our practice of psychotherapy and spirituality.

TRANSPERSONAL AND THE PROPENSITY FOR SELF DELUSION

An area of confusion arises, unconsciously, when the transpersonal is *naively* understood as an ill-defined divine psychological force that has a conscious intention that communicates itself through dreams, synchronicities and the circumstances of our lives. While this is very close to the Jungian understanding of the relationship of the ego to the Self it is also in danger of distortions that Wilber (1995) has some harsh words on. Wilber distinguishes between pre-rational (infantile) and trans-rational (transpersonal) states of awareness. The essential idea is that since pre-rational and trans-rational experiences are both non-rational they may be easily confused. This is called the 'pre/trans fallacy'. In this, early infantile feelings and needs are not distinguished from legitimate transpersonal or 'spiritual' experiences. Examples of this are found in the work of Freud and Jung. While Freud interpreted trans-rational experiences as a yearning for infantile regression and so saw the tran-rational as pre-rational, Jung idealized infantile undifferentiated consciousness as a precursor to mystical states of union and so confused the pre-rational with the trans-rational. Thus Freud fell into the reductionist position and Jung the elevationist position. Wilber says (1998, p. 90),

> For most of our modern era . . . the reductionist stance has prevailed – all spiritual experiences, . . . were simply interpreted as regressions to primitive and infantile modes of thought. However, as if in over-reaction to all that, we are now and have been since the sixties, in the throes of various forms of elevationism (exemplified by, but by no means confined to, the New Age movement). All sorts of endeavours, of no matter what origin or of what authenticity, are simply elevated to trans-rational and spiritual glory, and the only qualification for this wonderful promotion is that *the endeavour be non-rational. Anything* rational is wrong; *anything* non-rational is spiritual.

As is evident from this, transpersonal psychology can be most in danger of the Jungian and New Age mistake. However, to be fair to Jung (1963, p. 179), he does emphasize that in dealings with the mercurial and tricksterish nature of the unconscious it is important that the ego, as our conscious differentiating and rational self, be the final arbiter. Here is an important basic truth. In all spiritual traditions, along with methods of spiritual development there has simultaneously developed a process of highly rational and critical questioning and testing of beliefs and altered states of consciousness. Adepts over the many years have realized that the path beyond the rational, into 'spiritual experience', is littered with delusions that the naive and sentimental will always fall into. This is because, as with all other areas of our lives, it is very difficult not to simply colour our experience with unconscious complexes that distort perception with the defences that the ego has developed along its path of individuation. Thus, for example, the frail ego that desperately needs to feel important, (and safe), will too easily interpret feelings of grandiose union with the universe (*while avoiding individual people*) as a spiritual event when it is really no more than a defence against the danger and pain of intimacy. Welwood on this,

It is certainly true that many people take refuge in meditation or spiritual groups as a way of escaping from the normal developmental tasks of growing up. A certain kind of self-deception is common among such persons: exposure to the great ideas of the spiritual traditions may cause them to imagine themselves to be more detached and enlightened than they actually are. They may become inflated and carried away with themselves, or else emotionally flat, lacking colour or personal warmth. (Welwood 1983, p. 51).

Our propensity to fool ourselves with a fantasy of spiritual development hiding the more mundane reality of just acting out our complexes was once powerfully brought home to me during a meditation retreat. After several days I was in great mental distress from uncontrollable agitation that made concentration very difficult. In my mind I comforted myself with the thought that when the practice begins to work it brings up energetic disturbances. Thus my fidgeting became a sign of spiritual progress! That night I dreamt that my Buddhist teacher entered my room and brought me sharply back to reality by saying that it was not a sign of the practice working but simply my own mental chatter.

The problem of misinterpretation of experience is very real. Dreams, omens and signs are notoriously difficult to understand and the instant understanding is probably the most susceptible to self delusion. To the contrary, there is a great need to pause, consider, stay with and entertain uncertainty. It is because of this that it is virtually essential to have another person who is outside of our complexes help in the interpretation of our dreams and other unconscious phenomena. With another, who is not blind in the same way, it may be possible to see around the rim of light the ego casts and peer dimly into the shadow. However even this has limitations and participation in a dream sharing group will show the alarming (and rewarding) truth that no single interpretation or interpreter ever sees the whole. As we return again and again to the symbols new meaning unfolds. For this reason Jung was able to speak at the end of his long life of dreams he had had as a boy and still find in them new insights of value. Perhaps had he simply grabbed at the first easy understanding, that had confirmed the unconscious needs of his ego, this rich feast of gradually unfolding significance would have been lost. As it was, he described a way that at least tries to balance the imaginal and the rational so that neither should rule and in so doing harm the process.

To the rational safeguards of considered slow appraisal and the dialogue with another who is outside of us we may also add a third that is connected to the sensation function, the function opposite to intuition. Jeffrey A. Raff (1997), offers the idea of the 'Felt Vision' which effectively described the experience of vision accompanied by (often acute) sensations in the body. Following conventional Jungian understanding Raff says that an archetype functioning destructively within the unconscious, (because it is frustrated), may be turned to creative use once the ego connects with it, that is, gives it personal expression. When this occurs there is frequently a corresponding bodily experience that mirrors the psychological shift. Indeed this 'felt vision' may be more sensate then visual. Furthermore *it is the presence of the physical sensation that is the guarantee of the authenticity of the vision.* In effect what is being said is that while it is easy to imagine great transformations, only when it registers on a bodily level will it be real. He says (1997, p. 89):

The hallmark of a felt vision is creation and transformation. Knowing this permits one to evaluate one's own experience as well as another's to determine if indeed it is a felt vision. Is the experience transformative? Has one changed as a result of it? No matter how small a felt vision may seem, if it is genuine, one has changed. The greater the experience the more profound the change. As one gains experience, one can ask whether the other [the archetype/shamanic ally] has changed as well. Has my ally changed in some way? Is the archetypal figure I have encountered different? In the felt vision the seer is transformed while transforming the seen.

This powerful notion of the reciprocity of the ego and archetype both, reflected in the mirror of the body, touching and effecting transformation in each other, connects with the idea of the 'felt sense' that we will extensively visit later. This indicates that the reality of experience is confirmed and consolidated when it is felt in the body as well as the thoughts, emotions or fantasies. If we are not to delude ourselves by mistaking wishful fantasy for a real opening beyond the limits of ourselves, a transpersonal experience, this final confirmation is *almost* unarguable when used alongside careful thought and the Archimedean point of another. Yet almost can never be perfect!

TRANSPERSONAL AND THE FEMININE PRINCIPLE

The term 'transpersonal' has come to be associated with values such as compassion, generosity, non-judgement, honouring and caring. With methods that rely heavily on creativity, visualization, active imagination, dreaming and the arts. In the language of Jungian typology its superior functions are intuition and feeling while its less developed functions are thinking and sensation. The archetypes that most inform it are the Self and the anima, particularly as the Great Mother. The Self because of the concern with wholeness, balance and meaning. The anima because of the appreciation and preference for imagination, fantasy, intuition, and diffuse consciousness. And the Great Mother because of her omnipresent bounty and nurture, qualities frequently linked with the transpersonal. (Often conveniently forgetting her ravenous shadow.) Qualities that lie in the shadow of either of these typological positions or outside of these archetypes have been seen as somehow 'non-transpersonal'. These would include many qualities that have traditionally been ascribed to the masculine principle and the Hero, notably, focused consciousness, analytical thinking, a preference for sequential, hierarchical structures and a valuing of empirical and sensate fact. However while the idea of the transpersonal is naturally a synonym for the Self, it would be very limiting and distorting to also associate it exclusively with the feminine principle at the expense of the masculine. Thus if the transpersonal is an image of wholeness, it must include and combine both the qualities of the masculine and feminine principles; mother and hero, focused consciousness and the imagination, facts and fantasy, separation and relation, thinking and feeling, intellect and the heart. While this is obvious once stated, because of the imbalance within our society and the compensatory culture around transpersonal psychology, the unconscious inclination is to emphasize and concentrate on the feminine qualities and so lose the balance necessary for realizing the archetypal propensity for wholeness where both are equal and in equilibrium. To be whole, transpersonal psychology needs its phallus.

TRANSPERSONAL, PARENTS AND HOME

A third area of confusion occurs around the projection of the parental images. Perhaps because transpersonal psychology in England has drawn heavily on Jungian psychology which in turn draws from Romanticisim and Christianity, there is a possibility that God, a benevolent, protective and nurturing force, *unconsciously* conceived or felt as a celestial parent, becomes transferred into the notion of 'The Transpersonal' as a good father or (more likely) mother. When this occurs we form a relationship to our fantasy of the transpersonal that in effect compensates for early traumatic experiences of parental absence or maltreatment. Here the transpersonal is experienced as loving, caring, guiding, all knowing, wise, having our best interests at heart and we as lost unless we can identify and come into harmony with what is required of us. We may feel we have come home. I believe it was this that Freud observed and named as a regressive tendency while failing to realize that something real existed beyond the neurotic. Here the child archetype is heavily in evidence when we live in an emotional world that revolves around the belief that if we get it right we will arrive at a safe (omnipotent) place. A typical belief in this category is that psychological work will stave off accidents and physical illness, a belief that has little evidence in reality. While this emphasizes the truth that psyche and soma affect each other it ignores the equal truth that conscious people and great spiritual teachers all die of physical ailments. However, because we can not exclude the dark side of either the parental archetypes or the archetype of the child, there comes a time when the parent or childish emotional needs are rebelled against by the individuating ego. If transpersonal psychology is unconsciously identi-fied as a parent, holding the parental projection, this will be experienced as stifling and will have to be rejected so we can grow beyond ourselves and it. While I understand this from comparable firsthand experience, to throw the baby of transpersonal psychology out with the water of outgrown projection, still seems a great pity. It would be much better to withdraw the projection and continue the relationship on a more mature level. Of course this process is not unique to transpersonal psychology, any organization or person, secular or religious, may hold child/parent projections which will finally need to be withdrawn.

PSYCHOTHERAPY AND SPIRITUALITY

Transpersonal psychology both accepts the reality of altered states of consciousness, including and particularly, 'spiritual' experiences, and also encourages participation in practices, such as meditation, to gain a deeper understanding of our nature and our place in the world. This is not to say that psychotherapy and spirituality are the same nor that their techniques or methods produce the same results.

John Welwood (1983) has suggested three ways in which psychotherapy and meditation differ. The first concerns *expanding or letting go of identity*. Psychotherapy works within a model of identity development, within this model suffering is conceived as a failure to achieve stage appropriate qualities, for instance, initially, a separate identity and then an ability to properly relate. Here, healing is a mixture of adapting to the limits of reality while realizing as much of one's potential as is possible. Conversely the practice of meditation assumes a healthy self and then proceeds to the profound understanding of this self which involves letting go of fixed patterns of identity. Suffering is the ignorance of being trapped within the desires that the separate identity generates. Healing becomes liberation by the realization or inhabitation of non-dual consciousness.

The second difference is *the building and dissolving of meaning structures*. In psychotherapy we constantly move towards understanding our lives in a meaningful way. It is no exaggeration to say that the difference between a devastatingly painful experience destroying or enriching us is mainly found in whether we have managed to find a positive, creative meaning within it. By an ongoing process of identifying meaning we build a sense of self moving through the world in a purposeful way that has individual significance. Against this meditational practice and theory is absolutely disinterested in meaning because meaning is viewed as a way in which the ego maintains the fiction that it is a separate and self existing entity. From the perspective of meditation practice, experiences of meaningfulness and meaninglessness are identical: both rest on the illusion of a self going somewhere.

This links to the last difference, *goal orientation and letting be*. Psychotherapy always has a goal even if it is only to finally stop. Apart from this we speak of therapeutic objectives, working through, growth and transformation. All of these perceptions are based on moving from a less to a more desirable state. Against this meditation must be goalless, it has to truly be a meaning-free activity that goes nowhere. If it is not it may become an extension of the ego's need to make everything into an extension of itself and thus, rather then dissolving its separation, secretly strengthen it.

There are also some shared areas. In the same paper Welwood identifies the quality of *maitri*, or unconditional friendliness. In transpersonal psychology we link this to the compassionate observer. In practice this is the essential ability to not judge one's ideas, feelings and actions, particularly when they first become conscious, but rather let them be with a kindly acceptance that does not make us wrong for having them. Without this gentle acceptance it is impossible to let ourselves come out of hiding and so begin to learn something of who we are. Frequently I have observed that we have two levels of emotion. The first is a critical, self destructive 'voice' that persecutes us for feeling as we do, and beneath this is the more fundamental emotion. For instance, 'I feel bad for being so angry'. Unless one can let go of the the super-ego/judge it will be impossible to explore the more primitive and energetic primary emotion. Maitri then, is the unconditional friendliness that we extend to ourselves during the explorations of therapy and also as we sit in meditational practice. It is not to be confused with a defensive separation from one's feelings by observing them from a disconnected distance. Maitri in therapy provides the necessary safety of the vessel of transformation, and in meditation it is the gentle letting be of all thoughts and feelings as they rise, continue and dissolve in consciousness.

A second shared area revolves around the similarity of relationship between the therapist and patient and the master (or teacher), and student. The activities of the earliest healers and holders of tribal memory and wisdom have devolved into the specialist activities of doctors (therapists) and priests. Because of this long experience we can speak of the archetype of the priest/healer and also its close relative, the wounded healer. As with all archetypal experience, there is a certain mixed blessing. On one hand the power of the archetype can add to the therapist's skill and so constellate greater healing, however against this is also the real possibility of the therapist becoming identified with and thus inflated by the archetype and so come to consider themselves the source of the healing rather than simply its witness. Those of us who bear the wounds of a frail ego that is easily overwhelmed by archetypal identification or who are narcissistically wounded and so susceptible to the need for grandiose self expression, will be in danger. Here, identified with the priest healer we may feel that our duties include becoming spiritual guide, meditation teacher and guru, the psychopomp itself. Likewise, inflation from identification with the wounded healer may cause us to the split the archetype (Guggenbuhl-Craig 1971), retaining being the 'healed' one and so feed upon those who are 'wounded'. Now that the roles of priest and healer have separated we, as therapists, are thankfully not responsible for the care of our patient's immortal soul, we are just therapists not shamans, yet to entirely ignore the place of the transpersonal is not our way either. How then do we get the balance right? Should we ever teach 'spirituality' in therapy?

Welwood, as psychotherapist and meditation teacher, thinks on the whole not because:

> A teacher in one of the meditative traditions, has typically undergone lengthy, intensive training and discipline, and has been allowed to teach by one of his own teachers, who has carefully tested his realisation. A psychotherapist who has not had such a training or testing could run the danger of confusing the two roles and become inflated by pretensions to a level of spiritual understanding and authority he may not genuinely process. (Welwood 1983, p. 53)

To this I would add that the internal dynamics of the two relationships are fundamentally different, the one providing a vessel for, if necessary, infantile acting out, while the second requires the presence of two adults at all times for it to work best. In therapy, while it may be appropriate to introduce information about meditation, to discuss experiences that come from its practice and to use techniques that approach similar states of consciousness (see Unconditional Presence later in chapter), finally it is best to leave psychotherapy to psychotherapists and meditation to meditation teachers.

However we can do *something*. While it is unarguably true that a psychotherapy that offers a *facsimile* of spirituality may do more harm than good, it is also true that patients will benefit from the therapist who can recognize a legitimate spiritual yearning, who has contact with the broader archetypal themes in their own life and so can constellate them in another, who has access to their own spiritual resources and who can stand out of the way of the natural and spontaneous spiritual unfolding found in some processes. In all of this the therapist has not become identified with the priest and remains the means by which the patient can discover their own way at whichever level they choose. Of course the fantasy that the therapist is neutral in the process is a nonsense. As we sit we continuously transmit information about ourselves and our beliefs, not to mention our titles with which we broadcast to the world, but if this can be woven into the fabric of discovery, giving the patient an edge against which to define themselves, rather than an example for them to copy, then finally, the presence of the therapist's personality will aid individuation and do no harm. Furthermore, there is a difference between a therapist believing him/herself to be a representative of the tradition with a duty to proselytize and one who quite simply accepts the reality of both the life of the soul *and* the spirit.

SOUL AND SPIRIT

Firstly let me say provocatively that I approach this existentially and so believe that these ideas arise from our attempt to understand and organize experience *rather than that they represent actual objective entities that would exist whether we named them or not.* Though universally found, and so archetypal, these notions are not consistent in their detailed content. People in different places simply believe different things. Perhaps because of this, we find that there are a very large collection of definitions that cluster under the skirts of each word. I have found the definitions gathered by James Hillman (1979) useful and offer them here, not to be accepted as a truth but as both an attempt to articulate psychological reality and as a starting point for further discussion. Hillman defines soul and spirit so.

Soul is a place of dark, dank depths. She is the valley where waters gather and flow making the land fecund and moist. As we move along the valley floor it twists and turns and so it is impossible to gain a clear overview of how things lie before us. Because of this, soul is associated with the complicated and obscure unfolding of the personal, the individual, the particular and the historical. Its concerns include imagination, fantasy, illusion and mirage. Down here is blood and emotion. Soul food, soul land, soul music and soul mates. Jung called this the anima, the feminine soul that also encompasses all these qualities and more besides, and recognized her as that place of otherness in his own depth that when engaged with, paradoxically, enabled him to become more himself. Personal experiences in the world, passionate engagement with the experiences of life, creates soul and soul making is the activity that life excels in. Even places and objects can have soul when in their energies and fabric they retain the record of inhabitation and use. The beautiful patina of a piece of furniture polished for hundreds of years carries all the hands that have loved and cursed it; the intimacy within a much used toy.

Personally I believe it is soul that is being acknowledged and named when the word 'transpersonal' is frequently used. Soul is the animating force within life, creativity, imagination, relationship and also transcendence. All qualities associated with the transpersonal. When we speak of the transpersonal in this way it is not so much about an experience that takes us outside of identification with our personalities but rather an experience that enriches and so broadens. As such it is an ego *expansion*, expanded by soul, but not an ego *dissolution*.

Spirit, on the other hand, is associated with high places, the tops or peaks of mountains. Traditionally this has been the abode of the Gods. Shiva and his Shakti on Kailash, Yahveh on Sinai, Zeus and family on Olympus, to name only the most familiar. Likewise it is to these high places that we resort when we wish to leave the clutter of the world behind us and approach the divine and transcendent. From this aerial seat we too can look out across vast distances where the small and finite things of the world melt into insignificance. Here we are absorbed in the non-personal, and by extension, the abstract, the ideal, the objective and the general. Here we feel cool and there are cold considerations. Every thing is refined. Our personal and individual identities drop away and are of no significance as do also the individual concerns of the world. For this reason Maslow called transpersonal experiences 'peak experiences' and Jung spoke of the spirit as animus, the mind of the masculine that loves logic, reason, fact and abstraction but is also concrete and real. And so we have two clusters of meaning, the first associating spirit with spirituality and the second, extending this, spirit with all that is non-personal and abstract.

From this we can see that psychotherapy, concerned as it is with incarnation into the world and a full sense of self, is a soulful event. Likewise, spiritual practice or discipline, with its concern of dissolving the separate self into the ground of being, is a concern of the spirit. Together they make a whole. The journey into and out of identification with a separate and personal identity. Another way to look at this, not as a journey of a lifetime, but as a continuous and ongoing process, is that each requires the other for its balance and completion at any and every point. In this way we can ask diagnostically whether someone has too little or too much soul or spirit, what side is over balancing and causing the other to be too deeply within the shadow.

THE TRANSPERSONAL AND THE SELF

The transpersonal psychology of Jung places the Self at the pinnacle of realization. For Jung it is the Self, as the image of God within the psyche, that the ego must come into conscious relationship to. It is the Self, who as a divine urge, starts the process of individual life, a process of soul making, and which is finally realized as the sum of all human possibility. It includes the possibility for a single human life to be touched and transformed by something greater than itself. It is the Self that the ego must realize encompasses it and it is the Self, that imbuing life with meaning and purpose, makes suffering bearable and a possible experience of transformation. Experience of the Self is awesome, terrible, delightful, renewing. It is to bathe and be made whole again. It is to die and be reborn. It is the inspiration and goal of all initiation. It is to this Self, projected out, that we pray, and it is in opening to this Self that we are touched by grace. Finally it is union with this Self that we all desire and yearn for as we are captivated by love, for it is in the inner lover, initially reflected in the outer, that we find our final completion. Thus all love is finally love of the Self.

This beautiful myth is rooted in and remains very similar to Judao/Christian belief. It is the love affair between the individual soul and God, an event in which each comes to know the other better through *relationship*.

When we speak of The Transpersonal, here synonymous with the Self, that is known through the ego/Self dialogue, the ongoing homoeostasis between conscious and unconscious sides of the personality, we are to all intents echoing the belief that we may be more fully ourselves by opening to a greater and wiser power. In this light we may speak of The Transpersonal (or the Self), having, perhaps, an overall plan, that is made apparent through dreams, synchronicities and the ordinary events of life. In these its primary activity of myth making is found. Out of the fabric of our small lives The Transpersonal, as archetype of meaning, weaves a cloth of purpose, significance and direction. It creates both an understanding of how we have come to be ourselves and also an imagination of the self we have yet to be. This Transpersonal way, a journey of soul making, carries values that are consistent with Transpersonal qualities. Typically they are thought of as wisdom, light, love and compassion. However, so not to conceive of The Transpersonal, the Self, as having no shadow, its dark side, when it is perceived as a threat to an over rigid ego, is terrible in its revolution, bringing destruction and suffering before renewal. By and large we refer to this vision of the transpersonal as a *noun*, The Transpersonal. It is a divine like object to which we are subject. When it is spoken of and evoked in its own language, the poetry of symbol and metaphor, we may just feel it whisper on our flesh like a light air, for this was its first known form, a wind blowing in the grasses, a spirit in the trees, neuma, breath of the unseen God.

THE TRANSPERSONAL BANDS AND THE TRANSPERSONAL WITNESS

The very personal feeling for the Self, described above, that metamorphosis into the The Transpersonal and the Transpersonal Self, known through the medium of relationship as the divine force in man and nature, is conceived in many ways quite differently by transpersonal psychologists in America. Dr Stanislav Grof, one of the progenitors of Transpersonal Psychology, a pioneer of early research on LSD psycho-therapy, and then later, the use of Holotropic Breath work, has charted many transpersonal experiences. Of all these states Grof says, during a transpersonal experience the

> common denominator ... is the feeling of the individual that his consciousness has expanded beyond the usual ego boundaries and limitations of time and space. (1967, p. 154)

What is important to recognize clearly here is that Grof is talking about transpersonal *experiences* that we may have as an extension of normal consciousness. Here 'trans-personal' is used as an *adjective* describing those experiences that are felt generally as an expansion beyond self, time and space. By referring to the 'transpersonal area of the unconscious' and also speaking of a 'profound transcendental experience of an ecstatic and integrative nature' he seems to suggest that while transpersonal experiences give access to areas of the self previously unknown (unconscious), the final content and outcome of that experience is not just *trans*-personal but *post*- or *supra*-personal. The experience is not only of going beyond the usual limits of consciousness but of individual selfhood finally dissolving. Thus he appears to create a hierarchy of experience in which the transpersonal realm expands from being unusual personal experiences to the highest experience of personal transcendence, a going beyond the personal. No mention here of a Transpersonal Self with which we can connect and be informed by, but rather a more abstract and clinical anatomy of consciousness. Of the highest realm of experience he says,

> The void appears to be emptiness pregnant with form, and the subtle forms of universal mind are experienced as absolutely empty. (1967, p. 205)

and thereby echoes the ultimate Buddhist realization that is not about relating to a place of wisdom so that our individual journey through the world might be clear, but the Eastern ideal of finally dissolving all personal identity back into the formless ground from which it appears to emerge.

Ken Wilber, an active voice in the exploration of transpersonal ideas, like Grof, imagines transpersonal experiences on a continuum between our usual consciousness and a 'state' he calls 'Mind' (Wilber 1975). He suggests a 'spectrum of consciousness' where transpersonal experience is placed at a point just short of a final spiritual realization of our real nature. In these levels of consciousness, the 'transpersonal bands', are found between the 'existential level', which I recognize as simply the state of consciousness most psychologically mature adults exist in, and 'Mind', which is the ground that non-dual consciousness reveals. Wilber says Mind is,

> our 'innermost' consciousness that is identical to the absolute and ultimate reality of the universe. (Wilber 1975, p. 106)

and,

> Mind is what there is and all there is, spaceless and therefore infinite, timeless and therefore eternal, outside of which nothing exists. (p. 106)

And from Mind emerges the transpersonal band,

> where man is not conscious of his identity with the All and yet neither is his identity confined to the boundaries of the individual organism. (p. 108)

The transpersonal band is practically developed by a technique of disidentification with the contents of the ego that in turn is a transpersonal experience in itself. Wilber suggests two levels of mysticism (1975, p. 123). The first he calls *lesser mysticism* that is very closely linked to the idea of the compassionate observer that we looked at when considering Maitri, unconditional friendliness. He says that once we start looking at the previously unconscious patterns that drove us we simultaneously start to be free of them. This step in consciousness he calls a 'supra-personal or transpersonal witness' that is,

> observing the flow of what is, without manipulating it. (1975, p. 121)

As such it is both an immediately accessible and essentially important transpersonal experience *that far outweighs in importance more exotic and sensational experiences*. Here we should note that 'transpersonal' is no longer generalized trans-rational experience but more specifically a perspective derived from the technique of disidentifying with the contents of consciousness while one continues to actively observe them.

Transpersonal witnessing is a *position* of witnessing reality. (Wilber 1975, p. 124, italics mine)

The second stage he calls *true mysticism* which is the experience of the end of dualism, agreeing with Grof, that beyond transpersonal experiences, or a transpersonal witness, exists something greater which is not only a final 'level' but also the real ground on which everything rests. Not a place where one witnesses reality but where one *is* reality. The first retains vestigial subject/object dualism, the second does not. So, in conclusion, we have transpersonal areas of experience and a transpersonal position of consciousness, the witness, both of which lead to the Mind, the ground of being. This is further found in the work of Frances Vaughan.

Vaughan (1986), freely draws upon Wilber's work and adds a much more personal feel to it. She also sees the area of the transpersonal as existing somewhere between the usual identification we all have with our personalities, the ego and the unconscious forces of the shadow, and the 'Mind' of Wilber's conception, which she calls the 'Absolute'. She sees the 'transpersonal self', as a bridge between these two, linking them and providing a means by which the energy of the Absolute may become manifest in the personal. She says,

The transpersonal self thus serves as a bridge between existential self-consciousness and transcendental unitary consciousness where no separate self-sense remains. (Vaughan 1986, p. 44)

The transpersonal self does have specific qualities.

As limitless transcendent being, it partakes of infinite wisdom and compassion, understanding, allowing, and forgiving all things, without exception and without reservation. As manifestation of Absolute spirit, it is capable of unconditional love. (p. 42)

Yet strangely this experience, which has drawn the most extreme descriptions of bliss, love and light, is also said to be 'nothing special'. To bring this state into being, 'to awaken to the Self', it is necessary to disidentify with the contents of one's personality and become their observer. This is not to repress emotion and so loose it, but rather to disidentify with it while remaining conscious of its presence. Vaughan says the:

expanded sense of self that results from practising disidentification is appropriately considered transpersonal, rather than impersonal, since it is manifested in and through the personal, and yet transcends it. (p. 44)

This is important because it leads into practices of Focusing and mindfulness that we will explore later. Here again is the notion of Maitri, the compassionate observer linked with the transpersonal witness, which as a step of self-reflective consciousness, is a step so profoundly important that it creates the 'transpersonal self', a self that is connected to the Absolute, and which enables the personal self finally to dissolve into its original pure self-less nature. From small self to transpersonal self to no-self.

John Welwood (1977) agrees with a transpersonal level of consciousness that is wider than the confines of rational thought, that is brought into being by the practice of mindfulness or witnessing, and that gives access to feelings of wisdom, bliss, compassion and equanimity. This transpersonal sphere, or experience, is a:

> transitional phase between totally open, unconditional awareness and a separate self-sense. (Welwood 1977, p. 164)

He then adds new material when he suggests, that if looked at developmentally, it is from this absolute, non-personal state, that the rudimentary sense of self begins to emerge and that this non-personal state can be felt, when paying very close attention, as background life, the 'sheer vividness of being-here'. An energy that underlies and surrounds the levels of personal and ego focused experience. This is an alternative explanation to the more usual theories of developmental psychology because, while quite similar in its notion of an undivided consciousness that divides into object relations, unlike them, it starts from the radically different premise that views this division as a kind of delusionary imagination that obscures the true nature of consciousness, that is, its ultimate indivisibility. Only Jung comes close to this with his notion of a Self and individuating ego whose goal is finally to return consciously back to the Self. Finally, Welwood, with Wilber and Vaughan, understands the ultimate realization as the experience of:

> pure, immediate presence before it becomes differentiated into form and subject duality. (Welwood 1977, p. 166)

Using Buddhist language he describes this open ground as : 'primordial awareness', 'original mind' and 'no-mind'.

And so we have two quite different ideas that revolve around the understanding of the Self or The Transpersonal or the transpersonal self. Essentially the first understanding places the Self, (and The Transpersonal), as the central force and emphasizes a relationship out of which meaning evolves and this alleviates suffering. The second understanding places a transpersonal self as a state of consciousness, in the penultimate place to spiritual illumination, yet not identified with the contents that we recognize as ego. It becomes a position of observation that initiates and facilitates the necessary abilities to bring about spiritual realization that is identified by entering non–dual consciousness and it is experience of this that ends suffering. Wilber here is keen not to diminish the notion of the transpersonal while remaining adamant on its relative position. He says,

> This is not to denigrate the position of the transpersonal self or witness, for not only can it be highly therapeutic in itself, but it can frequently act as a type of springboard to Mind. Never the less it is not to be confused with Mind itself. (1975, p. 124)

While the second position often includes ideas of archetypes and the collective unconscious, all derived from the Jungian theories of the first, essentially it is not rooted in European thought but that of the East, particularly, though not exclusively, Buddhism. Because of this the notions of the compassionate observer, unconditional friendliness and the transpersonal witness all link to the most basic yet profound meditation technique, called in the Buddhist tradition, mindfulness, that in many traditions acts as the foundation of practice. However, for transpersonal psycho-therapists, it is important to realize that both areas of experience are present and powerful within the individual. Paradoxically, we can and do simultaneously experi-ence our lives as meaningful (or meaningless), and also derive a sense of meaningfulness from involving ourselves in practices that are designed to question and dissolve the very Self that yearns for and creates meaning. A yearning to dissolve the individual identity at both individual and collective levels, ego and archetype, small *and* large self. In my experience the balance of these two fundamental myths changes over the course of a lifetime. In the earlier years, while we are making a place in the world, the first is strongest because it favours individual identity, while later, once the rewards of this fade, the second appears like water in a desert. Of course this is not true for all, but for some, at some point, acceptance of a world without meaning, not meaningless but meaning free, may be a relief.

BRIDGING THE WORLDS IN THREE STEPS

In this next section, following Welwood's ideas closely, we will see how a bridge may be made between psychotherapy and meditation/contemplation, and how, though the two are quite different and serve different ends, the former may lead into the latter. Here we borrow a basic assumption from Buddhism, that the diagnosis and healing it offers for the cause of suffering is among the most profound and all pervasive. It observes that ultimately suffering is caused by attachment to and identification with a separate self in dual consciousness, here called primary dualism, and that this suffering will cease when the separate self recognizes its non-dual nature and ends its primary alienation. Put simply, complete healing is nirvana. This view we will explore as we go along.

   What follows is a description of three levels of consciousness (although the last may not strictly be called a level but more accurately 'the ground'), and how each impinges on the practice of psychotherapy. But firstly a word on language. In writing this the word consciousness has developed a number of different and complex meanings. In the first I use it as a synonym for concepts about the fundamental 'stuff' of reality, supra-consciousness, in Sanskrit this is 'citta', which translates as 'mind', in the sense of Buddha or enlightened mind, the Mind Wilber refers to above. It is this consciousness that *appears* to divide when becoming identified with the ego. In the second, more usual meaning, I have used the word 'conscious' as an equivalent to 'being aware' and so have said 'selfconscious' or 'being conscious' or the opposite, 'unconscious'. Here con-sciousness refers to the ego's ability to be self reflective and exercise the very divided consciousness that the first category defines. Next comes the technical psychother-apeutic usage of the 'conscious self', the ego and the field it exists in, and those repressed or undiscovered aspects of the self, 'the unconscious' or shadow. And finally, closely related, I have seized with pleasure on the word 'presence', a position of relaxed attention found in mindfulness, but more of this later!

1. PREREFLECTIVE IDENTIFICATION, BEING ASLEEP

As we have seen earlier, the consciousness of the neonate slowly forms islands of personal experience that finally coalesce to form a separate ego. These islands of experience are made from the interactions between the infant and her physical and emotional environment, the world of her mother. Each interaction serves to create and establish contents of consciousness that progressively become identified as 'myself'. This identification of a self is automatic, an archetypal disposition, and requires no reflection. As we have also discovered this self gradually effects, through the process of individuation, a series of separations, that finally create a conscious independent identity that is alone and therefore capable of relationship. In practice this appears as the endless communications within the primary carer and baby relationship that later broaden to include others.

In this ego unfolding we virtually see the reversed process of liberation from dual consciousness. Here undivided consciousness appears to begin division and form a separate identity firstly in the moment and then through the apparent continuum of time and space (Donaldson 1992). With each object relation, incarnation becomes more solid as qualities and attributes that I imagine to be myself, self-representations, build and multiply. In the language of myth, this devolution of consciousness is symbolized as the moment in which the Hindu god Shiva and his consort, Shakti, step apart from their mutual embrace and regard each other. In this act of self awareness the world is born. This idea is perhaps also to be found in our own creation myth where likewise an act of self consciousness causes the first couple to separate from the original perfect state of the garden. For the child, loss of her Edenic oneness happens slowly and it is only as she approaches and enters adolescence that the mirror of self reflection is handed over by others to her so that she may hold it herself. This is the point where self reflection, the facility to be self aware, to stand at a distance and observe objectively, to divide ourselves and the world we experience, evolves.

Paradoxically, it is the work of psychotherapy to facilitate this process when it becomes stalled. Though this is in effect aiding the cementing of consciousness to the small sphere of ego, of colluding with the illusion that we are the contents of our consciousness rather than the consciousness itself, this is absolutely necessary because unless we can do this first then all else is likely to fail. It is a fact that an ego that is too fragile, that is vulnerable to the inundations of its repressed shadow contents, will not be able to withstand the tensions of willingly surrendering itself. Only a healthy ego, grounded in the instinctual, can make the journey of transmutation. Thus in therapy we first and foremost assist in the development of a self and then self awareness. Those who come with a weak or fractured identity we help find a strong individuality and those who unconsciously dwell in a state of unreflective alienation from themselves we help find the strength to be self reflective.

Lastly, although I have shown here how the state of prereflective identification fully wakes into divided consciousness, self awareness, at adolescence, it would be a mistake to imagine that this awareness continuously persists. A cursory glance at the world will show that for most of us, continuing in a state of consciousness that is largely unself-reflective is the norm. While we retain the ability to look upon ourselves as an object, dispassionately, much of the time this is allowed to slip beneath the waves of awareness. In its place we continue to allow ourselves to be defined by our own unconscious complexes, those around us and the forces in the world we inhabit. Many of these influences are not benign; if we are unaware of where we really stand and who we actually are, we may be swept along and join acts of collective fear that profoundly harm those involved. As therapists, who represent the values of awareness, we must especially try not to go to sleep but remain awake to the responsibility of consciousness.

2. REFLECTIVE ATTENTION, WAKING

This level is made up of two steps, the latter of which represents a diminishing separation between the observer and the observed that we described emerging above.

Conceptual reflection

At the birth of this ability we become able to step back from ourselves and become the object of our own awareness. We become self aware. As well as having emotions and feelings, we can also reflectively think about them from a distance and in so doing take the first rudimentary step of disidentification. Yet by this means we repeatedly divide the field of consciousness into a series of me/not me experiences, each with an attached value, that appear to make consciousness, now identified with the ego, stand outside as an observer. The subject/object divide, that starts at birth or perhaps earlier, may be called 'primary dualism': the world of observer and observed which is created and strengthened by the ego's ability to distinguish itself from other. This is important. Although divided consciousness is the generator of ego (and the associated suffering), it is also a means to start a process of self-reflection that may finally lead to a return to non-dual consciousness. Welwood quotes the Buddha on this. Divided consciousness is like using a thorn to remove a thorn.

In psychotherapy we hone this ability to a finer point. We take the raw material of feelings, emotions and fantasy and reflect upon their patterns, significance and meaning, using the tools of image, concepts and language. Our therapeutic means are talking and thinking about feeling and emotion. All psychotherapy essentially complies with this generalization. It matters not whether the work is of short or long duration, concerned with simply altering behaviour or the far greater achievement of individuation; in all cases understanding is achieved by reflection that articulates the *prima marteria*, the basic stuff, of the self. Even when, as in the techniques of transpersonal psychotherapy and others, we utilize the imagination and the image making facilities of the psyche, or shift the attention from *content* to *process*, finally, when we consider where we have come to, we speak ideas. Furthermore these ideas, conceptual structures that give access to the mystery of ourselves, may be entirely personal or part of a larger collective belief. Thus all maps, theories, beliefs and dogmas, whether they be political, religious or psychological, are attempts to understand experience in more coherent ways. This includes this whole book on transpersonal psychology.

For this divided consciousness there is an expensive price to pay. To understand this we need to first return to our European perception of the wound. Conventional Western psychotherapeutic understanding sees suffering as an integral part of being human, from which there is no escape. Psychopathology is the result of unconscious attempts to alleviate this natural pain by defence mechanisms that have become out of date and as detrimental as they are helpful. Typically they trap us in ways of being and feeling that are no longer appropriate for the stage of life we are at (see Chapter 4 'The Wound'). Psychotherapy seeks to help us face our deep fears and consciously feel them rather than resort to unconscious defences. The 'unhealthy suffering' of neurosis is exchanged for the healthy suffering of a psychologically mature adult. Of course this is an ideal picture and the reality is that we continue to find ways to deny and accept suffering. When it is particularly bad nature helps us and we tend to regress to earlier patterns of coping until we are stronger again (the retreat under the womb-like duvet, the bearable unconsciousness of a binge). Each takes us back into the Great Mother until, if we are able, we can later emerge, strong enough to go on. The 'break down to break through' (McCormick 1998). However, the goal remains the ability to hold our pain consciously and this is principally achieved by the enormously valuable developmental stage of stepping away from oneself and observing oneself objectively. This is what we mean when we say we are conscious.

Yet this is at best a half truth. It does not go deep enough. We are not in two parts, observer and observed, subject and object, and the very skill that psychotherapy values so highly, from the perspective of Asianic psychology, particularly Buddhism and Advaita Vedanta, is also the very thing that creates a more fundamental and all pervasive suffering that we in the West, as yet, have little collective understanding of (Engler 1984). In Tibetan Buddhism there exists a terrifying iconographic image that portrays all the various expressions of life held within the grip of Yama, Lord of Death. At the centre of life is shown a pig, snake and rooster pursuing each other in an eternal chase. These three creatures represent attachment, aversion and delusion respectively and symbolize the mental states that keep us endlessly within the repetitive patterns of suffering. Attachment to that which makes me feel secure, aversion to that which makes me feel afraid and the delusion that by achieving the first I may avoid the second. In this simplest of ways Buddhist psychology says that it is not just not getting enough of the right type of parenting that causes pain but that suffering stems from being a human ignorant of our true, undivided, nature. This deeper understanding sees the divided consciousness, that the emergence and development of a separate sense of self achieves, as the *ultimate cause* of suffering. Once we have such a self identity we become absolutely compelled to maintain it. All experiences that threaten it are defended against, while all experiences that strengthen it are sought after. This simple truth is absolutely profound, and operates at all levels, personal and collective. If we look deeply, it is unlikely that any of us will be able to find a single waking moment or instance when this was not and is not in operation. This state of continuous self-defence, the suffering of desiring or rejecting experience, occurs in a transitory world, that makes achievement of any stable, unchanging state impossible, so all and every attempt to reject or hold experience, to establish an unchanging self that is never threatened, is bound to fail. Caught in the impossible task of identifying with an identity that is perpetually in a state of transition we can only suffer.

Naturally this bleak perception is not normally conscious. Part of the healthy ego (from a Western perspective) is its ability to defend itself from exactly such fears of disintegration. Furthermore, much of our Western culture may be seen as a massive and sophisticated defence against such a view. Virtually everywhere I look I receive invitations to identify with someone, some group or some thing (often a product), and so reinforce my identity. I am this but not that. Yet at the end of all of this, the achievement of more identity brings no release, and often the most sane come to therapy requesting an answer to this existential pain. If we accept that the development of a self and the divided consciousness necessary to develop this are also, most fundamentally, the cause of a deeper suffering then we must find a way in therapy that answers this.

Phenomenological reflection

While divided consciousness is the necessary initial step on the path of self awareness it is also the cause of suffering. What is needed is a means to begin to close the distance between the observer and the observed. Phenomenological reflection, being aware of the movement and shifts in the energy of consciousness as it appears in the thoughts, emotions and sensations of the body, is a means to effect this. Welwood says that by using phenomenological reflection, the concepts, or ideas, about where we are and how we feel, are 'experience-near'. By this he means that we speak directly from the immediacy of our experience as it happens in the very moment of answering a question or making a statement. How do I feel?, I pause, feel in, and slowly answer directly from the experience of the moment. Subject and object remain but the reflective distance is marginally closed.

There are at least several technical methods that I know of that fulfil the task of beginning to diminish the gap between experience, raw and simple, and reflective observation, *without simply regressing back into prereflective consciousness*. Of these the techniques of Spot Imaging, developed by Barbara Somers and Ian Gordon Brown, and particularly Focusing, developed by Eugene Gendlin are central (see final chapter for technical details). Both techniques are able to help patients keep very close to the emotional and imaginal material of their primary process, the raw phenomena of experience. While Spot Imaging is particularly useful for contacting past experiences, or rather the *memories* of past experience, being in some ways midpoint between the techniques of Freud's free association and Jung's circumabulation of an image, Focusing deals more directly with what is in the present. However, if we imagine phenomenological reflection, with these two as its principle tools, as a bridge between the reflective methods of psychotherapy and the naked presence of contemplation, (final section), then Spot Imaging always leads back into reflection while Focusing may lead either to reflection or, the opposite direction, into presence. Because of this, here I am going to concentrate on Focusing alone.

Psychotherapy that uses Focusing, or other similar techniques, is not just interested in the content of the patient's experience alone, the story, but is also concerned with the process. To enter into this level of the work it is necessary to shift the attention away from *what* is said towards *how* it is said. In practice this is achieved by putting aside conceptual understanding of ourselves and in its place we focus upon direct experience. Simple observation is central and this supplies its own explanations. When asked how we are, most of us will answer from an already established 'history of myself' that has previously arrived at some sort of conclusion. We might say, (probably causing some surprise!), 'I am having a bad day with my fears about being swamped and it is bringing up all my mother stuff'. Here I not only have my emotion, 'swamped', but also an analysis of it, 'bringing up', and its aetiology, 'mother'. While this may be a significant reflective achievement it also takes me away from the immediacy of the moment, my body and my present feeling. In Focusing we resist this impulse to answer from the 'history', but rather focus upon what Gendlin calls a 'felt sense' that is a combination of both feelings, supplied by consciousness of our emotional self and physical sensation, supplied by consciousness of our body (Gendlin 1978). The felt sense is slow and takes time to be noticed. Initially it may be ill defined or indistinct. However by focusing upon it, as both a sensation and a feeling simultaneously, either a word, phrase or image may spontaneously emerge from the felt sense that accurately reflects it. When this occurs we may then experience a 'felt shift', which is again, a spontaneous shift in body/feeling/understanding that can come from the attentive staying with the energy of our present state. It is here that the choice of which side of the bridge to go to occurs. Usually, because psychotherapy is a dialogue between two people to establish an understanding of the self, the felt shift will be used to gain very precise and powerful insight into the material the patient has presented. However, Focusing may also be used as a meditative tool where one is not interested in the result but simply the movement of energy as it manifests from one form (sensation, emotion, or thought), to the next. To achieve this Welwood has developed the technique of Focusing by drawing on his understanding of meditation and calls this revised method 'Unconditional Presence'. (Welwood 1990, 1997). In this method the transpersonal witness, the position of disidentified, desireless and compassionate observation becomes central and so closely approximates the meditational practice of mindfulness that closes the subject/object divide further. We will come to this shortly.

3. NAKED PRESENCE, AWAKE

Here we move from psychotherapeutic technique to spiritual practice and the essential point in this next step of reducing the subject/object divide is that we no longer speak of reflection but witnessing. The difference being that reflection suggests involvement or dialogue while witnessing is a position of neutrality that does not enter into identification with that witnessed. Whereas before, in both conceptual and phenomenological reflection, the goal was a greater understanding of our feelings and our journey through life, here the goal is simply to observe whatever is without any intention to change it. This is sometimes called 'bare attention'. (Wilber, Engler and Brown 1986; Epstein 1995). This too proceeds by stages. Here it is simplified into three steps, the first two being the final phase of awakening, brought about by mindfulness, and the last, the awake state itself.

Mindfulness

Mindful witnessing, or more simply, mindfulness, is the quintessential Buddhist meditation method that further closes the gap between pure experience and the reflection of divided consciousness. To be mindful is to be aware in the present of exactly what is happening around us and within us. This apparently easy task is immediately found to be extremely difficult as anyone who has tried it knows. What we find is that within moments, distracting thoughts, feelings and fantasies have swept us away and often, very much later, we suddenly remember that we are meant to be present but have actually been elsewhere. We find that we are not masters of our own minds. Yet it is only by being mindful that we can come to observe our own nature and so know who we are. Mindfulness shows us our reality and cuts through the fantasies about who we would like to imagine ourselves to be. The self-concepts, the internal representations of ourselves to ourselves, are found to be a conglomeration of illusions. In this sense it is not dissimilar at first from the discovery of the shadow and can be very painful. However this is merely the first step and continued practice leads into profound meditative and contemplative states that have been charted very carefully by those who have developed them and have guided others.

Concentration, developing a calm state

Jack Kornfield, meditation teacher and transpersonal psychotherapist, gives precise instructions, about beginning the practice of mindfulness from within the Buddhist Insight tradition, that are invaluable for those who are intending to start practice (Kornfield 1993a). However there are small differences between various methods* and Welwood offers one that is primarily influenced by Tibetan Buddhist Mahamudra and Dzogchen teachings (Norbu 1984, 1986, 1989). Essentially, in all methods, it is first necessary to create an awareness of separation from the constant chatter of subliminal fantasies, emotions and thoughts, the stuff of complexes, that make up the ego identity. This is achieved by sitting in an upright position, straight but not tense, and continuously fixing one's concentration upon an object. This may be a candle, an

---

* Here I have emphasized the basic similarities between the Vipassana/Insight tradition and Dzogchen for the sake of the argument. However, more technically there also exist important differences between these two paths and indeed other Buddhist paths as well. Please see: Goldstein. J. (Summer, 1999), 'How Amazing!', *Tricycle, The Buddhist Review*, p. 30 and Norbu, N. (1984), *Dzogchen and Zen*, published by Zhang Zhung Editions, Oakland, California. Without diminishing the differences it seems to me that at the initial stages of practice they are a little academic and rather than get caught up in them it is better just to start.

image, a letter (for instance an A), or one's own breath or sensations. (The breath, sensations or the A are without any cultural or religious associations.) The purpose of this is to achieve an unwavering concentration that is not distracted by thoughts and feelings, leaving the practitioner in a tranquil thought-free state. By repeatedly bringing our attention back to the object of concentration we slowly shift our identity from being synonymous with the content of our thoughts and emotions to a state of awareness that while alert is quiet and not driven by the contents of consciousness. Initially it is very simple to momentarily become aware of ourselves but it is extremely difficult to continue and most of us when we first try are astounded at the level of inner 'noise' that our minds continually make. Try sitting now for sixty seconds without thinking and you will immediately understand. However with practice, by kindly and patiently refocusing the attention on the object of concentration, over and over and over again, maybe a hundred thousand times, we will achieve a deep, blissful state of calm.

However, Kornfield warns us that the state of blissful fixation, or samadhi, that concentration develops is only an expansion of the self, not its final dissolution, and as such, though it is the necessary tool to reach non-dual consciousness, it is important not to mistake it for the final liberation.

> They [blissful absorption states] are not the goal of spiritual life. In the end, spiritual life is not a process of seeking or gaining some extraordinary condition or special powers. In fact, such seeking can take us away from ourselves. If we are not careful, we can easily find that great failures of our modern society, its ambition, materialism, and individual isolation, repeated in our spiritual life. (Kornfield 1993a, p. 11)

To avoid this it is necessary to continue further.

Insight

Concentration and the calm state it engenders is none the less a product of desire, if only the desire to achieve and maintain it. If we are to take the final step between reflection and presence, divided to non-dual consciousness, we must have a means that is ultimately without any intention. We begin this when the focus of concentration becomes the mind itself, a presence of awareness where awareness becomes self-aware. This is the emergence of the transpersonal witness earlier referred to. The mindful witness that allows us to step back from experience without reaction or identification is achieved by relaxing the fixation upon the object of concentration and so allow the blocked thoughts to begin to arise again. However in this instant, instead of becoming identified with them, as before, one observes them coming into the thought-free space, continuing and disappearing. Here we have moved from being identified with the contents of consciousness to a broader consciousness that observes thoughts, feelings and sensations, as they appear from an empty ground, continue and then dissolve. Here common analogues are of watching from the bank a fish rising to the surface of the water, making a ripple and then going, or of gazing at an empty sky (consciousness) and seeing the clouds (contents of consciousness) move across it. In this way we continue until gradually we are capable of maintaining this level of awareness not only during formal meditation sittings but also while rising and walking and then all the more complicated actions of our lives.

Transreflective presence, the self-perfected state

This is the final stage where calm and insight join, and one moves from meditation, an intentional act, to contemplation, an effortless continuation within non-dual consciousness. This is called self-perfected, not because there is any notion of a self to perfect or a self that has become perfect, but simply because any movement in the mind stream instantly is known to be indivisible from the empty ground it rises from without any need for the practitioner to do anything. It does itself. Totally relaxed. This is the final sublime realization that Grof describes above where emptiness and form are one. This state, impossible to conceptually understand, for ever a secret to those of us who have not known it, is called the Great Perfection (Tib. *Dzogchen*) and represents the ultimate healing. One who has entered it fully is called a Buddha, an awakened one, who rests in naked presence (Tib. *rigpa*), a natural wakefulness or clarity that is free from dualistic perceptions or attachments.

Descriptions of this state are beautiful (if ultimately impossible to understand until experienced). Here I quote from Welwood who in turn draws from masters; the first concerns the fundamental unity of all things:

> The ultimate practice here is learning to remain fully present and awake in the middle of whatever thoughts, feelings, perceptions, or sensations are occurring and to recognise them ... as an ornamental display of the empty, luminous essence of awareness. Like waves on the sea, thoughts are not separate from awareness. They are the radiant clarity of awareness in motion. In remaining awake in the middle of thoughts ... recognising them as the luminous energy of awareness ... the practitioner maintains presence and can rest within their movement. (Welwood 1996, p. 124)

The point is that there is nothing to do:

> Here no antidote need be applied: no conceptual understanding, no reflection, no stepping back, no detachment, no witnessing. When one is totally present in the thought, in the emotion, in the disturbance, it relaxes itself, becoming open and transparent to the larger ground of awareness. The wave subsides back into the ocean. The cloud dissolves into the sky. The snake naturally uncoils. These are metaphors that say: It self-liberates. (1996, p. 125)

And finally should we wonder whether this will leave us fit to function in the market place:

> Nor is the relative duality of self and other in daily life a problem when one is not trapped in divided consciousness. One can adopt the conventional perspective of duality and drop it when it is not necessary. Then the interplay of self and other becomes a humorous dance, an energetic exchange, an ornament rather than a hindrance. (1996, p. 125)

While mindfulness is characterized by absence of intent, none the less dwelling in this awareness may spontaneously effect emotional structures in the mindstream. (In Buddhism the teaching is that to stay in the state of non-dual awareness is the means to ultimately purify all karmas; that a moment of rigpa is more powerful than a great deal of purification.) Welwood's psychotherapeutic method that draws on this practice and its unintentional healing is called Unconditional Presence.

UNCONDITIONAL PRESENCE AS A THERAPEUTIC TECHNIQUE

When I entered analysis I was surprised to find my analyst emotionally reacting to elements of the material I presented. At times he would become plainly agitated and angry. I quickly rationalized this to myself as *my* fault, it was my inability to feel properly that evoked this response. Now I know other. My pathology was actually revealed in the speed and ease of my willingness to make myself wrong to protect a relationship from which I needed love. In fact the more spacious acceptance of what I had found in my own shadow, during painful and prolonged purification practices, was more helpful. Becoming emotionally involved in wanting or rejecting parts of ourselves is ultimately unhelpful as it merely perpetuates the stance of an ego trying to convince itself of its invulnerable existence. The ability to accept what I found could have, in the hands of a wiser therapist, become the foundation of unconditional presence,

> the capacity to meet experience fully and directly, without filtering it through any conceptual or strategic agenda. (Welwood 1996, p. 119)

However it is not only therapists with their own emotional agendas that further alienate patients from themselves. In Focusing, with the best intent, when used in the service of the individual self, there is a desire to follow through to a resolution, to make things 'better'. Thus there is a bias towards *doing* that maintains the dualism of one who observes and that observed. Though this is better than conceptual reflection alone, this is still a subtle spiritual materialism because it feeds the desire for something other. This desire for change or improvement can disturb the deeper letting go that is necessary for moving from 'the realm of personality to the realm of being'. To facilitate this release it is necessary to move the focus from the desired goals of change to '*how-we-are-with-experience*' (Welwood 1996, p. 119), that is to broaden the focus so we are present with our awareness rather than the content of that awareness as mentioned above.

Welwood suggests that as therapists, the essential quality we can develop in ourselves and our patients is unconditional presence because it is the *most* powerful transmuting power there is. In therapy unconditional presence operates in those small moments when we come into direct, intimate contact with our felt experience. Its quality is *non-doing*, not inactivity, but rather, 'non-reactive and non-controlling', yet an active engagement with what is happening at each moment. It is mindful. To arrive at this there are four stages, the first three are very similar to Focusing while the fourth extends the method. Here I will paraphrase Welwood's own explanation.

1. *Enquire* willingly and openly into what is our felt experience. This avoids the immediate and automatic response that avoids a deeper reflection.
2. *Acknowledge* what our felt experience is. As therapist we may suggest, 'Notice what

it is like right *now* just to acknowledge what you are feeling'. And the answer might be after checking the felt sense, 'Yes, I feel angry here, and sad, and vulnerable'. This is to feel it in the body, to stay with the feeling, to name it, and to cut through the impulse to identify or act on it. This bare acknowledgement moves us from a passive to an active stance and creates immediately more freedom.

3. *Allowing* the experience to be there. Not acting it out, not identifying with it, (I am this feeling), not resisting it, (I am not this feeling). Rather, giving the experience time and space, holding it in awareness and softening around it. Sometimes emotions are very painful and create the feeling that we are going to be overwhelmed. To avoid this we harden around the experience and impose judgements that say it is bad or wrong to feel like this. If this happens, by breathing into the emotion, allowing it to expand fully while remaining aware of it releases the pressure of the resistance. This takes practice.

4. *Opening* fully to the experience. This is to be present with our experience, with emotions, without 'judging, explaining or manipulating'. It is simply maintaining a mindful awareness of their presence. What is important here is not the feelings themselves but rather *the act of opening to them*. The movement from identification to witnessing. Feeling something does not create wisdom but opening to it does. When our focus shifts from feelings as the source of pleasure or pain to a state of presence, we move from the personal sphere to the transpersonal. We move from being at war with our experience and the painful structures of self and other begin to break down. Unconditional friendliness arises from this shift. Awareness and loving kindness are the qualities that we deeply yearn for in all our relationships, parents, teachers and partners; here we begin to provide them for ourselves. Welwood says of this final acceptance:

To be unconditionally present with our experience is the simplest thing we could possibly do. It means being present to what is, facing it as it is, without relying on any view or concept about it. What could be simpler than that? And yet, what could be more difficult? (Welwood 1990).

HORIZONTAL AND VERTICAL SHIFTS IN PRACTICE

In practice this may be used repeatedly throughout a process of therapy and introduces into the therapy, with a minimum of therapist intrusion, an element that is truly transpersonal in that in the moment of unconditional presence we have entered into a relationship with ourselves that is no longer primarily involved in the maintenance of the ego project. When we work at either of the levels of conceptual or phenomenological reflection nearly all shifts will be horizontal because they are 'content mutations' that move from one emotion to the next. 'I felt angry but now I feel sad and this feels better, more real'. This shift is entirely at the level of the personality. However, when we can rest in unconditional presence, we effect vertical shifts which are a movement from the personality to a clarity of being. This can only occur when we drop the observer/observed position and stay within the energetic experience itself without becoming identified with it.

For my part I would add that unconditional presence may also effect spontaneous changes, horizontal and vertical felt shifts, when the patient is not actively engaged as the above technique demands. Obviously many of our patients are not at a place where this sort of technique can be used because it takes a certain amount of therapist–patient cooperation for it even to be tried. In circumstances where the patient has not given this degree of permission to work, where perhaps there is a great deal of unconscious acting out, the therapist can none the less maintain unconditional presence in his or her self during each session (or at least some part of each). In practice this will mean being mindfully present with both the material being presented and one's own inner responses. Here all desire to facilitate change, to make assessments, to prefer one experience over another, is exchanged for the ability to rest in one's transpersonal witness, unconditionally present. When this occurs I have noticed that something of it is quite automatically and unconsciously registered by the patient who then may, without knowing how or why, feel a little more spacious and connected in themselves.

Lastly it remains important to remember that psychotherapy needs all its levels, conceptual and phenomenological reflection and contemplative unconditional presence. The contemplative approach to therapy being more concerned with the presence of awareness than with problem resolution is contra-indicated for those needing a more robust ego; conceptual reflection and Focusing are better for this. Making this differentiation is important. Psychotherapy always starts and finishes with a return to the reflective level of dialogue where it is helpful to consider experiences, including the vertical shifts, because it integrates them into daily life. In meditation and contemplation, while this may achieve deeper, more prolonged experiences of undivided consciousness, as Jack Kornfield has described so well (1993b), it is easier to fail to integrate them. We all know of the great meditator who cannot have a relationship and does not know how to wash dishes. What is important is to get the balance right, soul and spirit in harmony.

Psychotherapeutically, mindfulness represents a very sophisticated tool which, if this argument is accepted, may finally bring an end to the most profound levels of human suffering. While using Focusing in its developed form we become mindful momentarily and approach a place in our technique where being with experience, without the need for interpretation or meaning, has a place. Practising mindfulness enables the therapist to experience nakedly (and not emotionally react) and this enables the patient to do the same. The patient's possible decision to pursue this experience and build upon it with formal meditation practice is the place where psychotherapy and spiritual practice begin to separate and as I have suggested, I believe psychotherapists are best if they do not confuse themselves with meditation masters.

CONCLUSION

This chapter has many subjects missing that one might rightfully expect in a chapter on transpersonal psychology and spirituality. However I have tried to stay firstly close to my own experience (in as far as I am able), and also present something that is simple, profound and I hope functionally beautiful. I believe that the wedding of psychotherapeutic practice and 'spiritual' development by the bridge of Focusing/mindfulness is one of the most important conceptual and practical tools to become available at this present moment. It takes the very old wisdom from the Asianic traditions, born of three thousand years' experience, and combines it with the very young but precociously bright insights of Western psychotherapy. Together, both traditions, share the compassionate concern to address and end human suffering, the pain that we all feel at different points in our own lives and when we view the pain of others. This suffering may initially and provisionally be relieved by developing a good enough personal identity that can find a place in the world that will satisfy its deep archetypal longing. However this respite is temporary and a more complete and lasting answer, I believe, may be found by addressing the psychological structures that involve us in the continuous tail-chasing of the pig, snake and rooster, attachment, aversion and delusion. A struggle that is at base about clinging onto the very same self that it is first necessary to establish in a healthy way. Abraham Maslow, a founding Father of transpersonal psychology, says on this:

> The goal of identity . . . seems to be simultaneously an end-goal and also a transitional goal, a rite of passage, a step along the path to transcendence of identity. Put the other way, if our goal is the Eastern one . . . then it looks as if the best path to this goal, for most people, is via achieving identity, a strong real self. (Maslow 1968, p. 114)

However, it is also important to remember that life seems to move along spirals, and it is a balance of soul *and* spirit, not first soul and *then* spirit, as if soul is something that can be completed. Kornfield, with his powerful background as a meditation teacher, believes that meditation alone does not provide all the answers, that we can be very mindful of our breath but totally unconscious of our emotions. When the spirit is strong but the soul weak then he recommends psychotherapy. At the end of the day we may need both.

> If we can't love well and give meaningful work to the earth, then what is spiritual practice for? Meditation can help in these areas. But if, after sitting for a while, you discover that you still have some work to do, find a good therapist or some other way to address these issues. (Kornfield 1993b, p. 68)

Finally it is not about the form of therapy or meditation but what happens within them, Kornfield again:

> Does this mean we should trade meditation for psychotherapy? Not at all. Therapy isn't the solution either. Consciousness is! (Kornfield 1993b, p. 68)

As for what the notion of 'transpersonal' stands for, ultimately it probably is not very important. We have seen several different meanings and surely there are more. What is important is that whatever our path or journey, that we move from just talking and thinking about it to *experiencing* it. Here experiencing does not mean having emotions about the belief structures that comfort, confirm and define our sense of identity, the spiritual materialism I quote Trungpa Rimpoche mentioned earlier. Rather it is direct experience of stepping out of identification with the contents of consciousness (which includes all of this here plus everything that has ever been thought, felt and said about spirituality), and entering firstly the conscious position of the transpersonal witness, and then the state of 'self liberation' where all dualism ends. Naked presence. To what extent this is possible is still unknown in the west (how many enlightened Westerners do we know!). Yet even the early stages reveal simple benefits, expanding our consciousness into insightful calm while connected to the earth and the heart. As we breathe mindfully in and out, the complex and often painful stories of our lives lose their compulsive quality. Wounds become transparent and less significant, forgiveness and generosity are more easily found. Anger and fear are less necessary. And so we breathe.

The Zen Master Shunryu Suzki says it best:

What we call 'I' is just a swinging door which moves when we inhale and when we exhale. It just moves; that is all.

REFERENCES

Donaldson, M. (1992). *Human Minds*. London: Penguin.

Engler, J. (1984). 'Therapeutic Aims in Psychotherapy and Meditation: Developmental Stages in the Representations of the Self', *Journal of Transpersonal Psychotherapy*, **16**(1), p. 25.

Epstein, M. (1995). *Thoughts Without a Thinker*. New York: Basic Books.

Freud, S. (1927, first published 1961). *The Future of an Illusion*, Standard edition, vol. 21. London: Hogarth Press.

Freud, S. (1930, first published 1961). *Civilization and its Discontents*. Standard edition, vol. 21. London: Hogarth Press.

Gendlin, E. (1978) *Focusing*. Everest House.

Grof, S. (1967). *Realms of the Human Unconscious*. New York: Dutton.

Guggenbuhl-Craig, A. (1971). *Power in the Helping Professions*. New York: Spring Publications.

Hillman, J. (1979). 'Peaks and Vales'. In C. Giles (ed.) *Puer Papers*. Dallas, Texas: Spring Publications.

Jung, C. G. (1956). *Symbols of Transformation*, vol. 5 of *Collected Works*. London: Routledge and Kegan Paul.

Jung, C. G. (1958). *Psychology of Religion: West and East*, vol. 11 of *Collected Works*. London: Routledge and Kegan Paul.

Jung, C. G. (1953). *Psychology and Alchemy*, vol. 12 of *Collected Works*. London: Routledge and Kegan Paul.

Jung, C. G. (1968). *Alchemical Studies*, vol. 13 of *Collected Works*. London: Routledge and Kegan Paul.

Jung, C. G. (1963). *Mysterium Coniunctionis*, vol. 14 of *Collected Works*. London and Henley: Routledge and Kegan Paul.

Jung, C. G. (1963). *Memories, Dreams, Reflections*. London: Collins and Routledge and Kegan Paul.

Kornfield, J. (1993a). *A Path With Heart*. London: Rider Books.

Kornfield, J. (1993b). 'Even The Best Meditators Have Old Wounds To Heal: Combining Meditation and Psychotherapy'. In R. Walsh and F. Vaughan (eds) (1993). *Paths Beyond Ego*. New York: Tarcher Putnam.

McCormick, E. W. (1989, 1997) *Surviving Breakdown*. London: Vermillion.

Maslow, Abraham H. (1968). *Towards a Psychology of Being*. New York: D. Van Nostrand.

Norbu, N. (1984). *The Cycle of Day and Night*. Oakland, California: Zhang Zhung Editions.

Norbu, N. (1986). *The Crystal and the Way of Light*. New York and London: Routledge and Kegan Paul.

Norbu, N. (1989). *Dzogchen, The Self-Perfected State*. London: Arkana.

Raff, J. A. (1997). 'The Felt Vision'. In D. F. Sandner and S. H. Wong (1997), *The Sacred Heritage*. New York and London: Routledge.

Shunryu Suzuki. (1970). *Zen Mind Beginner's Mind*. New York and Tokyo: Weatherhill.

Tart, Charles T. (1994). *Living the Mindful Life*. Boston and London: Shambhala.

Trungpa, C. (1973). *Cutting Through Spiritual Materialism*. Boston and London: Shambhala.

Vaughan, F. (1986). *The Inward Arc*. Nevada City: Blue Dolphin.

Welwood, J. (1977). 'Meditation and the Unconscious: A New Perspective', *Journal of Transpersonal Psychology*, **9**(1).

Welwood, J. (1983). 'On Psychotherapy and Meditation'. In J. Welwood (ed.) (1983), *Awakening The Heart*. Boston and London: Shambhala.

Welwood, J. (1990). 'The Healing Power of Unconditional Presence' Pilgrimage, *The Journal of Psychotherapy and Personal Exploration*, **16**(3), p. 2.

Welwood, J. (1997). 'Reflection and Presence: The Dialectic of Self-Knowledge'. *The Journal of Transpersonal Psychology*, **28**(2), p. 107.

Wilber, K. (1975). 'Psychologia Perennis: The Spectrum of Consciousness', *The Journal of Transpersonal Psychology*, **7** (2), p. 105.

Wilber, K. (1995). *Sex, Ecology, Spirituality: The Spirit of Evolution*. Boston and London: Shambhala.

Wilber, K. (1998). *The Essential Ken Wilber*. Boston and London: Shambhala.

Wilber, K., Engler, J. and Brown, D. P. (1986). *Transformations of Consciousness*. Boston and London: Shambhala.

CHAPTER 10

Specific Techniques

Editor's note: In this final chapter we will look at some of the specific techniques that may be used in practice. Val Davies gives the stages for Focusing that I described more generally in Chapter 9. This is very important. Claire Chappell shows how to use Sandplay, while I offer the very practical side of working with dreams, Active Imagination and Spot Imaging. Philippa Vick has the impossible task of the Body in Psychotherapy and since this is a vast subject in itself, can only offer a small introduction. Three general points: firstly personal experience of a technique is necessary, doing something with someone that you have not done with yourself is morally dubious. Secondly, as with all techniques, they must grow organically from the work and not be forced in as an intruder; the worse cases of this will actually be harmful, particularly those that expose a weak ego to uncontainable unconscious forces. If in doubt do not do it. Thirdly, the most important 'technique' is our own quality of consciousness. If we are mindfully present and do nothing else we will do a great deal more than someone with a bag of tricks and no understanding. I personally believe that the best technique becomes invisible as it sits seamlessly in the fabric of the therapy.

N.W.

FOCUSING

Valerie Harding Davies

Focusing, developed by Eugene Gendlin, is a powerful process enabling people to make changes. It does this by differentiating between our stories, the established understanding about our identities and their histories, and what truly '*is*'. Focusing is a process built on the assumption that the essential meaning that events and relationships have for people is contained within a 'felt sense'. The felt sense is a physical sensation that contains complexities of emotional information. It is different from a specific emotional response such as hurt, fear, anger, etc., because these are precise and immediately identifiable. The felt sense contains all the diverse implicit meanings that an experience holds and these can only be accessed and made explicit through an expression (via word or image) of the felt sense. Immediately a word or image captures the essential meaning, contained within a felt sense, the person experiences a sense of 'fit' and then a sense of movement or change as this clarification of meaning allows other meanings to emerge. (McLeod 1993 in References at end of this section.)

Gendlin (1978) emphasizes that the most important rule for therapists to observe when engaged in the focusing process is to stay out of the focuser's way. It is the client's body that knows where the crux of the problem lays and is thus the expert. Focusing enables the body, through the unfolding of words and images, to express its wisdom and begin the healing process. Some clients will naturally pause and consult their felt sense when asked about their feelings or an aspect of their lives, however most of us will not and we will need to be taught. Learning this technique is easier for some than others. In a culture that lives very little consciously in its body, learning focusing is an alien task. Yet persistence will have its reward.

The process can be divided into seven stages that eventually will run together naturally once the focuser has become familiar with the method.

1. Clearing a space

We start by asking a question. How are you? How is your life right now? What are you feeling? This will evoke a collection of concerns, areas of anxiety. Answers to these questions are not to be found in 'the story' that we carry with us about ourselves, but in the unclear, ill defined 'aura' that may be vaguely felt within the body response to the question. This is sensed perhaps in the chest, stomach or throat. Observe this, not entering in or identifying, but leaving a little space between. Once this is felt ask again and check if you sense something more elsewhere. And then again until complete.

2. Felt sense

Next select one area of concern or interest and continue to focus on it. An aura of feeling that conveys all its parts as a physical sensation within your body. This is still an unclear, defuse felt sense.

3. Handle

Next find the quality of the defuse felt sense. Allow a word, phrase or image to come from the felt sense itself. A quality word is something like, sticky, tight, stuck, heavy, full. It describes *precisely* the quality of the felt sense. Stay with the felt sense for however long it takes for the word, phrase or image to emerge from it. This is different from conceptually finding a word, from our story, and labelling the felt sense with it.

4. Resonating

Now go back and forth between the felt sense in your body and the word, phrase or image that has emerged from it. Check how they resonate with each other, have you found the exact match? You may find both felt sense and its word, phrase or image change as you do this. Continue carefully until they fit. An indication of this may be a small bodily sign, a sigh, a feeling of 'yes', a release. Give this time, stay with it, feeling it completely, physical felt sense and its expression.

5. Asking

It is possible that the release, a 'felt shift', in the previous stage, has already given you an additional deeper understanding of your situation. If not try asking the felt sense what it is about the situation that has caused the felt sense to be so. Ask open questions like, 'What is it about this situation that makes it sticky, leaden, annihilating, stuck, etc.?', or 'What is the named quality or image of this?', or 'What does this felt sense need?' It is important that the answer comes from the felt sense. If quick, rationalized answers come disregard these and return to your body and wait for the felt sense to answer. Give lots of time. A real felt shift comes when the answer comes from the felt sense. The 'ah, ha' moment. A sense of physical satisfaction, this is the truth of it, this feels right.

6. Receiving

Finally happily accept what has emerged, however small or large this shift may be. Therapist and client need to be still at this point so that a true receiving has time to take place. Frequently at this point there may be tears, sighs, physical relaxation, whatever.

7. Returning

It is important that time is allowed to move away from inner space and to return to the present and the room in which you are working. Therapists need to check with their clients that their communication with the felt sense is complete before inviting them to bring themselves back to the room.

Focusing is an important tool that it has a central place in many sessions. Once we have learnt the method, recognizing that it gives truer information then the dead constructions of the story, it becomes an invaluable resource for the universal question, 'how are you?'. We use it when we are stuck and when we simply want to know. We can repeatedly use it in the session or just once as the basis for reflection. Finding associations via focusing for dream images is particularly powerful. The association that comes is the one that carries the emotional truth.

Finally, my experience of sharing with another in this way has always been extremely humbling, rewarding, enlightening and mutually healing. There is something spiritual present.

REFERENCES AND FURTHER READING

Gendlin, E. T. (1962) *Experiencing and the Creation of Meaning*. New York: Free Press.
Gendlin, E. T. (1978) *Focusing*. New York: Bantam Books.
Kahn, M. (1996) *Between Therapist and Client*. New York: Freeman.
McLeod, J. (1993) *An Introduction To Counselling*. Buckingham: Open University Press.

SANDPLAY

Claire Chappell

Some of the most effective, moving and satisfying work that I have done has been with sandplay as the primary focus for creativity and communication between myself and the client. As with other therapeutic tools, no therapist should use this technique without having initially experienced the process themselves over a period of time. This section is only an introduction to working with sand, the beginning of exploring a medium for expression. To do sandplay justice needs much more space than can be given here, and I hope this brief description of the process encourages you to explore it further.

Sandplay is a powerful method of psychotherapy. It is literally a 'hands on' approach, involving practical, creative work in a sandtray. The process is simple. The person at the sandtray creates three-dimensional pictures in the sand. The pictures are made with the hands which become the mediators between inner and outer reality. When creating these pictures our whole being is involved, the body, imagination, soul and spirit.

The therapeutic process of sandplay was developed by Dora Kalff from Margaret Lowenfeld's 'World Technique'. In Sweden, and more recently in Japan, it is used as a diagnostic technique in child psychiatry. In this country it is usually used as part of therapeutic sessions.

Sandplay is often a silent activity. The client creates and the therapist witnesses the creation, in silence. There are no clever interpretations to be made by the therapist either during the making or after. The healing and transformation comes from the interaction between the imagination and the body of the client and the process being witnessed of that process by a compassionate other. One client told me that it was like 'making dreams in the sand'. The technique it most resembles is working with dreams where there is a threesome, the client, the therapist and the dreamer, and here it is the client, the therapist, and the dreamer in the sand.

Requirements

Two sandtrays measuring 57 × 72 cm and 7 cm deep. The tray is not a perfect square. Ruth Amman (1991, p. 18) maintains, 'Because of the inequality of the measurements the rectangular shape creates tensions, unrest and a desire for movement, a desire to go forward'. This means that the client will 'finally find his centre, his personal circle, in the rectangle of the tray.'

The next requirement is a selection of objects all easily accessible. Some objects can be in drawers or boxes, so that the client can explore and find out what is available. The collection of objects should have a mixture of natural objects like shells, stones, rocks, wood, twigs and feathers. There should also be miniature man-made objects and figures, such as people from various countries and cultures, both historical and mythical, and people doing tasks like doctors, policemen or farmers. Houses, buildings, sacred buildings, religious symbols, miniature trees, plants, flowers, marbles and coloured glass stones can be included. Miniature animals, both domestic and wild, known or unknown, are important. I work with both children and adults and so I have figures from some of the modern myths, like Star Wars and characters from cartoons. It is not possible or even necessary to have 'something of everything'. Part of the process is to encourage the client to invent, create and make their own world from what is available. What really matters is not the number of objects but their variety and their symbolic value. It is important that everything is not just beautiful, friendly and light. There should be some dark, ugly and fearsome things available too.

The client is given no instructions: s/he is able to express what is spontaneously accessible within the session. Figures do not have to be used. Some clients only ever make sculptures with the sand. There is no right way to play in the sand, there is only the play itself.

How to start

Although I work with adults and children, within the context of this book I am writing only about working with adults. From my experience I find that the invitation to use the sand can be given at any time, at the beginning of a session, in the middle or when the talking appears to be 'getting in the way'. It really does seem that sandplay 'can reach the parts other therapies cannot reach'.

The role of the therapist

The therapist is primarily there to bear witness to the creative process. I usually sit alongside and a little behind the client; in that way I do not interfere with the client's space. I draw what is happening in the tray, as the client creates it. That is my most important task, to watch, to listen and to write down what happens during the process. I label the objects as the client labels them. If a client chooses a wooden house and calls it 'the office', then that is what I label it and how I refer to it. When the tray is complete and 'finished' according to the client, I take photographs of the tray from different perspectives. I give the client copies of the photographs at the end of our work together.

There are a few don'ts. When the client is working or if later they are talking about the process, do not put your hands into the tray, do not touch or point to the objects. The client has created their own sacred space and the therapist must respect that space and not intrude. Do not make interpretations; let the client make them.

After the tray has been finished the therapist can ask the client to comment on the tray. Is there anything they want to say, what did the process feel like? When they look at the tray from a different position is there anything else they notice? How do they feel now? The client may want to take time to talk about the sandplay or may wish to leave it alone and talk about it at a later time. After several sessions in which sandplay has been a part or the whole of the session, I have a 'review session'. The client and I agree a date and then together we look at the photographs and the client tells 'the story of the trays'. This is a wonderful time for the client to make connections, explore the meanings of the trays further and to share new insights or ideas.

REFERENCES AND FURTHER READING

Amman, R. (1991) *Healing and Transformation in Sandplay*. Illinois: Open Court.
Lowenfield, M. (1979) *The World Technique*. London: Allen and Unwin.
Weinribb, E. (1983) *Images of the Self*. New York: Sigo Press.

DREAM RECORDING

Nigel Wellings

This section shows how to use dreams practically as a central part of the therapy.

Recording the dream

Dreams need time, I like to know if the session will be spent working primarily with the dream so as to give adequate space. Some people bring a flood of dreams and others fragments. The first presents a problem of choice and the second the belief that there is nothing to work with. With a flood you will need to choose one or two that have particularly moved the dreamer. Or, with a vast dream, parts that are particularly powerful. Do not choose ones that apparently confirm a conscious position. Though they too will in fact compensate consciousness, they may be more difficult to understand than one that is plainly disturbing. The problem of fragments is often one of censorship, the belief that this is not an important dream. Work with it fully and you will both be amazed by what is inside it. Often the shortest are the most powerful. To discourage censorship I make a point of saying that everything is to be recorded even if it is only the vague sense of a feeling or image.

To record a dream you need to ask the patient to speak it slowly and to be in feeling contact with what they say. You then can write what they say, word for word if possible (you may need your own shorthand for this). Write the dream text in ordinary pen, leaving plenty of space between the lines. If they go too fast you may slow them down politely and gently.

Next ask if the dream means anything to them. Their own interpretation is important, it empowers them by recognizing they are the expert on themselves and shows you areas they may have missed. You can also ask for a title as this will show what they feel is essential.

Next gather associations. Simply ask what each image suggests or reminds them of. This is fun and playful as well as serious and sometimes painful, it needs a light touch to let the unconscious through. Write these in a coloured pen in between the text.

You now have text and associations. Often simply by doing this connections may be made and the meaning become clearer. Ask what they now understand. This is also the point to reflect back the associations and suggest connections that may have occurred to you. These are merely your ideas and not truths that the patient must accept or be labelled as resisting. You will often be wrong. From this themes from the work may unfold and a general reflective dialogue ensue. Sometimes this is the place for amplificatory material, you may suggest a connection or perhaps suggest something that could be followed up. Do not flood the patient with long mythical stories that bore them or burden them with the brilliance of your interpretation. Let them make connections, you can nudge but not push. Be able to back down.

You may work in this way all the time or occasionally. What is important is that the dreaming touches the dreamer's life and is not used as an escape. Used as such you both have a powerful tool and a place of wisdom to refer to.

The first dream

From this it may be possible to make a prognosis for the course of the therapy. I ask at the initial meeting if the patient dreams and if so did they dream last night. This signals the central importance of the dream and also elicits the first dream. If they do not dream I suggest that they very probably will once we start and this frequently is enough to get a 'non-dreamer' dreaming. It is impossible to make generalizations about the first dream, only reflection, experience and work with a supervisor can be of specific help, but as a rule of thumb, dreams that have a very negative outcome and which appear to be connected to the prospective therapy could reflect either an anxiety or even a possibility of the work being of little value, or worse, a harm. Take such a dream seriously and if there are other factors that make you suspicious of starting work then you may use this as a deciding factor. Conversely, optimistic dreams that have a sense of opening are a very favourable indication.

Also in the first session I ask that the patient records their dreams in a dream book/ psychological journal immediately each morning. Reading from this ensures that the dream is not changed with time.

The dream sequence

A therapy without dreams is like steering by the compass while with dreams we steer from a detailed and precise map. Dreams reveal the shadow, reflect changes in the conscious position as they occur and also communicate and offer corrections when not fully understood. Paying attention to central themes enables us to understand what is of primary importance and watching the changes in these themes enables us to assess and focus the therapy as is appropriate. Images that do not change or become more insistent and frightening may well be representing material that the dreamer is failing to hear. Images that were initially frightening and then transform into something helpful may represent an integration of shadow material. Again generalizations have little value, however the stuff of fairy tales and myth does show clearly the archetypal themes and patterns that run through most of our material.

The final dream

This may reflect the work completed and the next step on the journey. When a patient suggests ending I usually ask that we include their dream opinion in this. Often ego and shadow hold different views and if the whole person is to decide it is necessary to consider both sides. Also, sometimes I think the patient should continue and am surprised to hear that their unconscious does not agree and it is time to stop. In all events I am most satisfied when a dream clearly reflects and supports an ending.

FURTHER READING

Bosnak, R. (1998). *A Little Course in Dreams*. Boston and London: Shambhala.
Hall, J. A. (1983). *Jungian Dream Interpretation*. Toronto: Inner City Books.

Matoon, M. A. (1984). *Understanding Dreams*. Dallas, Texas: Spring Publications.

Von Franz, M. L. (1970). *Interpretation of Fairy Tales*. Dallas, Texas: Spring Publications.

ACTIVE IMAGINATION

Nigel Wellings

Active imagination is a technique for building a bridge between conscious and unconscious mind, ego to shadow. C. G. Jung developed it during the height of his own encounter with the unconscious and went on to offer it to his own patients. It is not to be confused with guided imagination, because we do it on our own without the participation of another, nor with meditation, because this has a different aim, nor visualizations that serve the ego's ends.

The unconscious loves ritual. Because of this before we start active imagination we may mark it ritually, perhaps by lighting a candle, lighting incense, sitting in our special seat, whatever. The important point is that we signal to ourselves that this is an important and serious occasion where we are preparing to open to something larger then ourselves. As with an experience of grace, we can not call the unconscious to order but we can offer a space where the numinous may choose to enter. An attitude of mindfully curious, kindly acceptance of whatever occurs, something or nothing, is essential.

There are four stages to the exercise.

1. It is first necessary to quiet the mind's chatter. Quite simply if we sit to do active imagination and find that we are caught up in thinking then we will not be aware. I have talked extensively in Chapter 9 'Naked Presence' about how we do this by using meditations that increase and perfect our concentration. Here we may use these methods again, breathing slowly and mindfully is particularly good. However, unlike before, here we are not interested in leading eventually to a state of contemplation.

2. Once we have quieted the mind, we allow the unconscious images to arise. This is quite tricky. Firstly the level of contact has to be deeper than simply semi-conscious thoughts circulating, perhaps containing much wishful thinking. To counter this we used the concentration initially. The next problem is that the concentration is too acute and an image floats to the surface but remains fixed or moving little. To solve this we must relax more. And, finally, the opposite problem to this is that the images come too fast, like an inner film, and we are not connected to them. To solve this we must focus more. Jung gives a good example of his first attempts in Chapter 6 of his *Dreams, Memories and Reflections*. We simply want to become sufficiently quiet and calm so that when we stop meditating we have both dropped our consciousness down, so that unconscious images may be contacted, and also are sufficiently mindful, so that we are aware that we are in contact and not simply sucked in and unconsciously identified.

3. Now we are in contact with the unconscious. This may frequently be with images

of characters that represent parts of our psyche. Sub-personalities may arise spontaneously or alternatively we may have dreamt of them previously and have entered the exercise with the intention of furthering the relationship. This is a common starting point. Whether that which is encountered is human, an animal or an object, new or previously known, it is possible to speak to it and to hear what it has to say. We merely have to start! I remember my first goes were rather self-conscious and I distinctly felt I was making up the answers but at a certain point the figure answered back quite autonomously and from then on felt like a distinct and separate person with whom I could meet and talk. An initial suspension of disbelief is helpful.

Once the dialogue and exploration is established it is necessary to record it in some form. Generally people choose to write down what has been said. This may be done while doing the exercise, like writing conversation in a play, or once the meeting is complete, from the memory of what has occurred. Try both ways and see what suits. You may also want to record the work in a painting or even with clay, music or dance. What is important is that it is given some physical expression that we can later return to and reflect upon. James Hillman, talking of his own attempts, said he wrote books of dialogue but then never read them, this of course is useless. Other problems are that the style and technique of expression becomes more important than the content or that the expression is given too little attention and is scrappy because we think it unimportant. Both attitudes are harmful.

4. The final stage is the integration of what we find into our lives. This is like achieving *The Task* in a fairy tale and so is central. A confirmation of this is that it is felt both emotionally and physically. The problem at this point is that we may have been doing the whole thing *as if* it were real with the hidden thought that it is only fantasy. This attitude guarantees we are not really touched by the work and ego defences that rationalize or disengage as a way of not feeling alienate the numinous power of the shadow. The whole value of the exercise is that it facilitates change by making contact with the shadow and this is bound to be difficult and uncomfortable at times. Not all initiations are fun.

As I have said, active imagination is done alone and then is brought into a session and further explored. It is used as part of the vocabulary of therapeutic technique. It is essential that the therapist does not make suggestions when the patient gets stuck but allows the patient to find their own way. This is the work, to struggle with that inside of us that unconsciously keeps us caught in old destructive patterns of being. To help is to infantilize. The therapist's place is to support integration.

Active imagination should not be used by someone who has a fragile ego, who suffers borderline ego states or has a psychotic illness. In all cases it could easily do harm.

FURTHER READING

Jung, C. G. (1963). *Memories, Dreams, Reflections*. London: Collins/Routledge and Kegan Paul.
Hanna, B. (1981). *Encounters with Soul: Active Imagination*. Santa Monica: Sigo Press.

SPOT IMAGING: THE NECKLACE OF LIFE

Nigel Wellings

The theory

Spot imaging represents the marriage of Freud's free association method that leads directly to the complex's and Jung's circumambulation method that remains close to the primary image. Like the first it has the ability to take the patient down into forgotten/repressed childhood memories or *seeming memories* and like the second it connects with the synthetic and teleological needs of the Self. So it is the best of both methods and furthermore it facilitates a conscious connection to the material at a *felt* level.

Aims

Transpersonal psychology accepts the premise that unconscious material has the ability to constellate situations that reproduce the circumstances of the original wounding; for example, the abandoned child as an adult chooses partners who always leave. Unless we become conscious of this we cannot make the choice to find a better alternative. Imaging enables us to do this by:

- Identifying wound patterns, complexes, habitual destructive behaviours.
- Deepening a felt connection to these and the emotional pain they defend against and simultaneously re-create.
- Allowing an experience of release, catharsis.
- Discovering how to integrate new understanding into everyday life, how to handle the wound in the best way and how to allow new energies to become conscious.

We are not trying to 'cure' complexes. If the complex is conceived as a wound that brings us our own individual way of being in the world and the repeated struggle with it, the means of incarnating our particular destiny, then the wound, the complex, is also the healing and as such is the most valuable thing for 'soul making'. While obviously not all suffering is good and most patients clearly want to feel better, it does remain true that someone who has been through much and *has made meaning out of it* does have a quality about them that is instinctively recognizable as good. Are we saying then that suffering when meaningful can become good?

The practice

The place for imaging is as part of a repertoire of therapeutic techniques and perceptions. Knowing when not to use it, as well as when, is part of its strength. It is not used when the patient resists, has a fragile ego structure or is already flooding the work with unconscious material.

The fundamental point is always *follow the energy* – all else follows from this.

An example session

Typically a patient will speak of an event, thoughts or feelings that are happening in their life. The therapist is in part listening to recognize *a point of entry* into the background, the shadow, of this description. This will be when some event, thought or feeling appears *highly charged* when spoken of, or alternatively, if the patient presents a *'flat'* description, when the therapist draws attention to something that may be charged but remains just beyond the immediate light of the patient's ego – perhaps something obviously painful but denied.

Once the point of entry has been identified the therapist may invite the patient to explore the material more closely. If this is acceptable, and the patient has absolute say, the patient will be requested to close their eyes and either *focus on a feeling, a body gesture/posture* or *find an image that represents the subject of conversation*. Which of these one asks for depends on the situation and is usually apparent and obvious.

Situations vary. A feeling is easily accessible for it is simply itself. Likewise, drawing attention to a gesture or posture is also immediate because of its simplicity of expression. However affect hidden within thoughts is more obscure and thus easier to deny. Certain types of people will find connecting with the feelings in the shadow more easy than others. For example, those with a schizoid, narcissistic, masochistic or obsessive wound, all of which feature keeping control, will not have immediate access to their feelings, while those with oral, symbiotic and histrionic wounds will seem to find it easier. Please note 'seem'. Knowing the capacity of the patient means not asking them to do something they are not yet capable of. Furthermore, in some circumstances it is essential that the ego defences be left intact, for example when a weak ego is threatened by the shadow with the danger of disintegration; under such circumstances this technique is contra-indicated.

Following feelings tends to lead to historical events. Images may lead to feelings which in turn lead to events. Body sensations may also lead to feelings that lead to events. Both images and body sensations equally carry unconscious material that first becomes conscious as emotion and then may be thought about. However there are no hard rules about what leads where. Images may also spiral into more and more images and then it is necessary to ground them in the body and life if they are to be real. A tendency to avoid either feeling by staying in image or image by staying in feeling should be noted as this can show either a hesitancy to be emotionally embodied or a fear of a greater objective reflection. Encouragement to do both achieves a desirable balance.

To continue: the patient now rests with their eyes closed and is focusing on the feeling they have just described. The therapist asks them to stay with this for a few moments and to give a description of what they are feeling while still keeping in contact with it. Something like: 'Just stay with that feeling and tell me what you find.' This is a skill: to simultaneously feel and observe. Once this is established the patient is asked if any situations, circumstances or events, that they may have experienced previously, come to them, that share in the same or similar feelings. Generally this leads to an event in the near or distant past. The patient is then asked to stay with the memory of this event and explore it fully via their different senses. What do they see, hear, smell, feel about the event? Also who is there, what is happening, how old are the participants, what are they feeling and doing, and so on? The aim is to inhabit the memory at a feeling level, connecting with material that may have been forgotten or repressed. When the scene is exhausted of affect the therapist asks the patient to stay with the principal feeling that has emerged and, once again, lead by this, wait for a second situation to present itself which is then explored as with the first. Then when this is exhausted the principal feeling leads to the next event. Thus the pattern becomes feeling, event, feeling, event, feeling, event, continuing until the conclusion.

An image for this is a necklace of beads. The cord connecting the beads is the feelings that lead down from conscious life into the inner world and then back up. The beads are the life events that are strung along the feelings and which the feelings penetrate and connect. Neither cord nor beads have purpose without the other. Feeling imbues life with meaning, and situations, events, material history embody feeling.

This process also works from the starting-point of the body. Here we start with staying with a body gesture, posture or sensation and 'see what comes up'. This will usually produce feelings, so we continue as above. So: body, feeling, event, and so on.

This process also works with images. Slightly differently, the patient is asked to close their eyes and find an image for what they have been describing. Here, instead of memories of events connected by feelings, the necklace, one may find a series of images connected by feelings that may embody events from the past (an image of a black hole that feels like my mother's death), but equally may speak of the present and future (a light on the horizon that gives me hope). Obviously, images, as precursors to feeling and experience, are particularly inclined to look forward. So: describing events, finding an image, feeling, image, feeling continuing. In some ways working with images is particularly important because it powerfully connects the ego to the symbolic language of the deep imagination and the healing that this can confer. In this way it reaches down through the personal unconscious and aligns us with our archetypal ground.

And lastly they can all be mixed. So: event, feeling, image, feeling, event, feeling, image, continuing up and down until the end.

The overall shape of the session is as follows. The patient begins the imaging sequence and perhaps travels through two, three or more vignettes. Typically they will open their eyes at a certain point which will indicate that they have returned to surface consciousness. At this point it is necessary to assess whether this represents the need to rest and assimilate the material or merely a momentary surfacing that may be redirected down again. If it is the first, then the therapist's task is to assist in the digestion, and if the second, to lead back down. Again typically there may be intermittent periods of descent and assimilation.

The therapist uses their voice and questions/directs to reflect this choice. To return, a quiet, non-invasive, neutral voice is used – 'shall we just close our eyes and return to that feeling?' – inviting a staying with feeling before resurfacing. Once the patient has resurfaced they may need a moment to recollect themselves. Here the therapist pauses, then uses a normal voice to help the return to a solid ego. Questions evoking feeling are now replaced with questions that require the patient to be objective about their own subjective material. Thinking, reflecting and meaning are central. As Jung says, individuation begins, not in experiencing affect, but in its objective perception.

This is achieved by asking the patient what they have seen in the material brought to light and what they make of it, how they think it might help and what it tells them, and how they may integrate it into their life. This is the final part of the session and it is important that the therapist carefully stage-manage the timing so that this last part is not rushed nor missed nor, to avoid this mismanagement, that the time boundaries of the session be extended so to complete.

At this point it is appropriate for the therapist to summarize the session and reflect on what the theme may have been within it and its connection to previous work. As with any interpretation, this must be offered, not force fed, and the response noted and considered. We are often wrong.

Diagramatically the session looks like this:

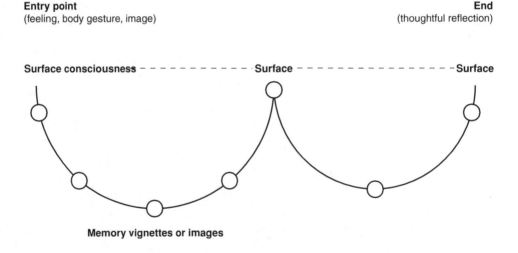

Figure 4 Spot Imaging

THE BODY IN THERAPY

Philippa Vick

This is an introduction to working with the body/energy. This powerful method requires both study and personal experience and so here I can only point out some starting places and where to go from there. The body has its own natural wisdom which is communicated through expression, movement, pleasure and pain. We need to hear this wisdom because the society in which we live primarily lives in its thoughts and is unconscious of the joy of being alive as physical beings. By listening and responding to our bodies we are more in touch with life and no longer entirely run by the mind's tendency to pursue disconnected desires. Now let us look at how these principles may be applied in therapy.

The body in process

The body is constantly in communication through facial expressions, tones of voice, movements and gestures, pathological symptoms and the patterns and rhythms of breath. This is a communication of the unconscious and unspoken life that opens the client to a bigger picture and builds bridges into who they actually are. This is not to improve the client but a recognition that we are already whole.

In practice I focus on the body when it is calling attention to itself or when I meet a client who is alienated from their body (nearly all of us). In the session I see when the client is noticeably gesturing, moving, is physically incongruent with what they are saying, or conversely, if they are unnaturally still. The techniques of spot imaging and Focusing both enable the client to work with their body's expression, not the content of their stories but rather how they are *in* their stories. The content of the story is called the primary process while the body/energy communicates the secondary process (Mindel 1984). To work with the secondary processes I draw attention to the body's expression and invite the client to slow down and become mindfully curious. This is essential because the body process works at a similar speed to the dream process and may not be worked with at the faster thinking speed.

For example, a client is huddling down while speaking. I ask them to notice how they are holding their body. We find it is held, contracted. I can then ask what the body is trying to do. Perhaps their body is trying to protect itself, to be smaller, not there. From this I would invite them to follow this process and simultaneously hear all the little signals within it. Not change it but enter in more fully. We may find that behind or within the contraction is not only fear but also the repressed desire to expand. With these two pulling against each other it is not surprising that the client lives in hover. Finally I would ask the client to consciously, and within their own control, experiment with both aspects of the energy movement, contraction and expansion, and to notice this movement in their everyday life. Not to change it but be conscious. Change then, if it occurs, will be spontaneous.

The client's answers come from their body, not the conscious ego (provided they have not answered too fast), and they now have an entry point to their secondary process and innate wisdom. For many of us this will initially be difficult because our heroic culture is dedicated to overriding most of these messages but by slowing and listening we can hear.

The body as history carrier

Let us start with another example. A client comes to their first session. I see someone who has a scooped empty chest that suggests undernourishment and their eyes appear big and helpless, looking to me for help. Their body may be thin and narrow, slumped, perhaps childlike, they breathe shallowly and have weak energy. Their story is full of emotional emptiness. All this may tell me that this person has an oral wound. That is, feelings about being undernourished, possibly from the first months of their life.

This physical/energetic, as well as emotional, presentation tells me immediately the background issues that we will be exploring. Our therapeutic relationship will revolve around barriers to receiving and feelings of having nothing to give because one is empty. Beneath this is a desperate need for love and care and also anger for not being nourished originally. Knowing this will help me not to get hooked into being the all nourishing therapist/mother whose food is rejected yet longed for, nor of falling into an identification where I too feel empty of anything good.

Once there is enough trust in the relationship we may begin to work with this. Perhaps I see that a subject causes the client to become more 'scooped', like an empty bowl. I can then draw attention to this in the way described above. In this way the unconsciously habitual physical structure that carries emotional memories may become conscious. In the example above part of the exploration would be to emphasize and exaggerate the body structure and to ask if what they found was familiar to them.

I do this because I believe that our bodies, their postures and structures, how we hold, move and breathe, reflect unconscious decisions we took in childhood about how to survive. These choices now show as chronic and stable patterns, that persist through life, and that are so much part of us that we are no longer aware of them. Now, in the present, if this is made conscious, we have an opportunity to reflect upon these decisions and how they adversely effect our lives.

In Chapter 4 on 'The Wound' we saw that specific psychopathologies may occur at different periods within the infant's development. These woundings also show in the body and its energy in specific ways. Reich, Lowen, Keleman and now Kurtz and Mindell have explored, developed and extended this understanding and it is from this perspective that I have been speaking. I can only touch on the complexity of this approach and for a fuller understanding it will be necessary to go to their work.

REFERENCES AND FURTHER READING

Keleman, S. (1975). *Your Body Speaks Its Mind*. Berkeley: Center Press.

Kurtz, R. (1970). *The Hakomi Handbook*. Boulder: Hakomi Institute.

Kurtz, R. and Prestera, H. (1984). *The Body Reveals*. San Francisco: Harper & Row.

Lowen, A. (1976). *Bioenergetics*. London: Coventure.

Mindell, A. (1984). *Dream Body*. London: Routledge and Kegan Paul.

Mindell, A. (1985). *Working with the Dreaming Body*. London: Routledge and Kegan Paul.

Further Information

The Centre for Transpersonal Psychology runs the following courses and services:

- Introductory workshops for those with a personal interest in transpersonal psychology.
- Seminars on various transpersonal themes, general and clinical, for psychotherapists, associated professions and interested others.
- A one-year, part-time Introduction to Transpersonal Skills and Perspectives for those who wish to deepen their understanding of transpersonal psychology and may be considering training.
- A modular, part-time Professional Preparation for the Practice of Transpersonal Psychotherapy. This leads to accredited membership with the CTP and registration with the United Kingdom Council for Psychotherapy.
- A referral service for those who are interested in working psychotherapeutically with a transpersonal psychotherapist or for those wanting supervision from a transpersonal perspective.

For further information contact:

The Centre for Transpersonal Psychology
86A Marylebone High Street
London W1M 3DE
Telephone: 020-7935 7350
Telefax: 020-7935 2672

Index